IMAGES
of America

OCEANA COUNTY
1850–1950

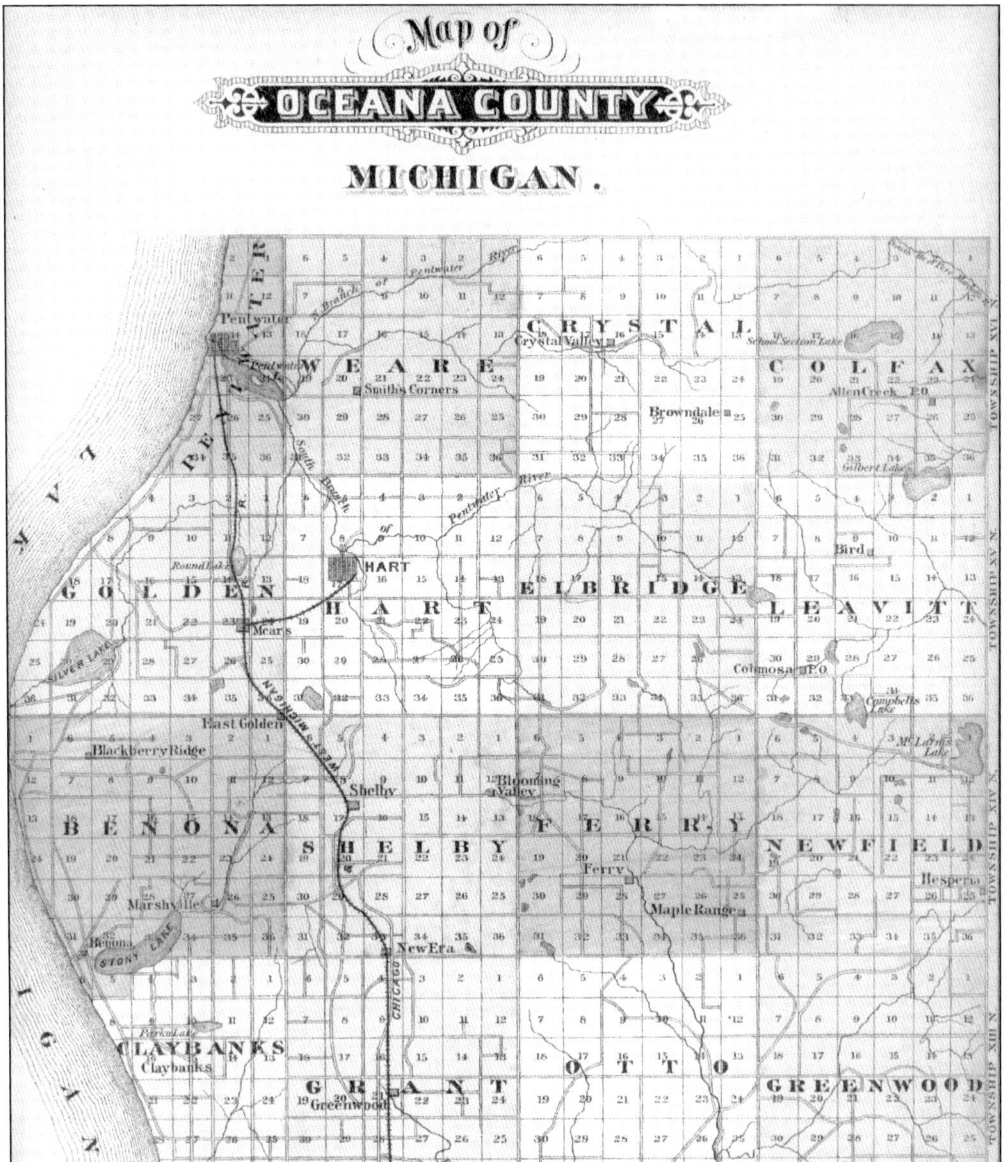

MAP OF OCEANA COUNTY. The 16 townships of Oceana County are clearly defined and laid out in this c. 1882 map of the area. The population of Oceana County increased to over 1,800 and was spread out amongst the eight organized towns by 1861 and by 1880. (Courtesy of the Oceana County Historical and Genealogical Society.)

ON THE COVER: **A BICYCLE BUILT FOR ONE.** The c. 1900 image is a street scene in the city of Hart. (Courtesy of the Oceana County Historical and Genealogical Society.)

IMAGES
of America

OCEANA COUNTY
1850–1950

David K. Petersen and the
Oceana County Historical and Genealogical Society

ARCADIA
PUBLISHING

ISBN 978-0-7385-9362-3

Published by Arcadia Publishing
Charleston, South Carolina

Printed in the United States of America

Library of Congress Control Number: 2011943820

For all general information, please contact Arcadia Publishing:
Telephone 843-853-2070
Fax 843-853-0044
E-mail sales@arcadiapublishing.com
For customer service and orders:
Toll-Free 1-888-313-2665

Visit us on the Internet at www.arcadiapublishing.com

I dedicate this book to my grandparents M. Earl and Laura Fern Purdy-Shaw. Their influence and love continue to guide me in my life.

Contents

ACKNOWLEDGMENTS

I would like to thank the Oceana County Historical and Genealogical Society for welcoming this project with open arms. Without their help and assistance, this book would not have been possible. Unless otherwise noted, all images appear courtesy of the Oceana County Historical and Genealogical Society.

Karen Urick and Ed Ricketson, among other volunteers at the society, were very helpful during the hours I spent reviewing materials and scanning photographs from between 1850 and 1950 for inclusion in Oceana County.

The Oceana County Historical and Genealogical Society is one of the few societies that truly live up to its mission statement of preserving the area's history and making what it has preserved available for the enjoyment and use by all. Oceana County should be proud of the society's accomplishments and rest assured that the family photographs, scrapbooks, and artifacts donated by residents have found a safe and secure home and are being saved and shared for the enjoyment of future generations.

I would also like to thank my editors at Arcadia Publishing—Anna Wilson and Liz Gurley—for their help and assistance as this edition of Oceana County history was being prepared.

I spent a number of years within Oceana County organizing and presenting drug prevention programs. I always enjoyed working there; the people have been open and supportive, and I felt connected to the area from the first day I was working there.

While I did grow up a little to the north in Ludington, I do have family roots that run deep in Oceana County as well. The Purdys and Tullers came up from Hillsdale County to Oceana over 125 years ago, and the Inman family followed a short time later. My maternal grandfather, Earl Shaw, and Archie Campbell drove Shaw's Harley up to Mears in 1919, where Shaw met his bride-to-be, Laura Fern Purdy. My paternal great-grandfather, Anton Edward Peterson, came down to Pentwater and opened a boat-building business, and my great-great uncles Louis Hartwick and William Tuller published *Oceana County Pioneers* in 1890.

Oceana County is close to my heart, and working on this book to tell the history of the area has been a joy.

INTRODUCTION

The area comprising the present state of Michigan was under the control of the British until 1796, a full 20 years after the Declaration of Independence was signed. When the Michigan Territory was formed in 1805, the United States of America was but an infant government in the eyes of the world, and much of what would become Oceana County was in a wild and undeveloped state.

On January 26, 1837, Michigan was admitted as a state into the Union after its southern neighbors. Ohio was admitted in 1803, followed by Indiana, and Illinois; even Arkansas was admitted before Michigan. It almost seems that in the states's westward march, Michigan was nearly forgotten, almost an afterthought. In 1837, few explorers of European descent had bothered to venture north. Most travel along the lakeshore at that time was done with the destination of Mackinac in mind rather than the unearthing of secrets within wild shoreline and the even more mysterious interior of Michigan, which many considered naught but a swamp, crisscrossed by deer runs and Indian pathways.

It was not until February 13, 1855, that the Michigan Legislature established the present boundaries of Oceana County and organized the first three townships, consisting of Claybanks, Stony Creek, and Pentwater. Oceana County was reputed to be named for the great freshwater ocean of Lake Michigan, but the great forest seemed to be an ocean itself, a never-ending sea of green gold for the lumber barons to exploit. The harvest of these mammoth stands of pines brought men, and then families, to the area to work and build their fortunes.

As with many of its immediate neighbors, Oceana County was forged from the exploits of trappers and lumbermen. It was sustained and nurtured by the farmers and businessmen who remained. They built communities on the pine-stumped fields left after the great stands of white pine were shipped out to build the ever-expanding cities of a growing nation.

The howl of the wolf, the beat of native drums, and the dense forests filled with white pine relented and gave way to the sound of the axe, the buzz of the saw, and the penetration of the light of the sun as it warmed the soil and sprouted the seeds of newly planted fields that had not felt the penetrating rays of old Sol for a hundred seasons.

At the time of the organization of Oceana County, there were but two small settlements: the first, the outgrowth of a small sawmill being near Claybanks, and the other being Pentwater. When the vote came to determine the location of the county seat in 1855, Claybanks was chosen over Pentwater, as it had superior numbers in population and was closer to the community of Muskegon, which was further developed and settled. Transportation, another consideration, was difficult, with most travel between settlements along the beach and by water.

In those early years of settlement, many communities sprang up around sawmills or well-traveled, wide spots in the paths along the lakeshore only to fade away again almost as quickly as they appeared. If luck was with them, the names that were given stayed in the memories and lore of the settlers and were remembered by those who came afterwards.

Post offices were often in the home of the postmaster, and the official designation often named the site after the postmaster, a Native American resident, or some other early settler or geographic feature in the immediate area. Names such as Alice, Allen Creek, Forest City, Pa Pa Me, and Cobmoosa were chosen for some of the more than 40 named sites in Oceana County.

All of these local sites contribute to the colorful lore and history of Oceana County, Michigan. The Oceana area grew slowly in those early years, and the conflict between North and South, that Great War of the Rebellion as it was called in those days, further slowed the influx of settlers and commerce. Though, what the war took away in those four years in volunteers and conscripts, it also gave back in an influx of new settlers once the war had ended. The nation again looked to the future of rebuilding and new growth.

Settlers began to flood into northern Michigan to work in the pinery and mills, cut shingles, farm, and begin new businesses to support the growing communities. Men who had seen the ravages of war and wanted to build their lives anew took advantage of the Homestead Act and staked their claims on virgin lands that they cleared with the hand axe and saw. They built their farms and raised their families in the new lands.

There was little land to be had in the old country, as it had been taken and held for generations. Much of Europe was living in a hand-to-mouth existence with many taking survival day by day. Being able to make enough to eat was, for many, almost an unattainable task.

The streets of America may not have been paved in actual gold, but the streets, even the dirt-covered ones, were paved with opportunity the old country families had not seen in 1,000 years. Classified ads touting the wealth to be gained by purchasing farmlands in Oceana County circulated throughout magazines and ethnic publications in the old country. Land-starved residents of faraway nations such as Germany, Denmark, and Sweden saw an opportunity and came to America to seek their fortunes and build their new lives.

One or two people from a community might come, but after settling into their new home, they wrote and told others, "Come to America!" In today's world, especially in America, we barely give a thought to commodities such as milk and honey, but to many in the world, milk and honey were the lifeblood that could sustain them and their families. They heard the message loud and clear from their new American cousins and came in increasing numbers, making the land of milk and honey their home.

The communities of Oceana County began to grow and prosper and, by the early 1870s, were in a full and unrelenting advance towards their future. As the trees fell and the pathways became better traveled, roads emerged, and with the development of roads within the county, commerce prospered and Oceana County grew.

After the pineries were gone and the mills closed, many of the little communities began to fade in size and from memory. Oceana, like many of its neighbors, had to find a way to remain viable. Living in "God's country" may feed the soul, but one must also feed their families. Having the dunes, lakes, and beaches were part of the answer, and Oceana County began to develop its tourism market. Today, it is an important west Michigan tourist destination.

One

Early County History

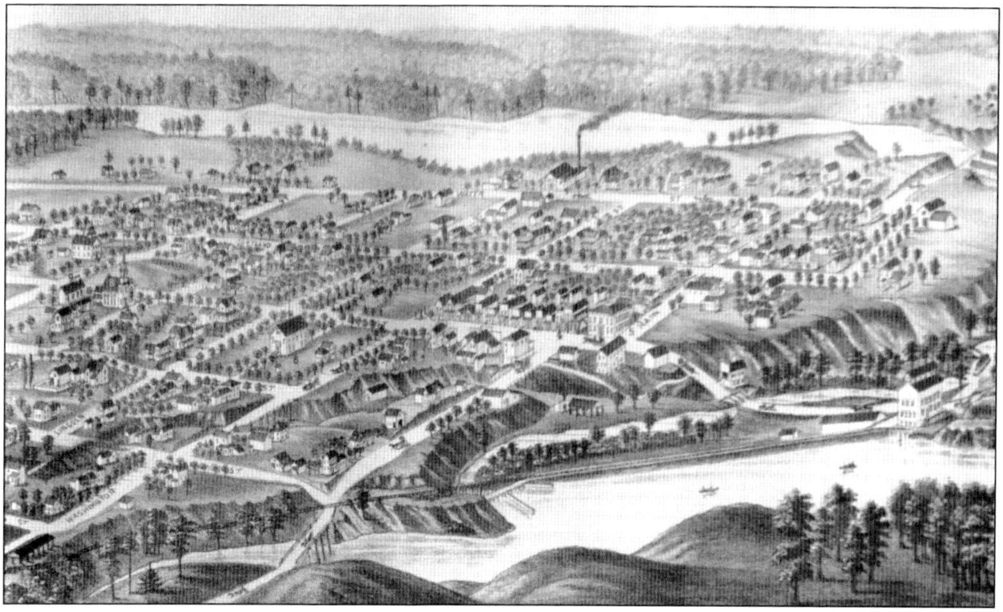

View of Hart, 1880. The village of Hart had seen considerable growth by 1880, as seen here. After the county seat was removed from Whiskey Creek in 1861, growth was slow in direct response to the War of the Rebellion and the resulting enlistment of 128 men (including 34 native residents). By 1864, there were only three buildings in the whole village: the newly built courthouse, Corbin's Boardinghouse, and a residential home.

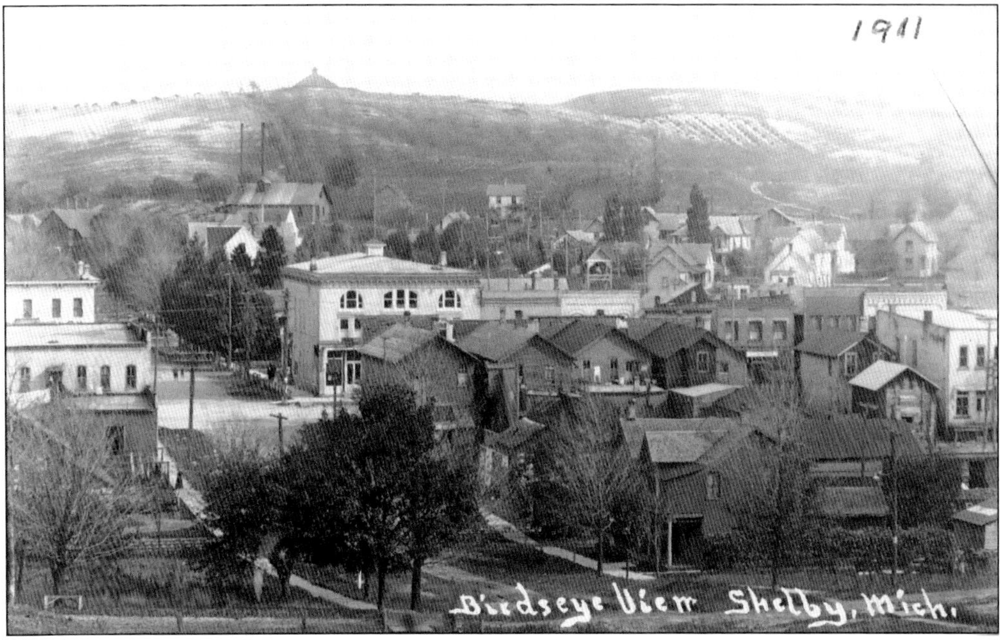

Shelby Village. First called Benona in 1862 and then Barnett in 1874, the village was incorporated as Shelby in 1882. Destined to fail, the little village was rescued in 1874 by numbers of passenger pigeons so great that they blackened the sky. The resulting boom from hunters and the harvesting of the flock brought resources and people to the area, and the village began to flourish.

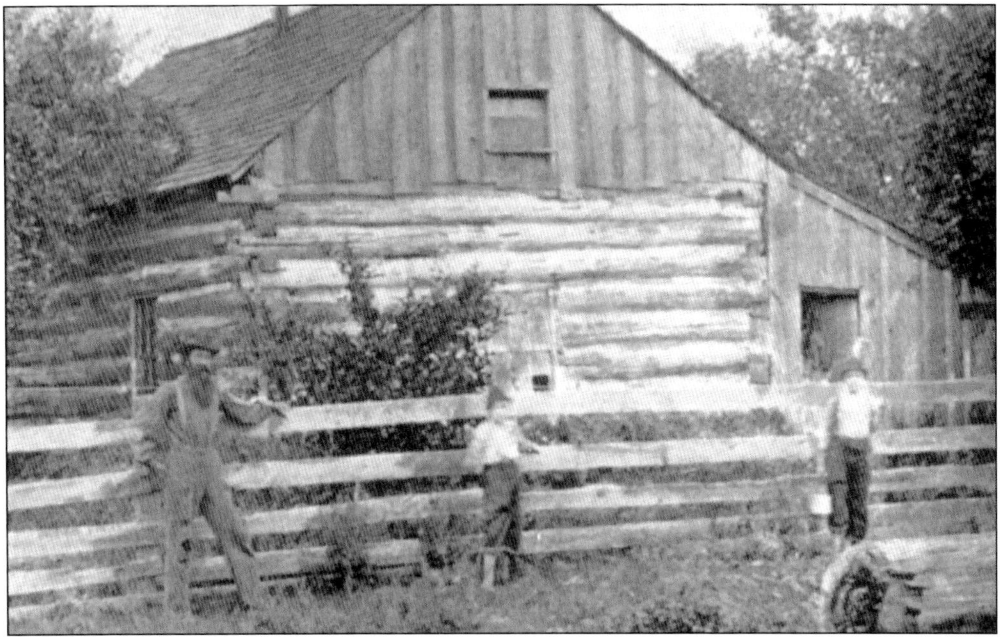

Oldest House in the County. This log home was built in 1850. James Gibbs settled here in 1857, at the time this picture was taken. In 1880, the structure was deemed to be the oldest house in Oceana County. One of the first tasks that fell upon the settlers was to fell some of the trees and make a small clearing to build a log home. There were no hotels, which meant there was no place to stay except for under the stars at night until they could erect some shelter.

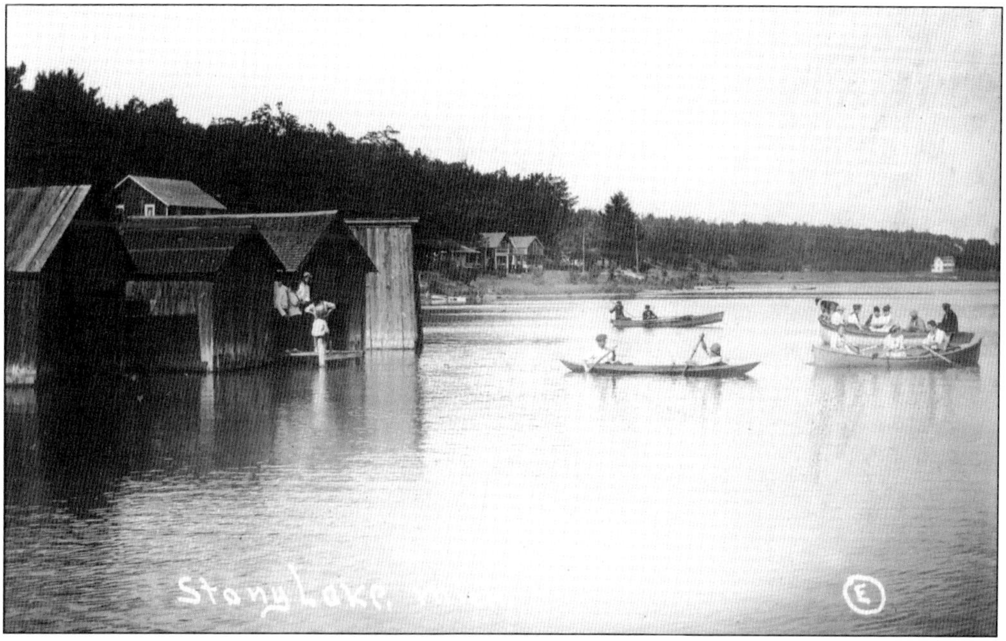

STONY LAKE. This vintage view of Stony Lake brings to mind the song "In the Good Old Summertime" and images of Victorian women, iced lemonade, and porch swings. The resorts of Stony Lake's past catered to world-weary travelers who looked for some escape from the big cities' noise and confusion, if only for a scant two weeks in July.

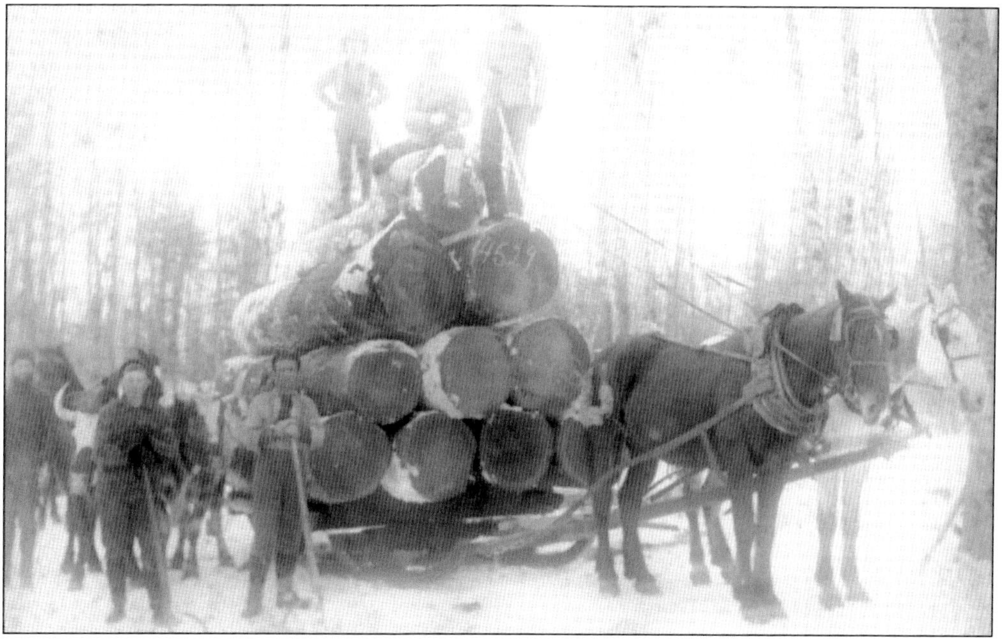

LOGGING IN OCEANA. Oceana County, in contrast, did not have rivers and streams large enough to carry logs to the holding ponds and mills, as did Mason to the north. The White River was dammed, and logs floated to Whitehall. Butters's Mobile & Ohio Railroad (M&O) carried logs north to Buttersville. Pentwater is the only village that was built with the benefit of a harbor for placing sawmills and shipping lumber.

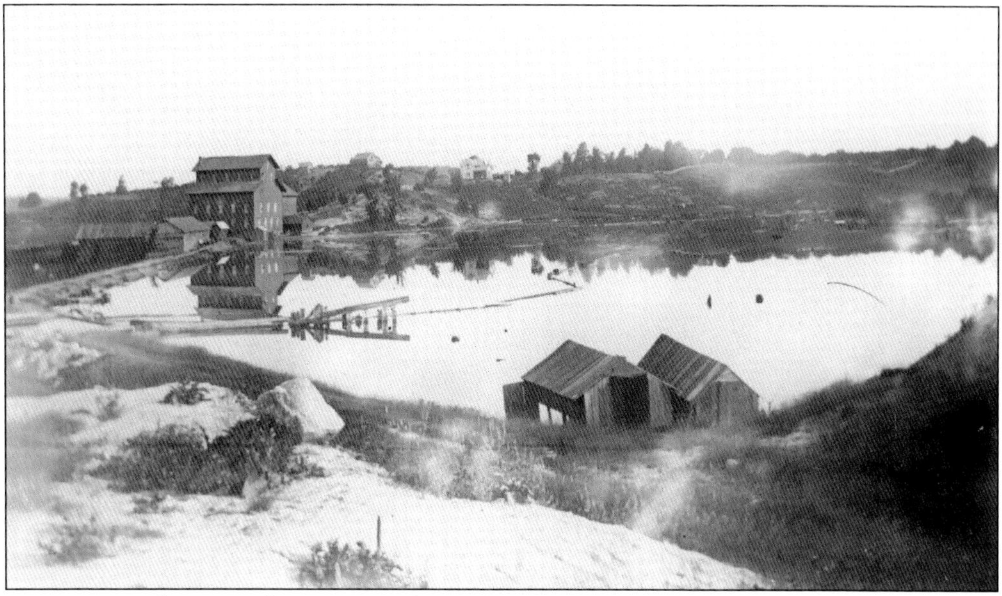

Hart Mill. The gristmill at Hart was located on the north side of the present lake and bridge and was originally built by Lyle Corbin and Ira Ford. The mill was known in later years as the Hart Roller Mill. The establishment of a gristmill was a significant draw to bring rural farmers into the village for news and supplies and to hunker down and "chew the fat."

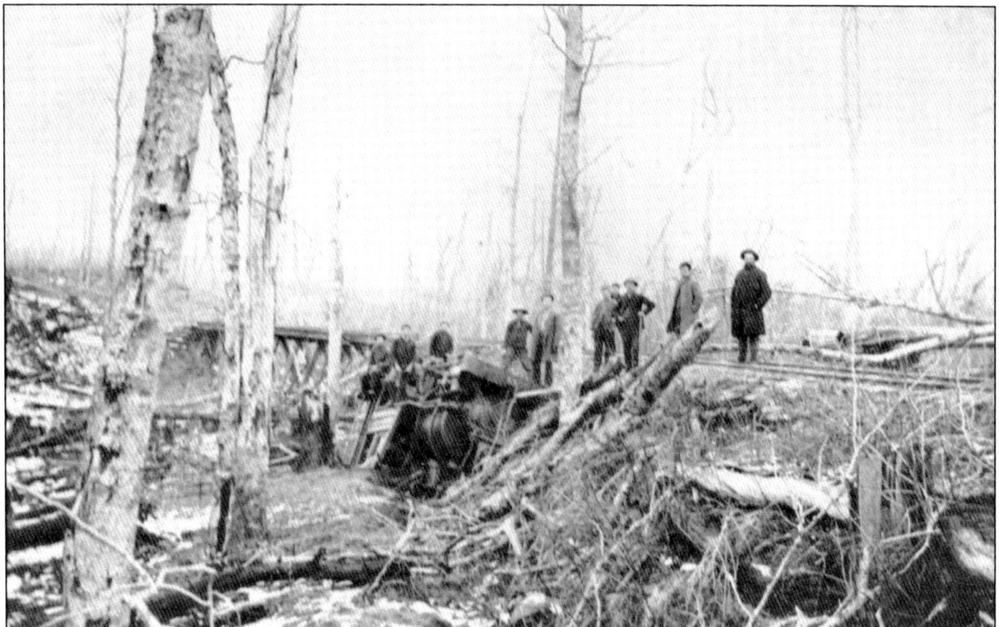

Staples and Covell Train Disaster. Considered the worst accident of its kind in western Michigan, the Staples and Covell disaster of April 9, 1894, left seven dead and two scarred for life. The logging train had dropped a load of logs at the rollway on the north branch of the White River and was returning. The train, running backwards down the track, struck a tree that had fallen, causing the train to jump the tracks and derail. The resulting accident burst a steam pipeline, and the escaping steam scalded all nine men.

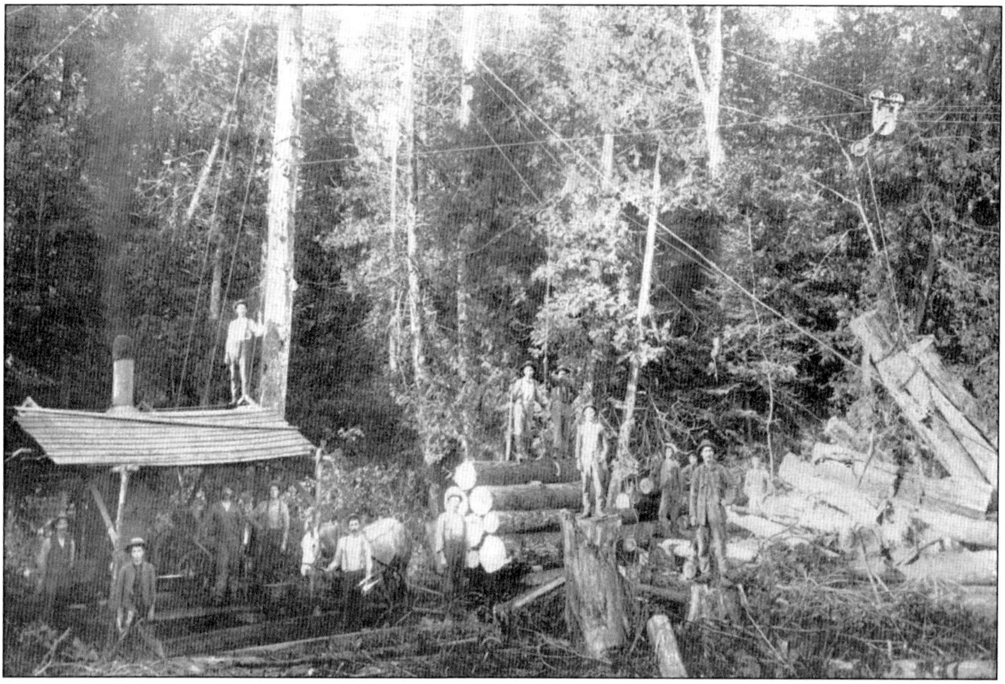

Steam Skidder Logging. Horace Butters held several patents in the lumbering industry, one of which was for a steam skidder that allowed easier transportation of logs overhead on cables through the swamps along rivers like the Piere Marquette or Pentwater River. The skidders increased their reach and ability to harvest logs that they might not otherwise be able to bring to the market.

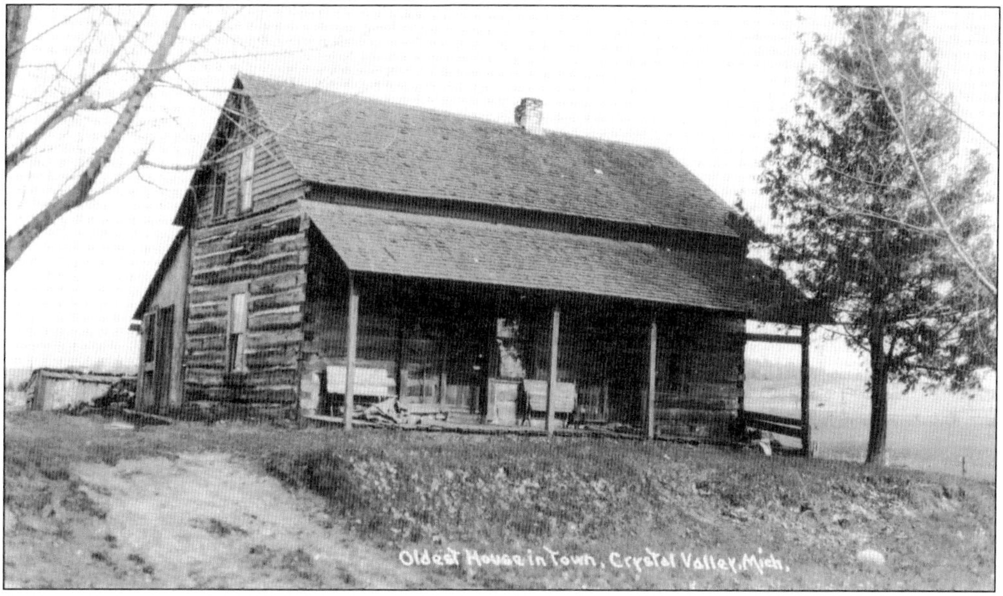

Oldest House in Crystal Valley. The old log cabin in Crystal Township was constructed by Jared Gay and his wife, Catherine, after they came to the Grand River Ottawa Indian's Reservation. Jared was the second blacksmith appointed by the government to provide services to the displaced natives. The Gays were the first permanent settlers of European ancestry in Crystal Township and remained there until 1902.

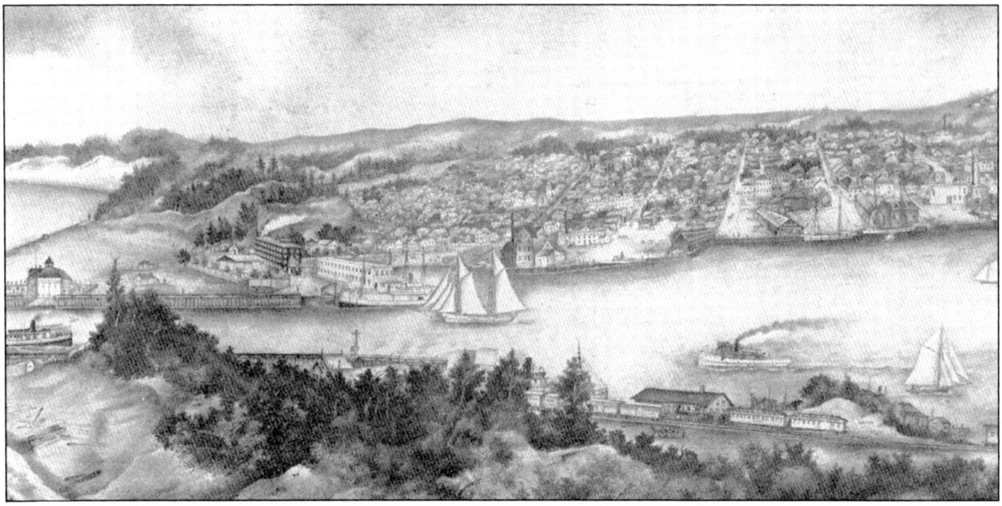

Bird's-Eye View of Pentwater, 1889. Pentwater was one of two original settlements in Oceana County, and in spite of its location on the only harbor in the county, it failed to secure the county seat in part because its northern-most position in the county placed it 16 miles farther north from Muskegon, which was the seat of commerce in the region at that time. Goods and people entered Oceana County through Whiskey Creek.

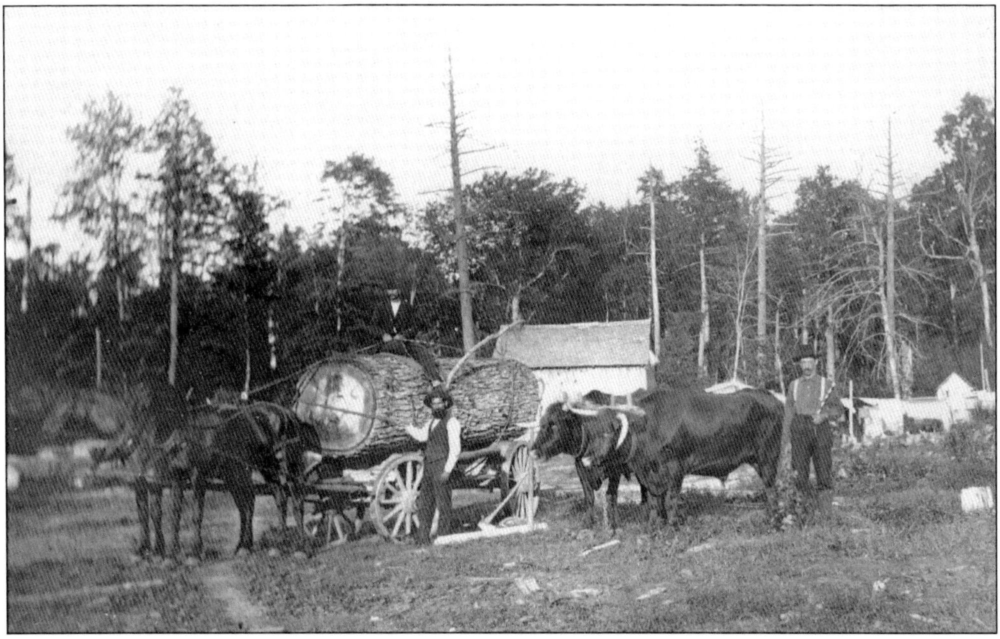

Sands and His Log. A Mr. Sands is seen here in this early photograph with a massive log being hauled to the mills. Oceana County, like many of its neighbors, got an economic foothold through logging operations that supported the early settlers and cleared the lands for agriculture. Many early homesteaders worked as lumberjacks during the winter months and farmed during the summers.

Two

Townships of Oceana County

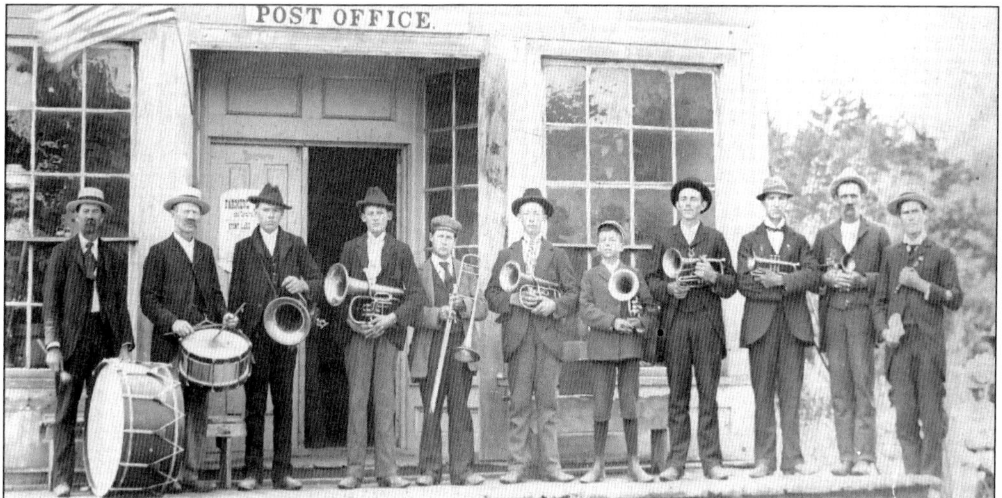

Benona Brass Band. Community bands were common during the days when people had to create their own entertainment. The community band can trace its history back to 11th-century Europe when waits patrolled the streets with horns. The bands today, however, are more in line with the bands formed after Adolph Sax introduced his new designs after 1840. Originally, in 1831, Oceana consisted of 28 townships and took in part of Muskegon, Kent, and Montcalm but not the present-day boundaries of Oceana County. Benona Township was included in Stony Creek, one of the three original townships when Oceana County was organized in 1855. According to state records, "The first township meeting was held at the house of Amos R. Wheeler, in April, 1855. Harvey Tower was Chairman, Warren Wilder and Estes Rich Inspectors of Election, and Malcom Campbell Clerk. The following officers were elected: Supervisor, Warren Wilder; Clerk, Malcom Campbell; Treasurer, James MeNutt; Justices, A.R. Wheeler, Jasper Thompson, Henry Harris and Estes Rich; Highway Commissioners."

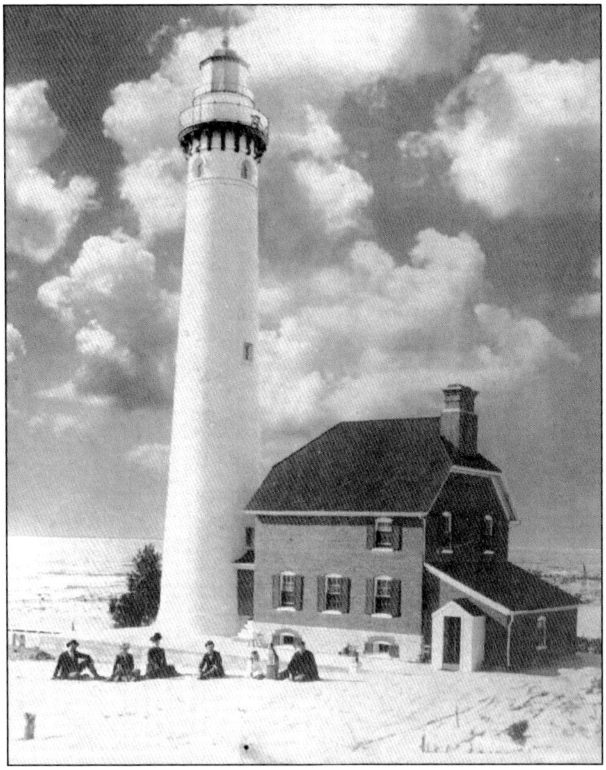

Little Point Sable Lighthouse. An agricultural community, Benona Township also is home to the resort community that sprang up around Stony Lake and the Little Point Sable Lighthouse. The wooden-hulled ships that plied the waters of Lake Michigan depended on the lighthouses for safe travel. In the event of a storm or disaster, rescues from the treacherous waters were mounted by the crew of the lifesaving station. Built in 1876, the lighthouse has been preserved by the Sable Points Lighthouse Keepers Association.

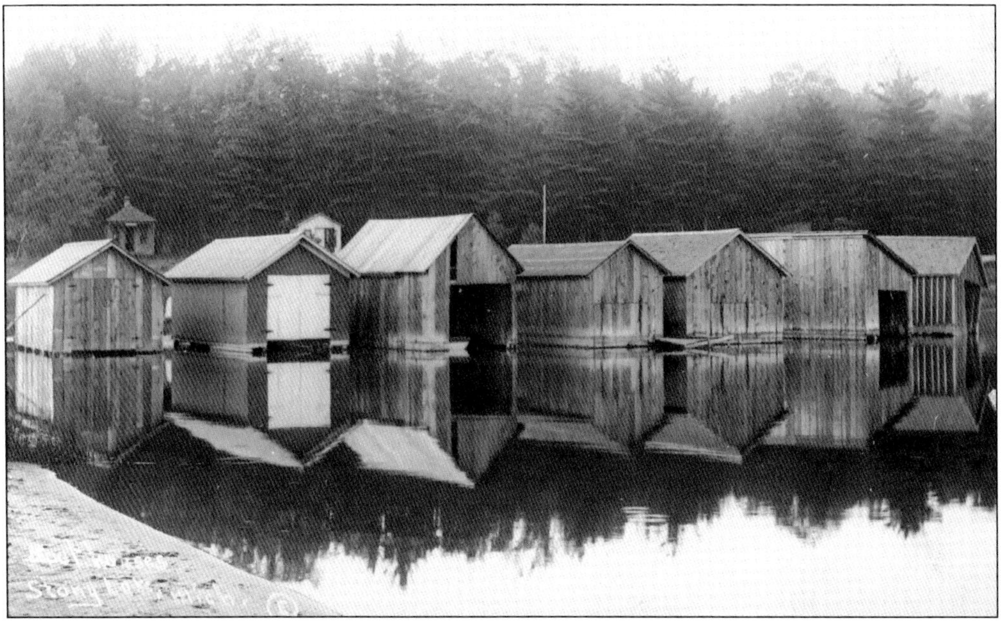

Stony Lake, Summer. After World War II, transportation and roads improved, and the resort communities developed quickly along Lake Michigan and around Stony Lake. Tourism became an industry of ever-increasing importance, and Stony Lake met with the approval of travelers seeking respite from the heat and drudgery of hectic city life as they relaxed with the cool breezes off of an idyllic lake in the north.

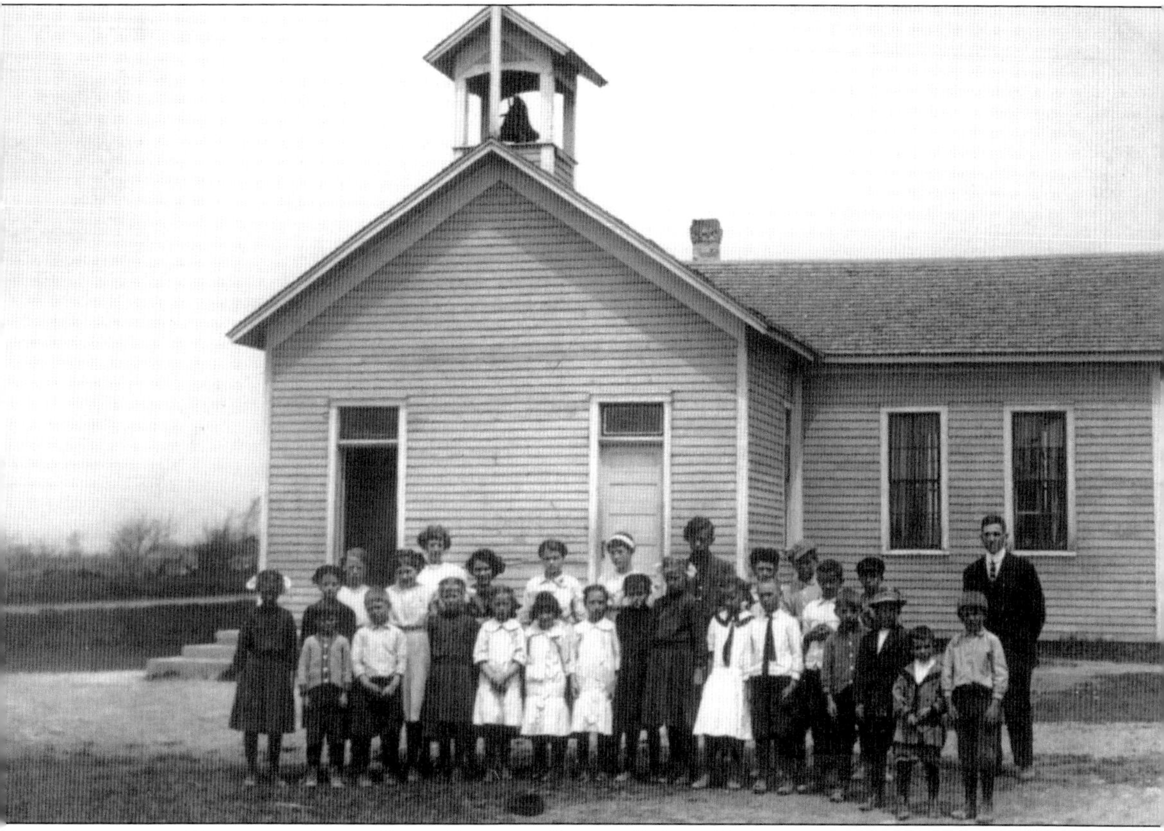

CLAYBANKS TOWNSHIP GIRDLE ROAD SCHOOL. The Girdle Road School was one of five one-room schools that operated in Claybanks until consolidation. One of the three original townships, Claybanks was an early powerhouse in the political development of Oceana County. The first county seat was established at Whiskey Creek and remained there until 1864, when it was removed to Hart. Claybanks became an agricultural center, and at one time, three post offices existed: Whiskey Creek (also known as Roseville), Flower Creek, and Holstein. The township shares Stony Lake frontage with Benona, where a thriving resort community was established. Other schools included Pine Grove, Flower Creek, Bradyville, and Green. Claybanks (named for the red clay banks) was organized by the Michigan Legislature on February 13, 1855. The first election took place on April 2, 1855. Alex .S. Anderson was elected supervisor, Timothy Brigham was elected clerk, and Thomas Phillips was elected treasurer. Claybanks Township was one of the three original townships in Oceana County, and Grant, Otto, and Greenwood Townships were set off from Claybanks. Initially, it seemed that Claybanks, the location of the first county seat in Oceana, would play a continued role in the governance of Oceana County.

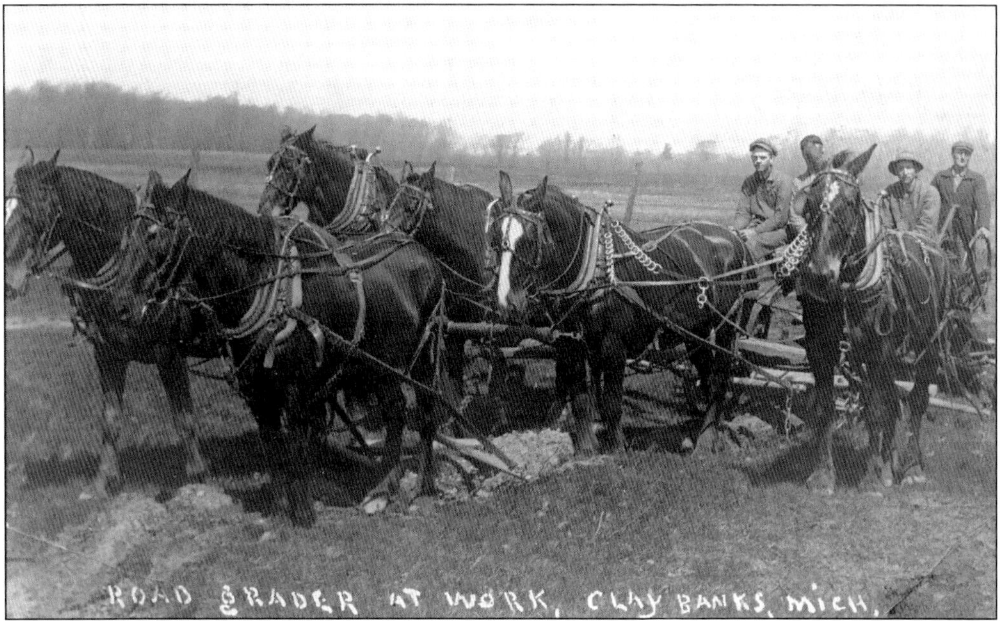

CLAYBANKS ROAD GRADER. In the early days of the county's development, creating a better system of transportation was of utmost importance. Being able to get goods to market and have them arrive intact without damage was crucial, especially in the fruit belt. Goods were perishable, and time was of great importance if the farmer were to make a profit on his labors; a good system of county roads was of tantamount importance.

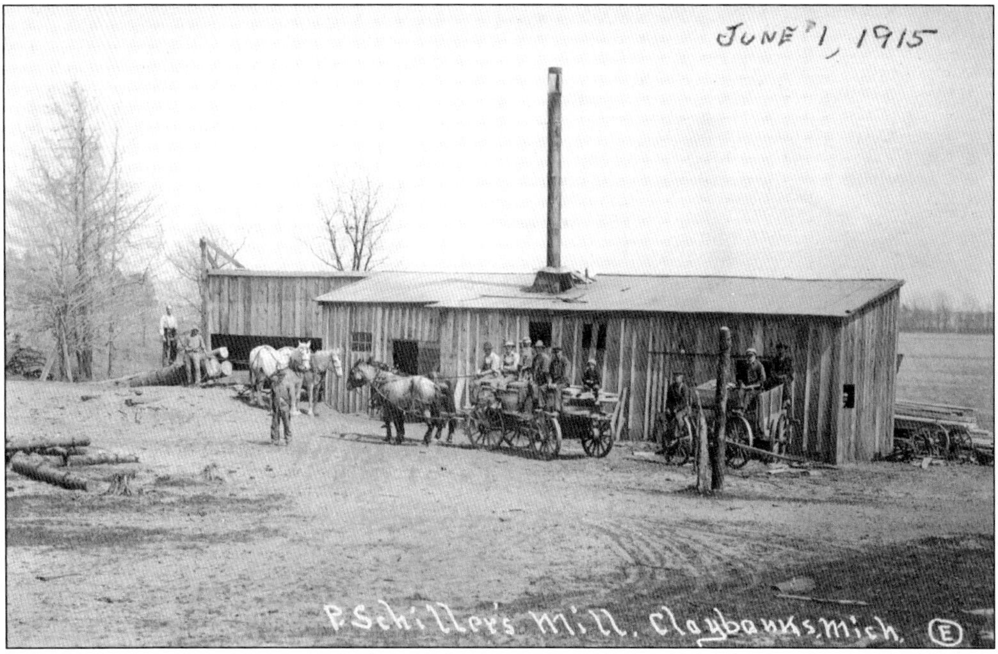

PETER SCHILLER'S MILL. Peter Schiller was born in 1872. The son of Adam and Theresa Schiller, he inherited lands purchased by his father, an early settler in the Whiskey Creek area. Peter operated the sawmill, but also, like many others in the area, farmed and maintained orchards during the summer and logged and ran the sawmill during the winter and spring.

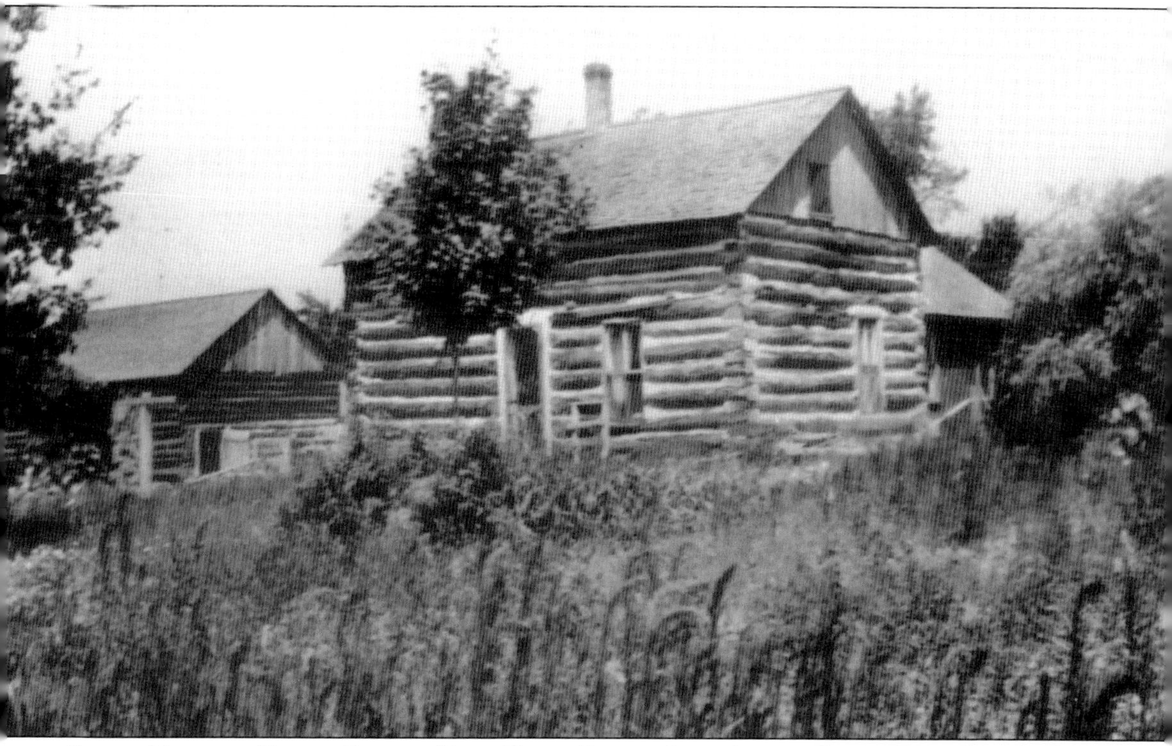

Colfax Township Potter Farm at Ruby Creek. During the early years, farmers burned much of the wood from trees felled during the clearing of their land. In 1895, Butters and Peters established the Colfax Camp and were cutting hemlock in the summer and hardwood in the winter. Many farmers sold their cut and scaled hardwood to Butters and Peters during the winter months to earn additional income. In 1868, the area known as Colfax separated from Crystal Township and, on April 1, 1869, organized as a new township, taking its name from the current vice president of the United States under Ulysses S. Grant (Schulyler Colfax). The influx of settlers that increased the population in that remote section of the county came in response to the Homestead Act of 1862, where a person could claim 160 acres of land and keep it if they lived on and developed the property for five years. After the war, western Michigan received many new settlers, often men fresh from the horrors of the Great War of the Rebellion, looking for peace and a new beginning in a new land.

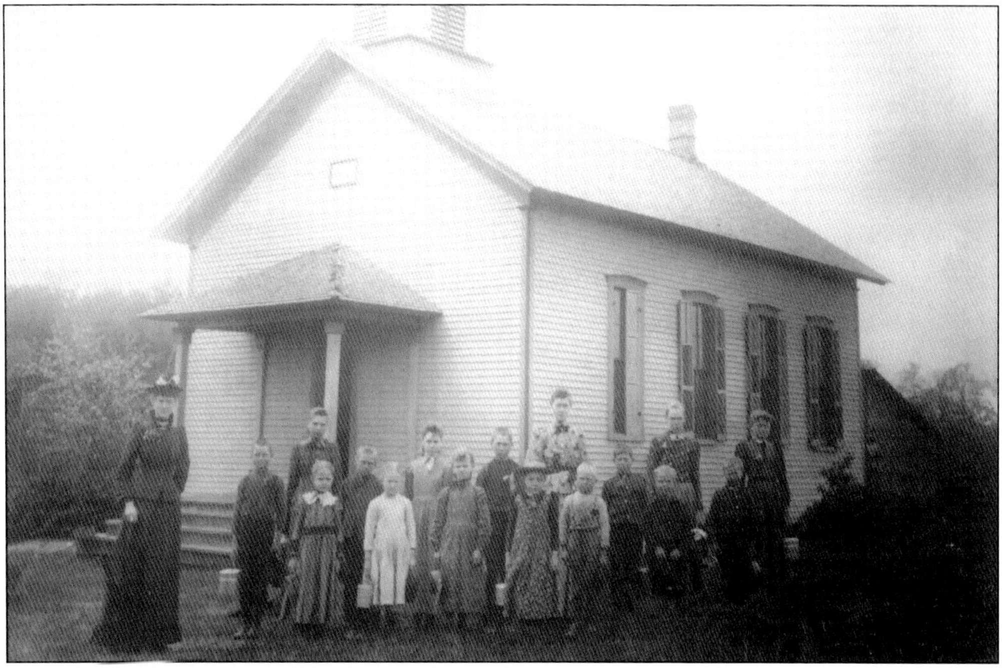

Colfax School Baldwin. One-room schools were plentiful and necessary in the rural areas. More than 80 such schools existed in Oceana County. Their placement was often dictated by which family donated the acre of land they were built on and if they were within walking distance for the students who attended. Contrary to grandparents' claims, getting there did not always require walking five miles, uphill both ways, in neck-deep snow.

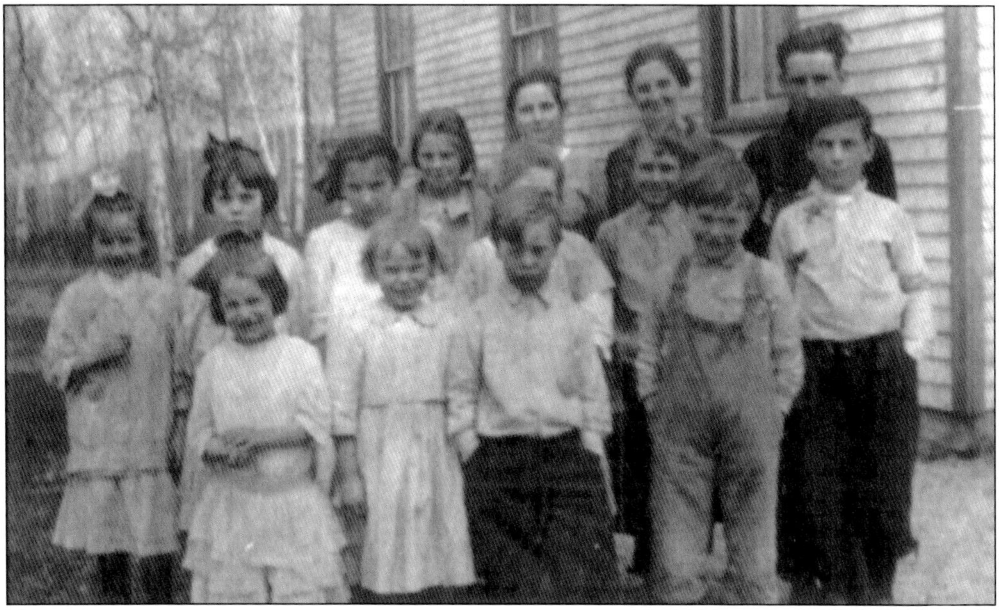

Ruby Creek School. By 1864, school districts had been organized along the lakeshore, and since community buildings were few and far between, the schoolhouse became a focal point in the community—a heart of the area where people would gather for dances, meetings, voting, and other activities that bound the residents together.

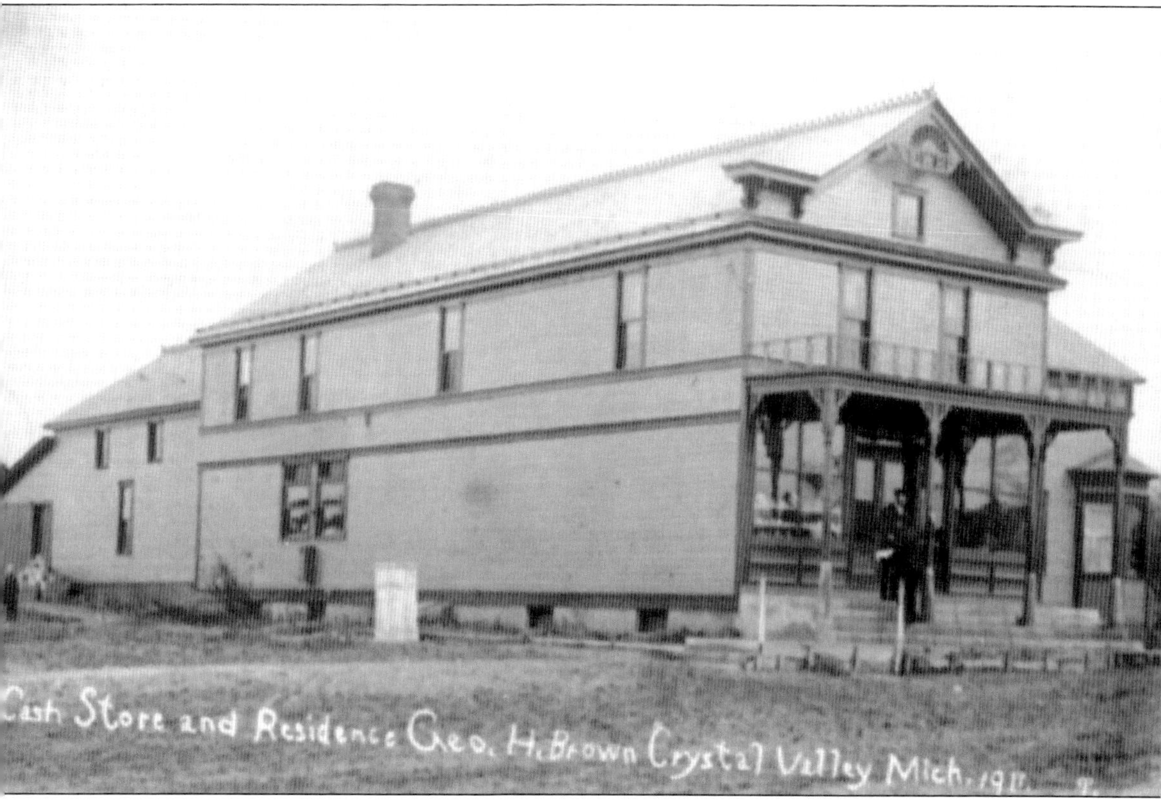

Crystal Township George Brown's Country Store. George Brown's Cash Store is seen in 1911. Crystal Township is a rural area 36 miles square and dotted with farmlands. The township has a current population of just over 800 residents. Its only present community, Crystal Valley, is unincorporated and located near Crystal Creek. Crystal Township, organized in 1865, was set off from Weare Township and originally took in the area that became Colfax in 1869. The new township included part of the reservation that had been established in 1855 for members of the Grand River Ottawa Indians. Many of the dislocated natives began to move into the area from 1856 forward and were passengers on the Propeller Mears. Buildings and meeting places were sparse in those early years of settlement, and meetings were held where any four walls and a roof would welcome them. The first meeting in Crystal Township took place in the government blacksmith shop, operated by Jared Gay, who was also the minister that provided services to the natives at the reservation.

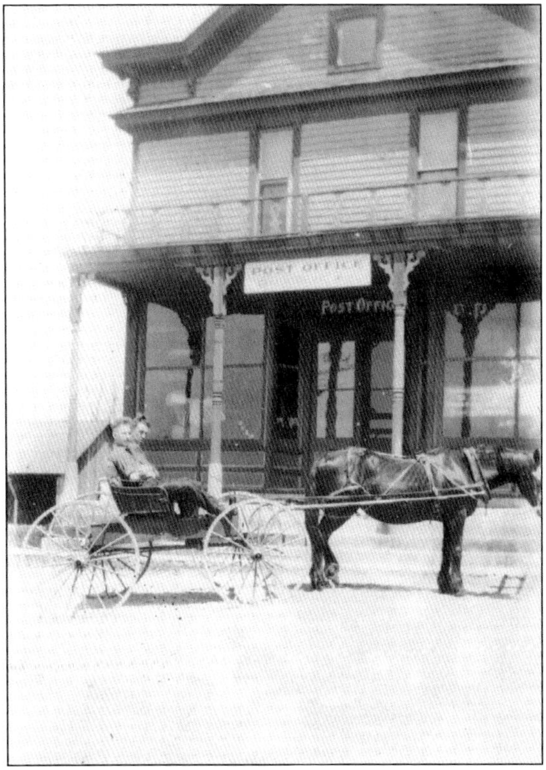

CRYSTAL VALLEY POST OFFICE. The Crystal Valley Post Office was the last to close in the township. The post office opened on July 14, 1871, and closed on February 28, 1954. Other areas represented by a post office were Peachville, on the Mason & Oceana Railroad line, and Woodburn. Catherine Gay suggested the name of Crystal in recognition of the crystal-clear stream.

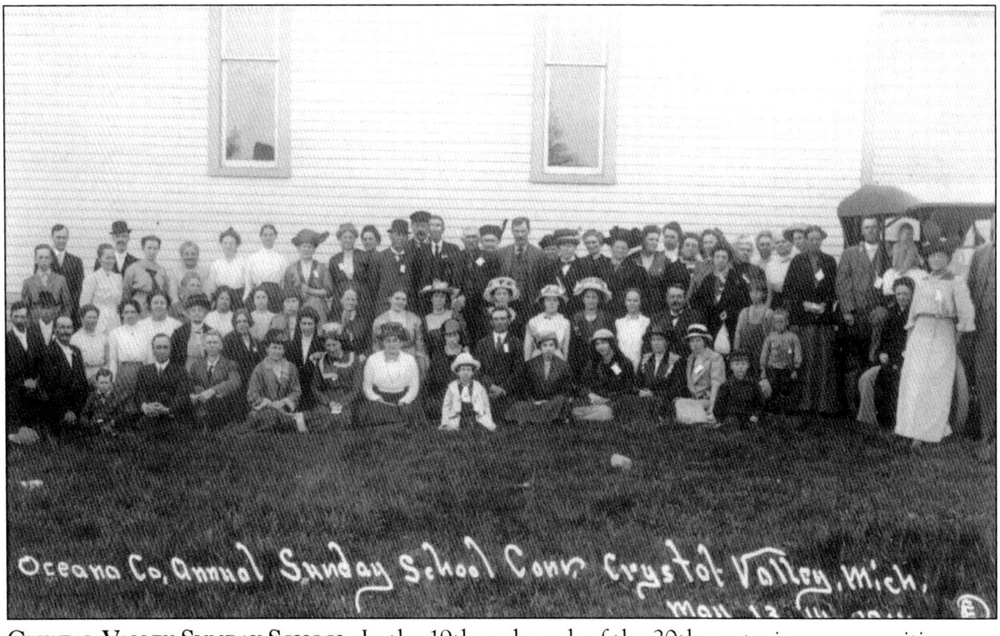

CRYSTAL VALLEY SUNDAY SCHOOL. In the 19th and much of the 20th centuries, communities were very close-knit. Church played an important role in the daily lives of residents, and attendance at church and gatherings that took place afterwards were opportunities for people to worship and catch up with each other. Families would don their Sunday best and spend their day of rest in the company of friends and neighbors.

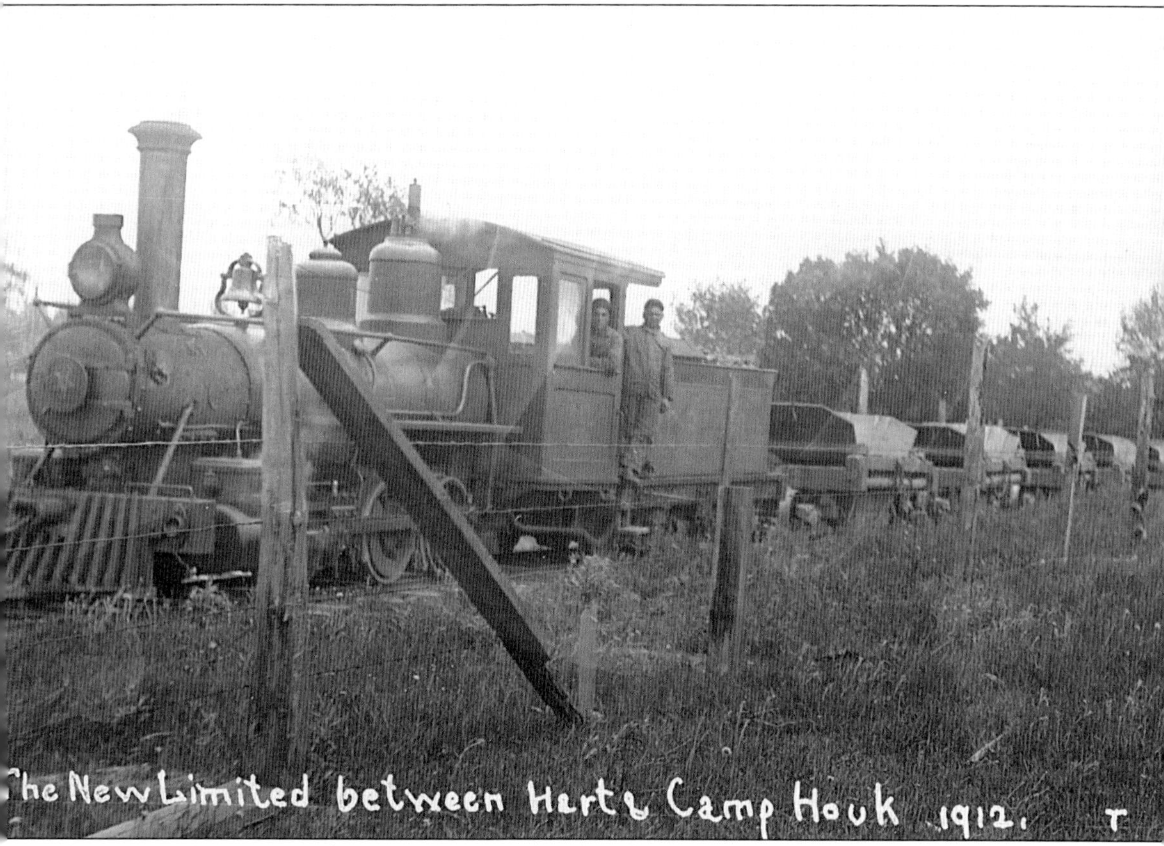

Camp Houk Reunions. The New Limited Railroad ran between Hart Michigan and Camp Houk, also known as Reunion Grounds. The camp was the site of Civil War encampments for those who served in the Grand Army of the Republic (GAR). Founded in 1882 and named after T.G. Houk in 1883, the site hosted reunions in the last week of August after the harvest was in.

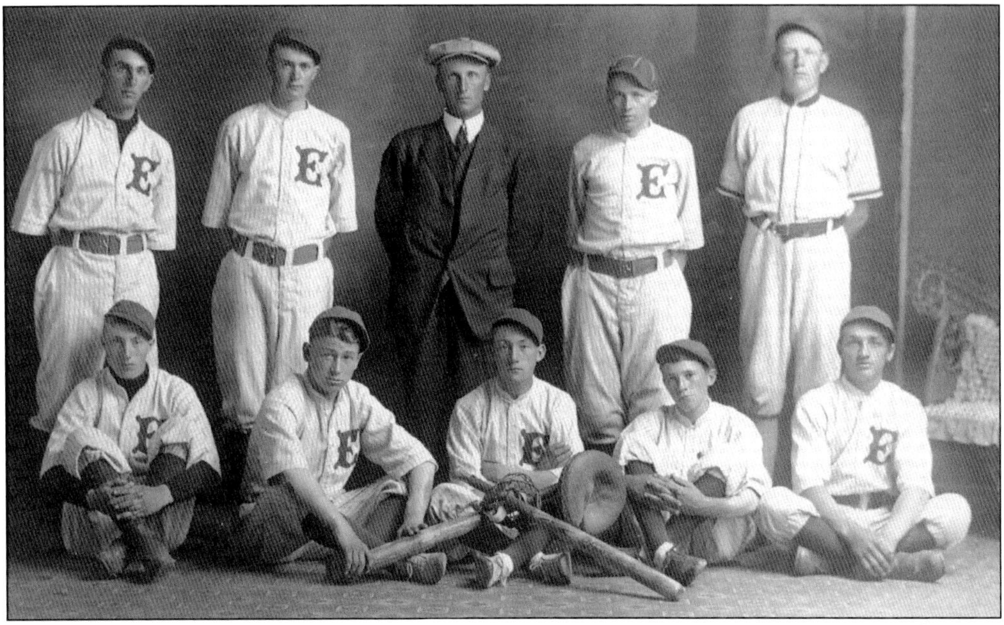

Elbridge Baseball Team. This is c. 1910 view of the Elbridge Baseball team shows them all decked out and ready to hit the field to play the Hart Invincibles. Every community had their own team, regardless of size, and they played regularly during the season with some friendly neighborly rivalry.

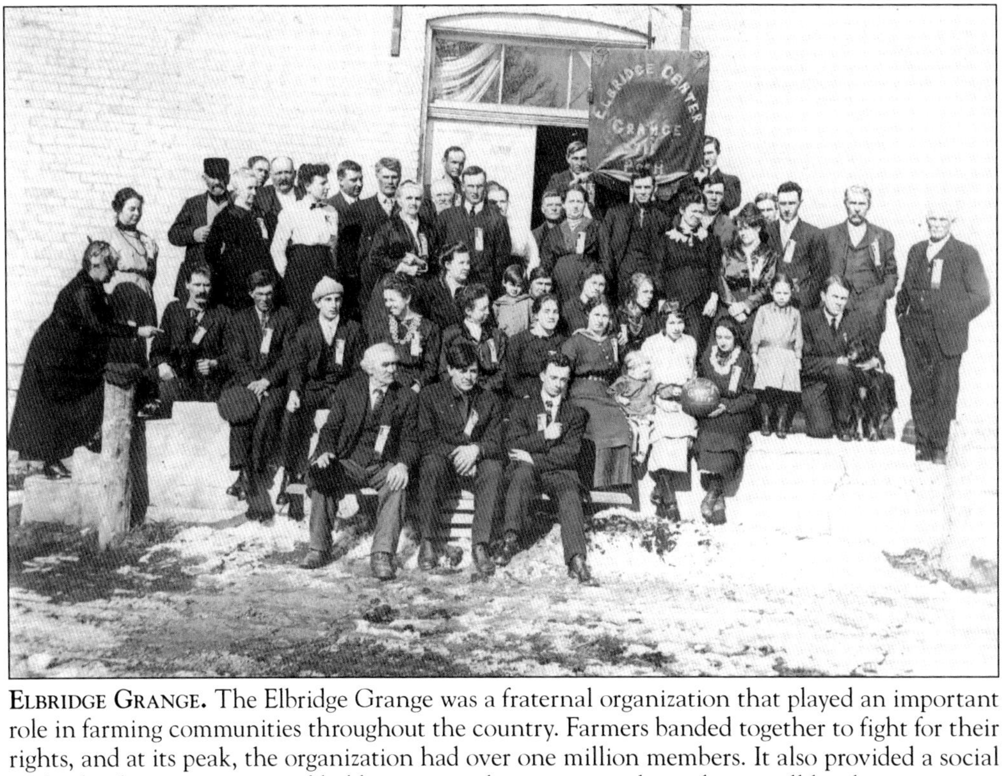

Elbridge Grange. The Elbridge Grange was a fraternal organization that played an important role in farming communities throughout the country. Farmers banded together to fight for their rights, and at its peak, the organization had over one million members. It also provided a social outlet for the community and held women and teens as equal members at all levels.

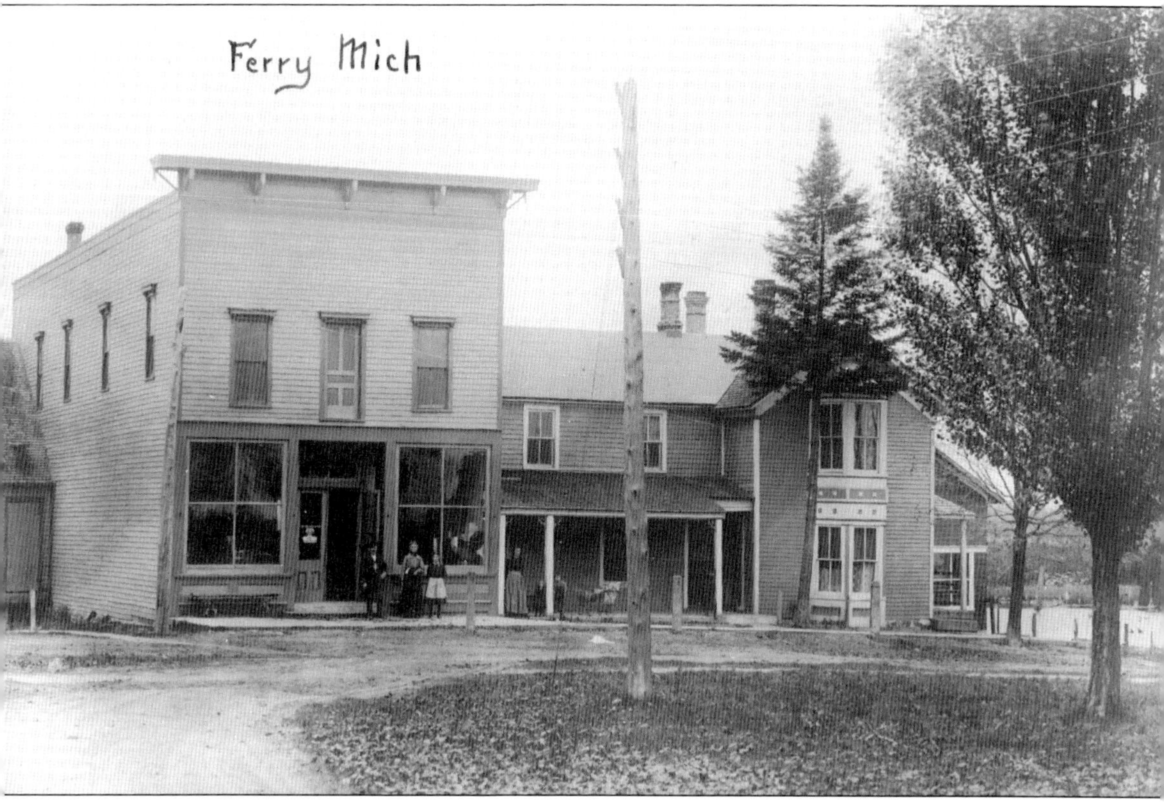

FERRY TOWNSHIP. The township originally split off from Otto as Reed Township in 1858 by a petition submitted by the Elnathan Reed family. Although the first to settle in the area in 1957, Elnathan Reed remained until 1875, when he sold his properties there and moved back to New York State. The name of the township and village was soon changed in honor of Sen. Thomas W. Ferry. Ferry, a reverend, and his family had been early developers in the area, having purchased land near Stony Creek as early as 1847. By 1849, the reverend and his son Thomas had purchased 1,300 acres. In 1850, they established the first mill in Oceana County, and within two years, Reverend Ferry's son Thomas had made the decision to run for senate, so the family liquidated their holdings in the area. Ferry Township is primarily an agricultural and rural community located south of Elbridge.

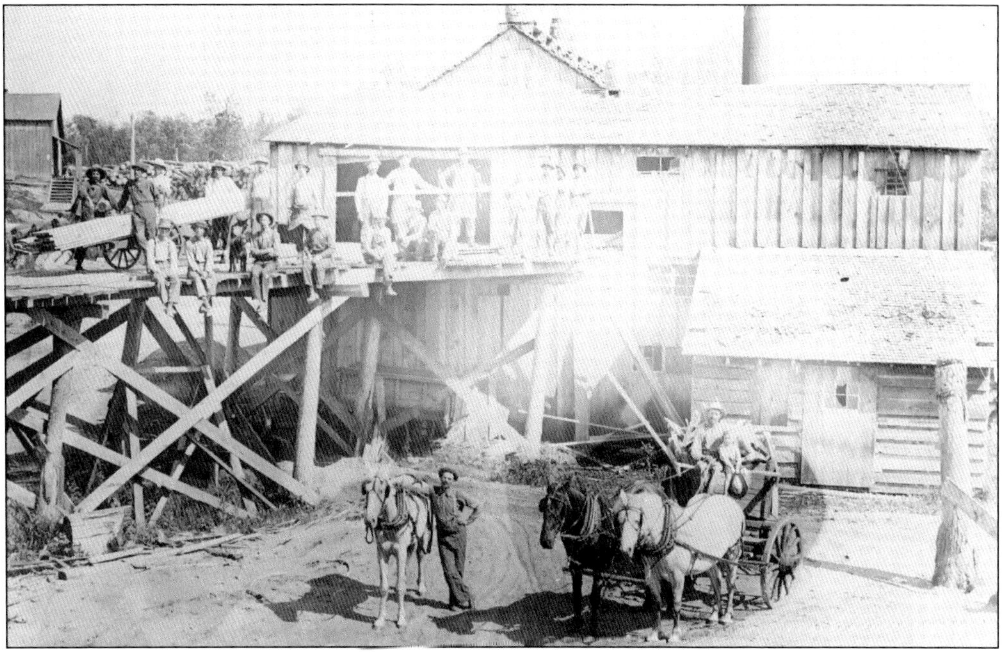

SAWMILL AT FERRY. The eastern and northern portion of the county were said to be populated with white pine, and the areas nearer to the lake were hardwood stands of Beech and Oak. Sawmills sprang up throughout Oceana County, and as timber was harvested, orchards and farms took their place. Often because of the fire danger, barrels of water would be filled on the roofs of mills such as this and could be tipped when water was needed to help contain a fire.

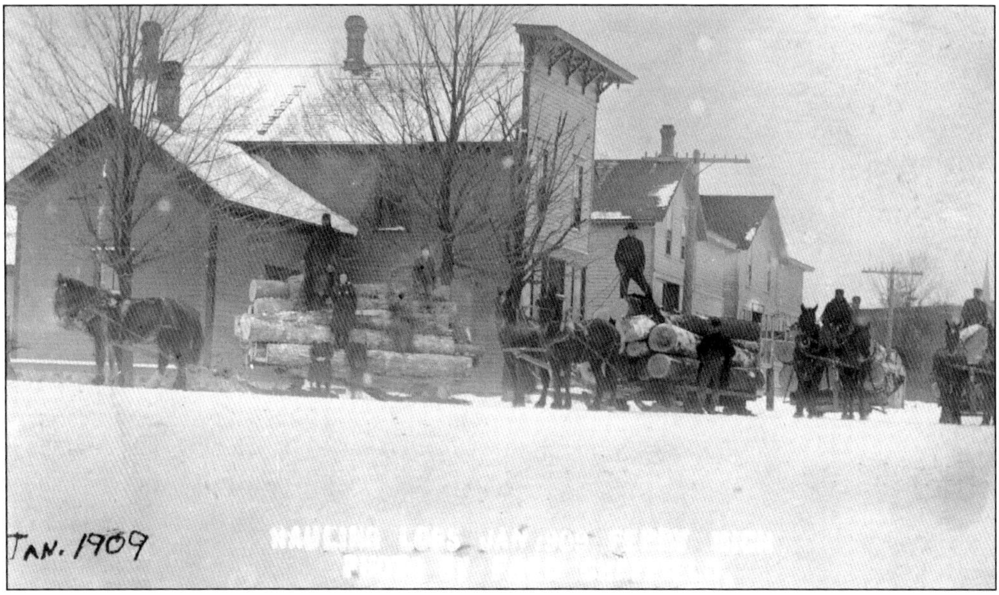

HAULING LOGS AT FERRY. In this 1909 photograph by Fred Chatfield, one can see clearly how logs were transported in the winter months. The ice and snow made it easier to move the large logs to the mill on sleighs. Summer transportation of the logs was much more difficult until Silas Overpack of Manistee invented his Big Wheels and Horace Butters of Buttersville invented his Steam Skidder.

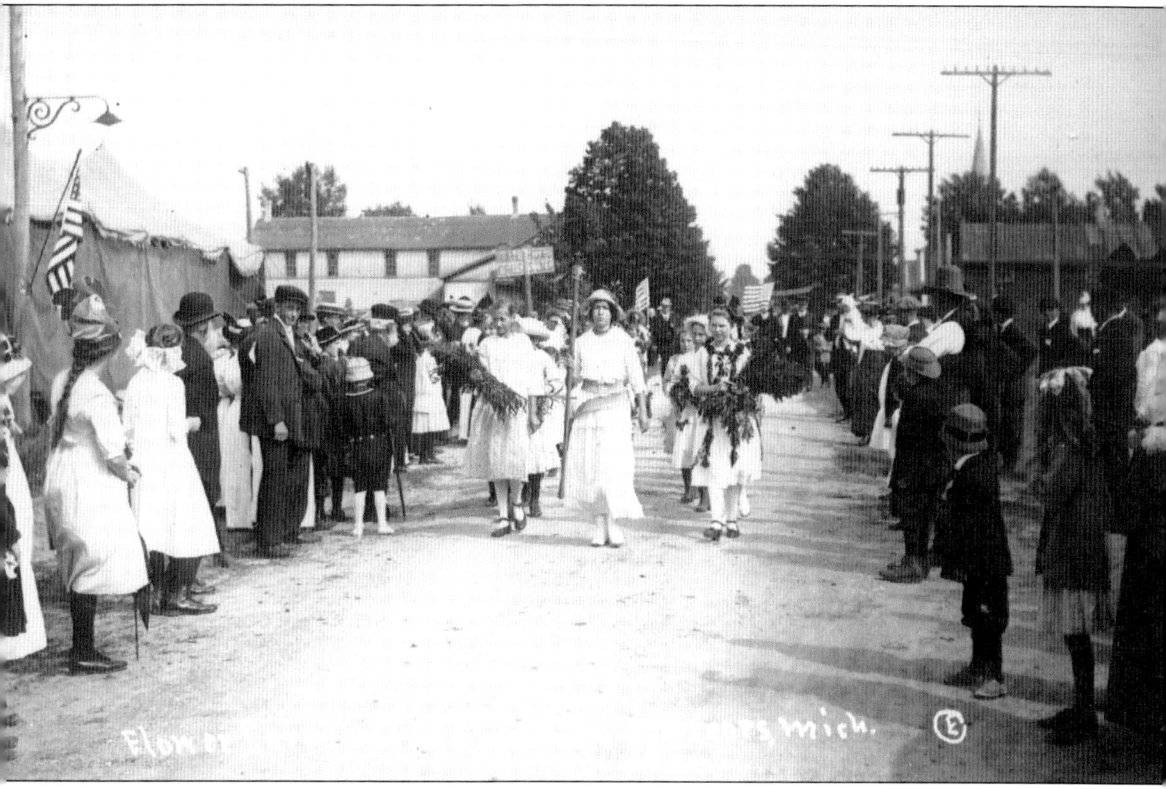

FLOWER CARNIVAL, GOLDEN TOWNSHIP. These young ladies are marching down the lane in this c. 1910 view of the Flower Festival. Alice Wright Fuller is to the left of the woman in the hat with the staff. This image was taken by Oceana photographer Harlo Elliott. Mears hosted the annual Golden Fair in the fall, in which all township schools would compete to create the best display. Originally split off from Hart Township in 1864, and named Golding after the mother of William Haughey, an error in spelling resulted in the township retaining the name of Golden. Primarily a logging and an agricultural community in its early development, Golden is home to the village of Mears and Silver Lake. The area surrounding the lake has prospered as a resort community and has many recreational outlets, including the famous Mac Wood's dune buggies, which lease a portion of the Silver Lake State Park and offer rides in the scenic dunes. People travel from great distances to have access to the dunes in the all-terrain state park at Silver Lake and drive their own buggies on the dunes overlooking Lake Michigan.

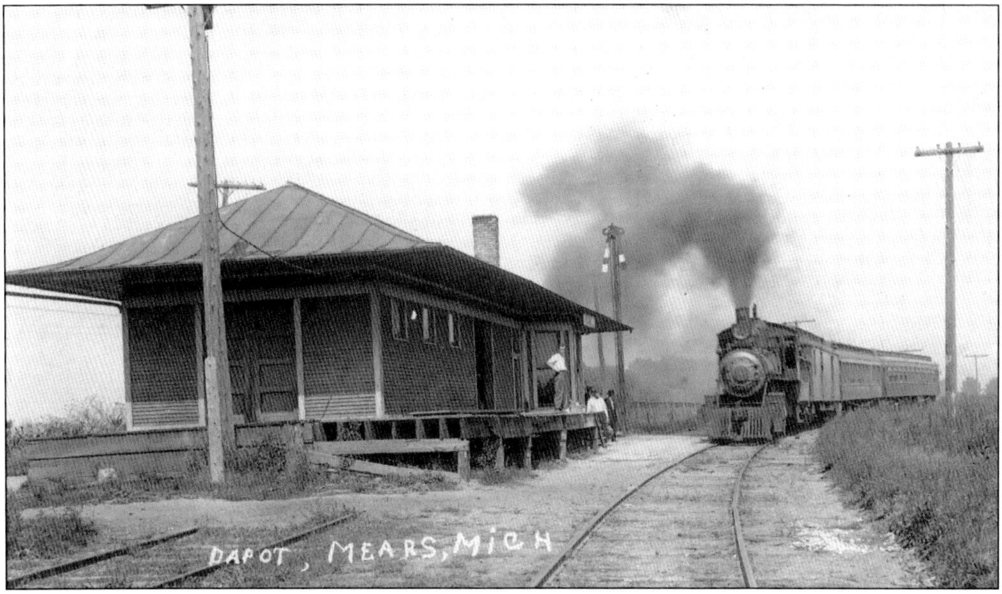

MEARS TRAIN DEPOT. Mears had a rail line and depot before Hart, and in an effort to stave off continued attempts by Charles Mears and pressure from Shelby and Pentwater to have the county seat removed from Hart, businessmen there donated $12,000 to build a railroad spur to Hart. The arrival of the railroad in Mears helped to firmly establish the community and was responsible for much of the growth and development.

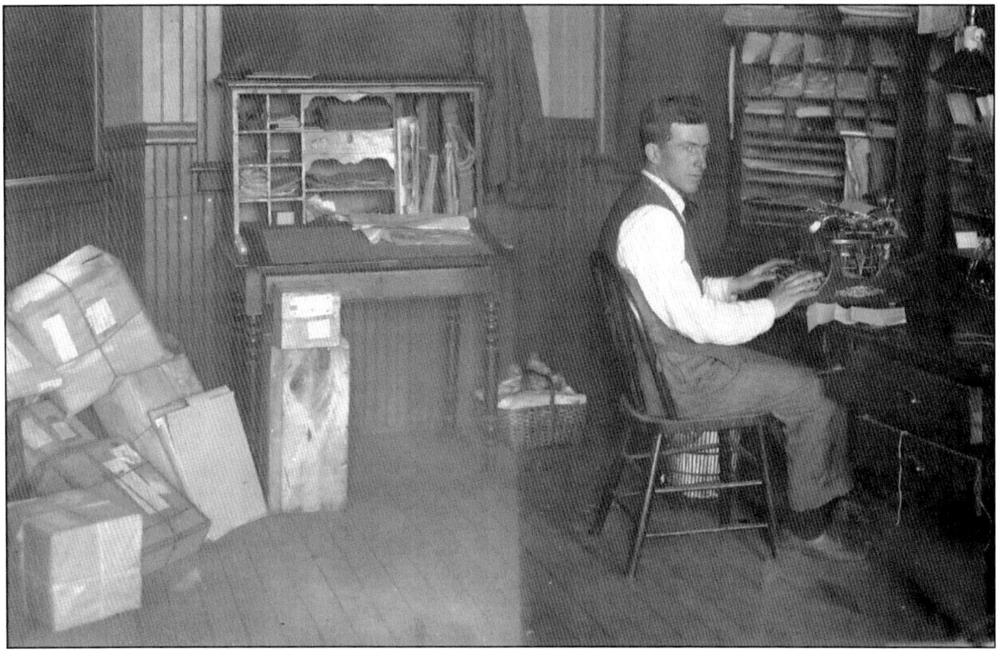

INTERIOR OF MEARS DEPOT. Photographs of the interior of train depots are rare. The depots provided a place where passengers could purchase tickets and freight could be loaded and unloaded on the platform. Most every town, village, and spot on the line had a depot, although many were crude and without amenities. While many disappeared with their communities, others remained as landmarks.

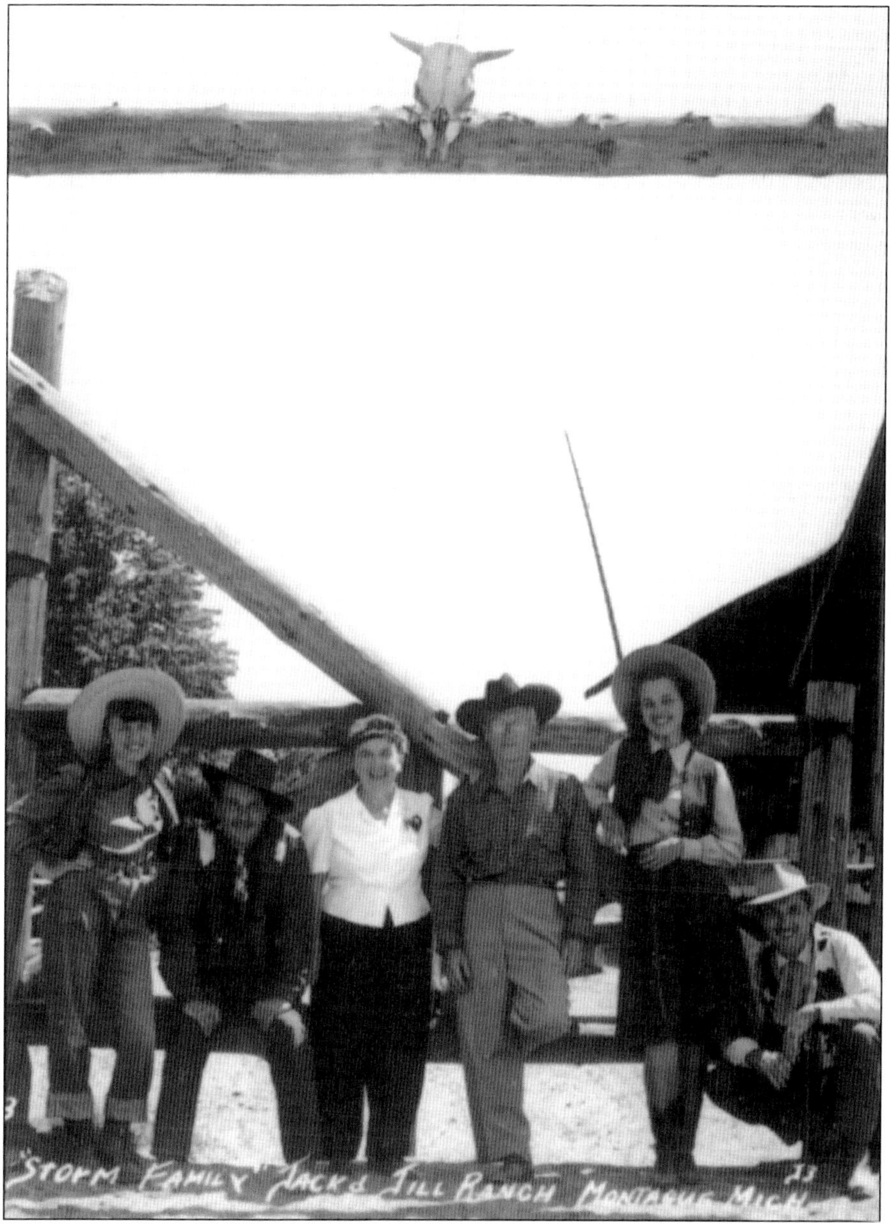

Grant Township Jack and Jill Ranch. The Storm family is shown here at the Jack and Jill Ranch around 1950. Originally a Girl Scout camp, George Storm made a decision to convert the camp to a resort in 1937. The resort became a local landmark steeped in the memories of visitors and employees for decades. The Double JJ Resort has been a part of the Oceana County tourist scene for over 70 years. The first permanent settler in Grant Township, Fernando Seaver arrived in 1851. The township itself (as Grant) was not organized until 1866. The timing of the organization and subsequent naming of many Michigan communities after the Civil War retain names given in honor of major figures in the War of the Rebellion. Grant Township was so named after general and soon-to-be-president Ulysses S. Grant in 1866, in part because some of the settlers had fought in the Great War of the Rebellion under Grant. The first township election saw Oliver White elected as supervisor, Jason Carpenter as clerk, and Henry Turk as treasurer.

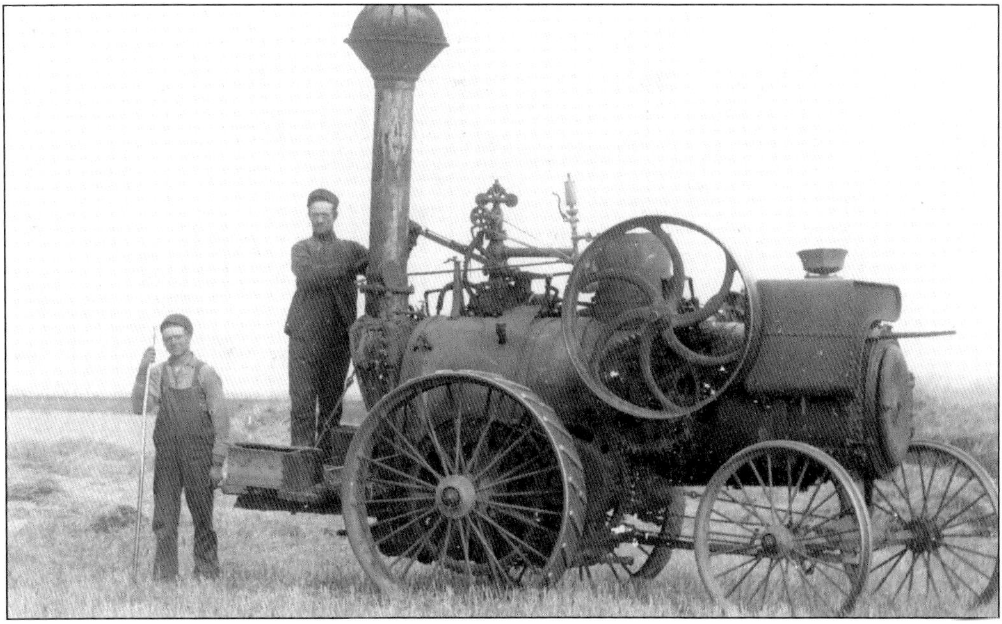

STEAM TRACTORS BRING CHANGES. When steam tractors such as this came into the farming community, production increased and the plowing of fields and harvesting of crops started to become more mechanized. The steam-driven tractor was doomed though, as the ease of use of gasoline-driven tractors became a dominating factor in the market. Steam did find its niche in driving threshing belts, further displacing the use of horses in day-to-day farming.

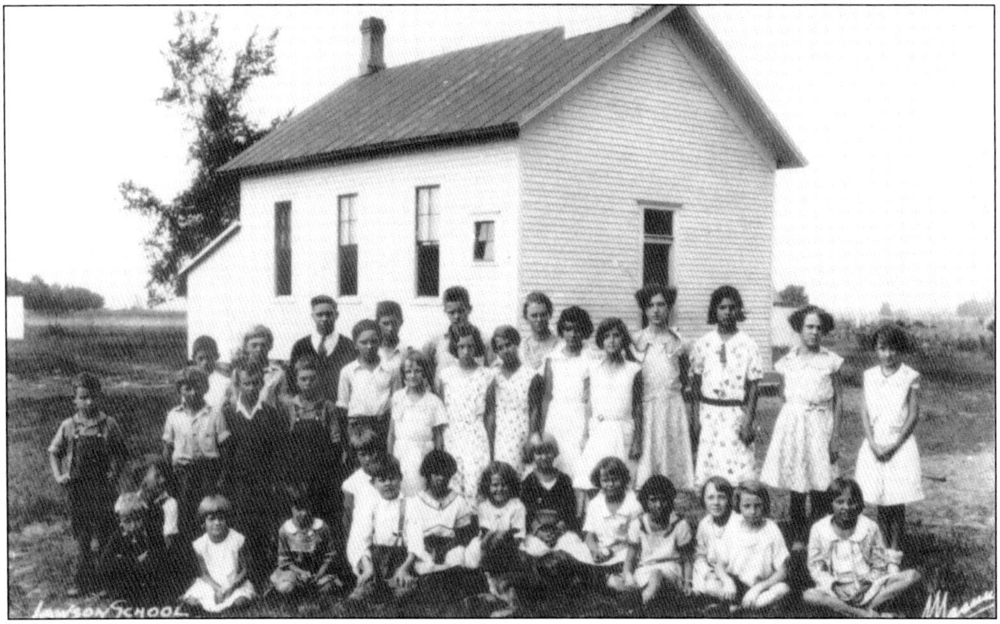

LAWSON SCHOOL ASSEMBLY. Students and their teacher are assembled outside of the Lawson School, just outside of the village of Rothbury, around 1925. Originally known as the Mears School (after Albert Mears) when organized in the 1870s, the building was replaced in 1888 and remained in use until 1951. The name was changed to Lawson School after Phillip Lawson purchased the land surrounding the school building in the early 1900s.

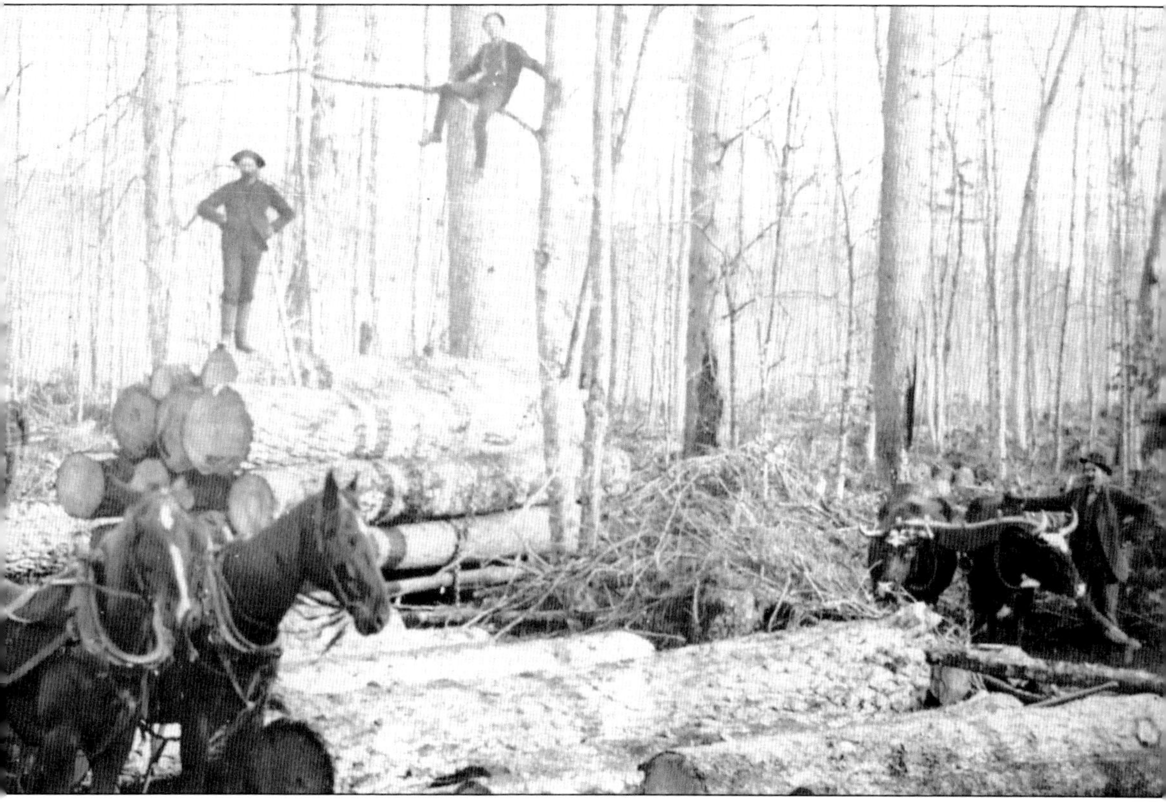

GREENWOOD TOWNSHIP LOGGING. Soon after Henry Clark settled in 1855, loggers started moving north into the rich timberlands of Greenwood Township. The township of Greenwood was the first township organized on February 1, 1858, by the county supervisors, and on April 5, 1858, the first meeting was held at the home of William Wilson. (Elbridge was organized the same day.) The election results included Oliver Swain as supervisor; Cyrus W. Bullen as clerk; C.B. Moe as treasurer; O. Swain, Nelson Wright, C.W. Bullen, and Amos S. Wright as justices; Benjamin Ish and Samuel C. Wood as directors of the poor; Lachlan MeCallum, Lyman Brown, and B. Moe as constables; and O. Swain and N. Wright as school inspectors. The township is home to Forest City, Hazel Grove, and Krain City, all communities that either never prospered or never came to be, such as Krain City. There were two names submitted for consideration in naming the township, with Greenwood winning over Oliver. At the time Greenwood was organized, it was somewhat isolated, and settlers had the option of coming into the township through Newaygo overland or by having pole boats bring them down the White River.

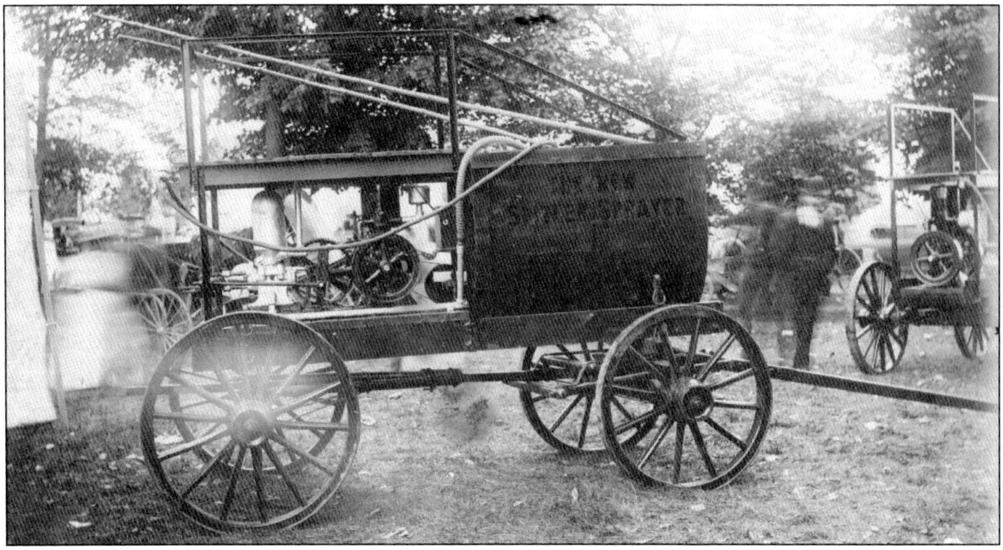

COLBY SPITLER AGRICULTURAL SPRAYER. The Colby Spitler Company of Hart touts its new sprayer to help mechanize and simplify the care of local orchards. By the 1890s, most aspects of mechanizing farm duties were being developed. Fewer man-hours were required to produce crops, as the cream separator was in wide usage, steam tractors were beginning to replace raw horsepower, and by 1910, gas-powered tractors were common. Farmers readily utilized new forms of mechanization and commercial fertilizer to improve yields.

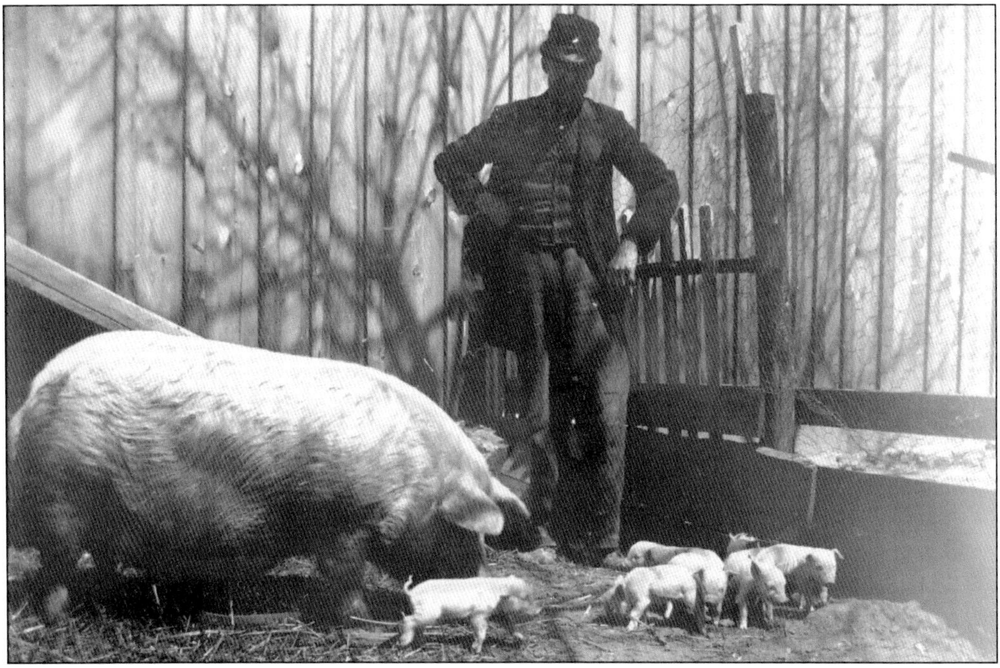

FARMER AND HIS PIGS. The first purebred Essex hog was brought into Oceana County by H. Tower in 1868. Livestock was an important piece of the agricultural commodities in the county, and some farmers were known to have paid as much as $1,000 for a purebred sire. Sheep raising was also on the rise. In 1882, one herd of 1,000 sheep produced 3,275 pounds of wool, which brought in $1,000.

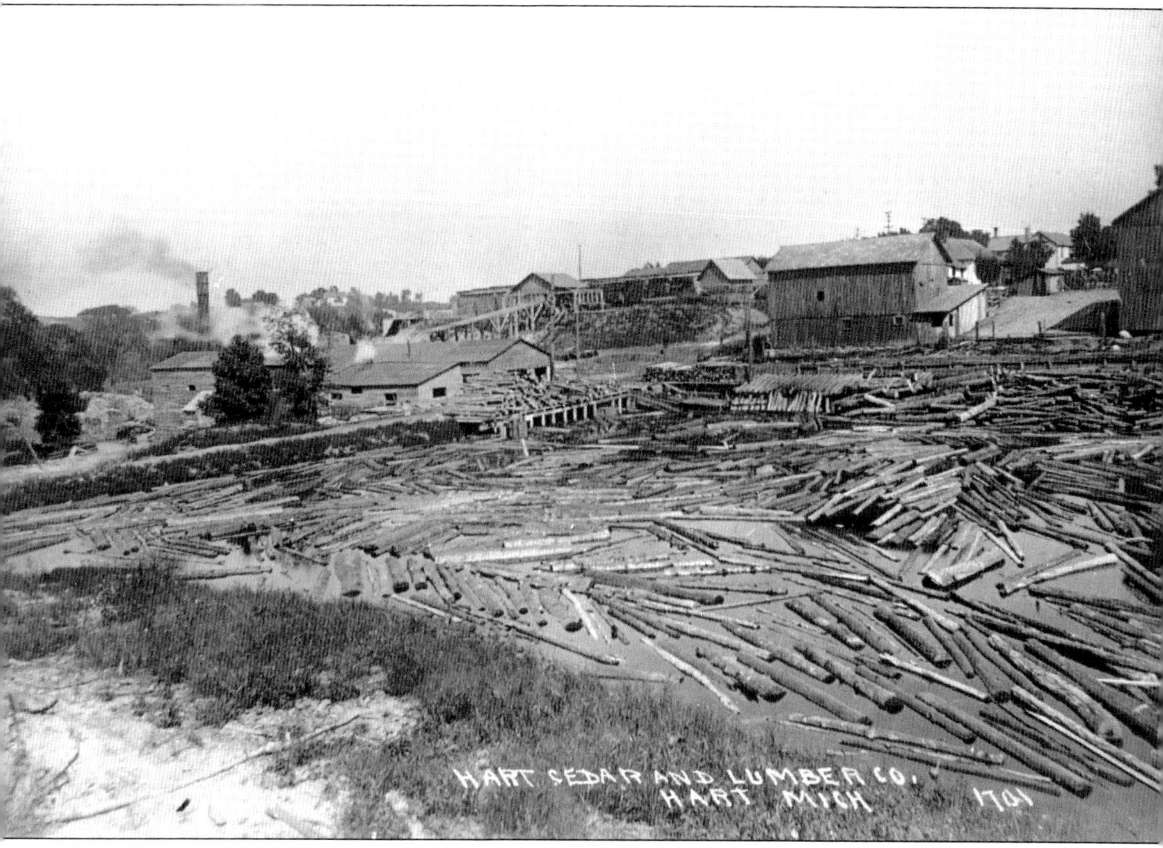

HART CEDAR AND LUMBER COMPANY. The Hart Cedar and Lumber Company, located just north of Main Street in Hart, has a full holding pond of lumber ready for the sawmill. A curious fact is that logs would pile up on each other in the lakes and ponds and drive full logs down into mud, where many remain to this day. In 1860, an application to form Hart Township was approved by the commissioners but not without contest, as a group of Elbridge residents petitioned to have the vote to create the township rescinded. The township of Hart was organized on April 9, 1861, and the first election was held at the schoolhouse, where A.W. Peck (supervisor) and C.W. Wilson (treasurer) were elected to office. By 1869, all 16 townships in Oceana County were organized under their current names and boundaries. The village of Hart did not have a hotel until 1883, but by 1889, Hart had two opera houses: the Palmiter and the Slayton. In 1893, an ordinance was passed to prohibit swine, sheep, cattle, horses, and mules from running free on village streets.

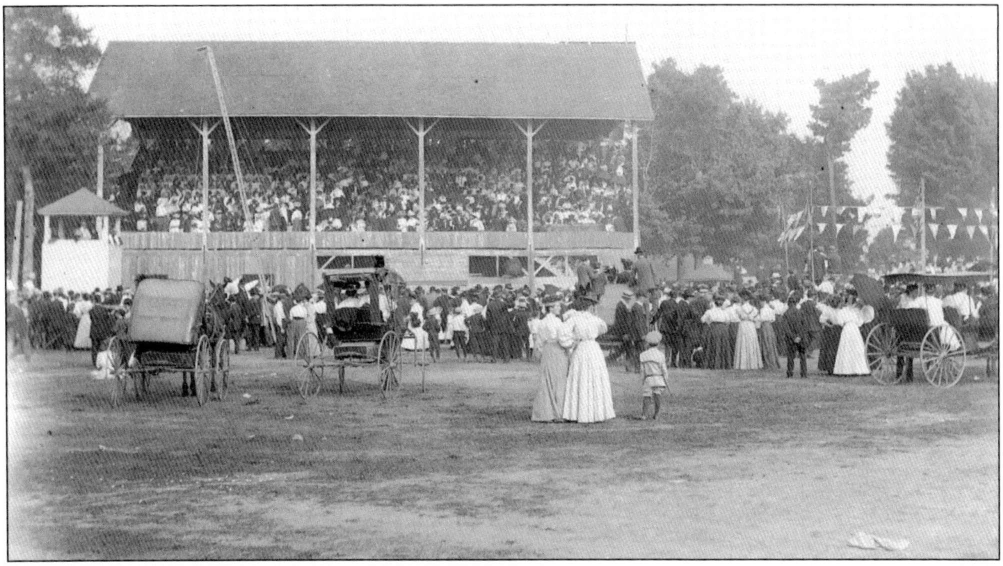

Hart Fair Draws a Crowd. The Oceana County Fair board was organized in February 1870, and the first fair was held on September 24 and 25, 1872. The grandstand is filled to capacity as the crowd awaits a well-anticipated event (possibly baseball) in this c. 1903 view of the fairgrounds. The Oceana County Fair continues to draw large crowds every summer for the exhibits and rides.

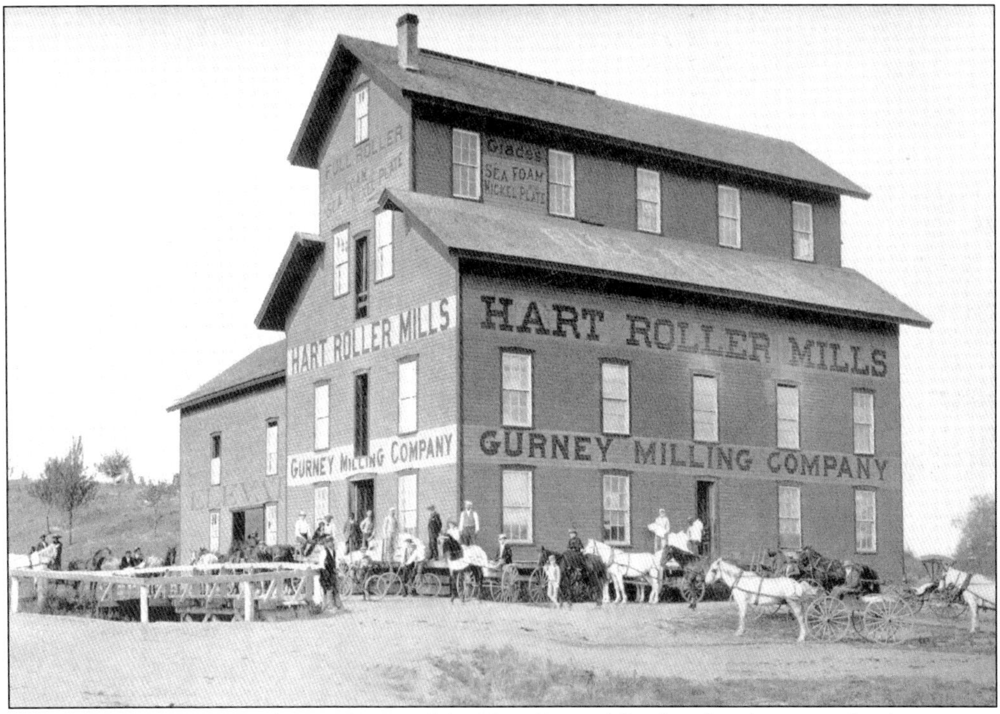

A Gristmill Portrait. The employees of the Hart Grist Mill take a break to pose for the camera. The gristmill existed before the birth of Christ and underwent few changes in 2,000 years, coming into the 19th century. The term *Miller's Toll* refers to the percentage of the ground flour or corn that was kept by the miller in lieu of wages. This arrangement worked well in an era where coins and currency were often scarce.

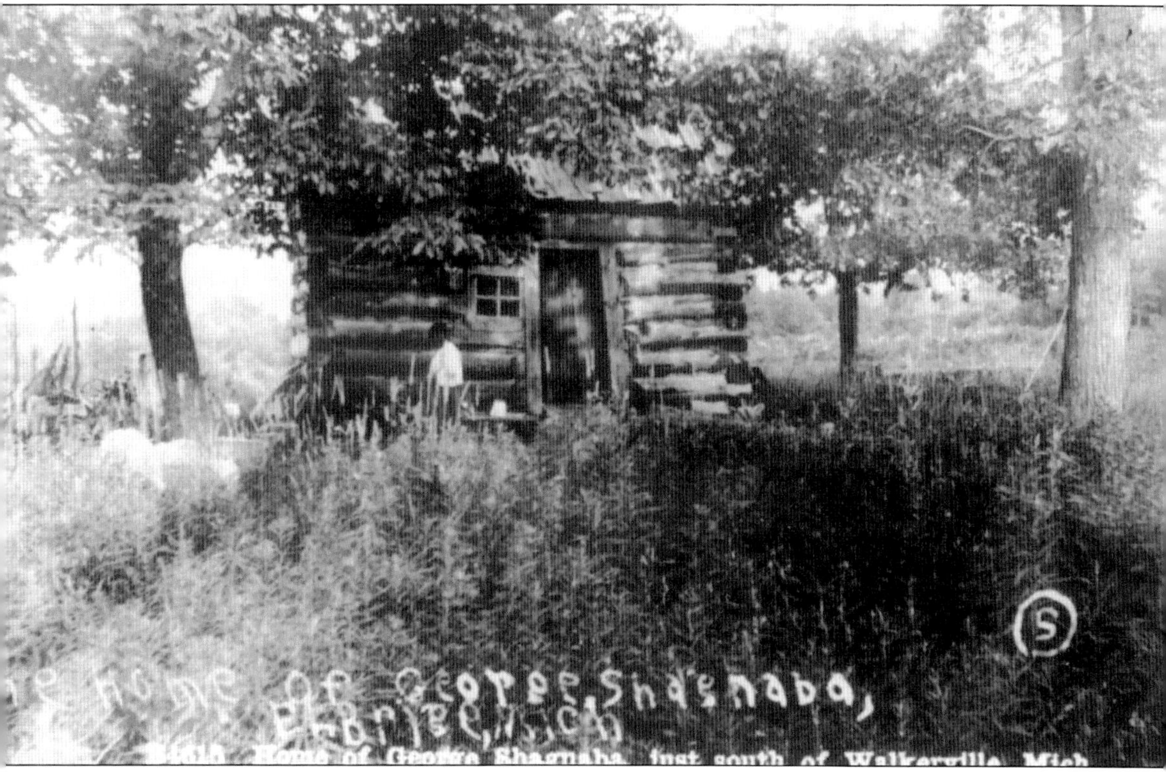

HOME OF GEORGE SHAGNABA. Hazen Leavitt was the first settler of European origin to come to what would be named Leavitt Township. Hazen arrived in 1864 with his wife and young son Worter. After the establishment of his homestead, Hazen took his grain to the gristmill at Shelby, a round-trip journey that took three days. Leavitt Township was organized in 1866, and the first election took place the following spring at the home of R.R. Sorter. That first election saw Vincent E. Clark elected as supervisor, Valentine Carpenter as clerk, and Rufus J. Carpenter as treasurer. In 1883, Fayette Walker platted the village of Walkerville in spite of the odds against him for being successful. Nearby, a general store had already been established, but once platted, Leavitt was able to begin selling lots, and a village was born out of the sand and swamp. The rustic log home of Native American George Shagnaba is located just south of Walkerville, Michigan.

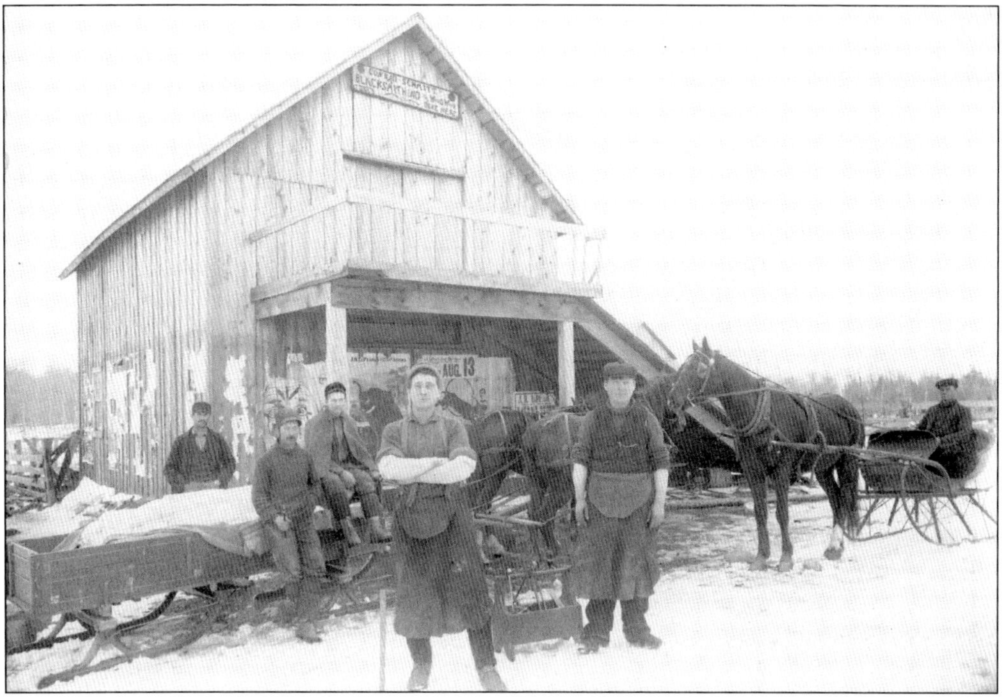

CONRAD SCHMIDT BLACKSMITH SHOP. The blacksmith was an important person in every community they set up shop in and provided a needed service to local farmers and businessmen. The blacksmith's skills were critical in that they could generally repair anything made of metal. They kept the farmer plowing, horses shod, and wagons rolling. It wasn't until after the horseless carriage came about that blacksmiths started to fade from the landscape.

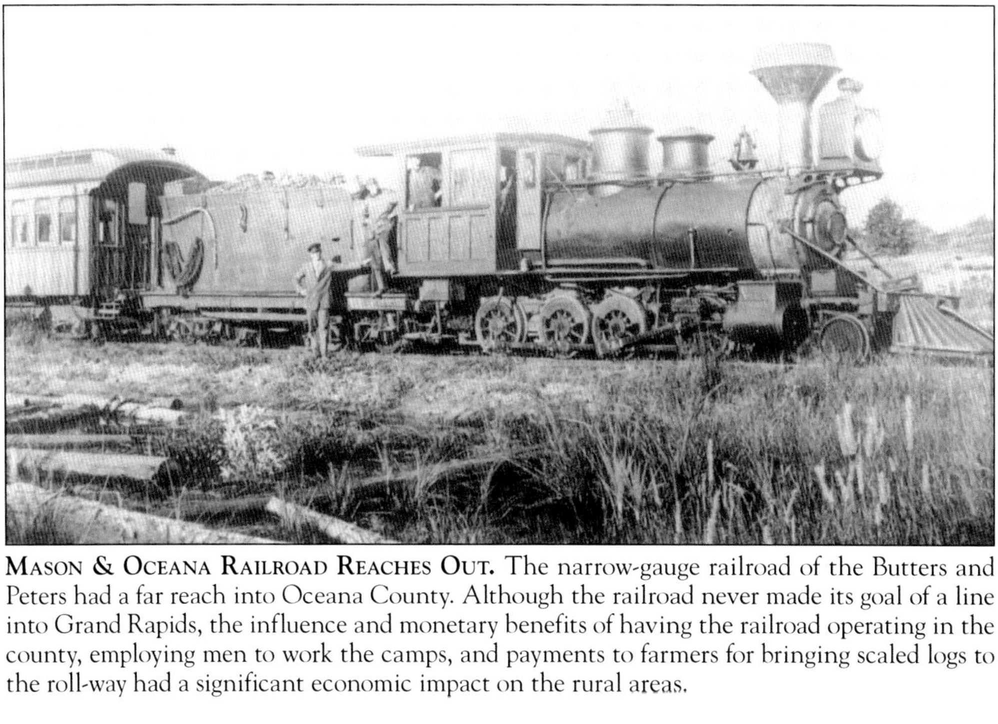

MASON & OCEANA RAILROAD REACHES OUT. The narrow-gauge railroad of the Butters and Peters had a far reach into Oceana County. Although the railroad never made its goal of a line into Grand Rapids, the influence and monetary benefits of having the railroad operating in the county, employing men to work the camps, and payments to farmers for bringing scaled logs to the roll-way had a significant economic impact on the rural areas.

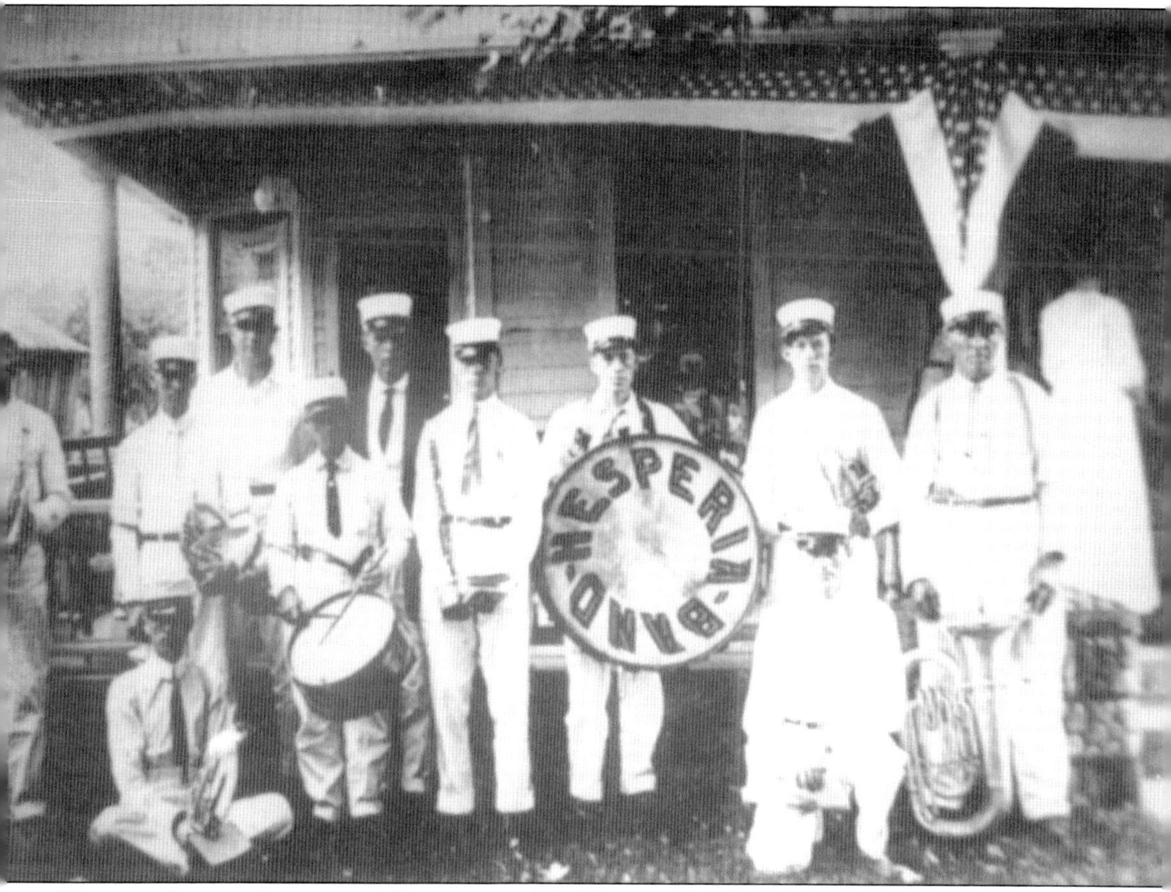

HESPERIA BAND IS ASSEMBLED. This picture of the Hesperia Band was taken in front of the home of Etta Seymour on Division Street in Hesperia. During the Industrial Age, hours were long and hard; not much time was available for recreational pursuits. Many mill owners, however, came to support the idea of the community band as a means of a positive pursuit that provided employees with a much needed respite from the grueling hours and demanding work they were subject to. One of the interesting oddities about Hesperia is that it was built on the dividing line between Oceana and Newaygo Counties. The first log house in Hesperia was constructed on the Newaygo side of the dividing line. The first settler in Newfield Township was Booth Perry, who came about 1857. He cleared his land and, shortly afterwards, sold out. He returned in 1858 with two friends from back East: Alex McLaren and Patrick McFarland. At the time that they purchased land in 1858, the selling price was 75¢ an acre. A 160-acre homestead could be bought for $120.

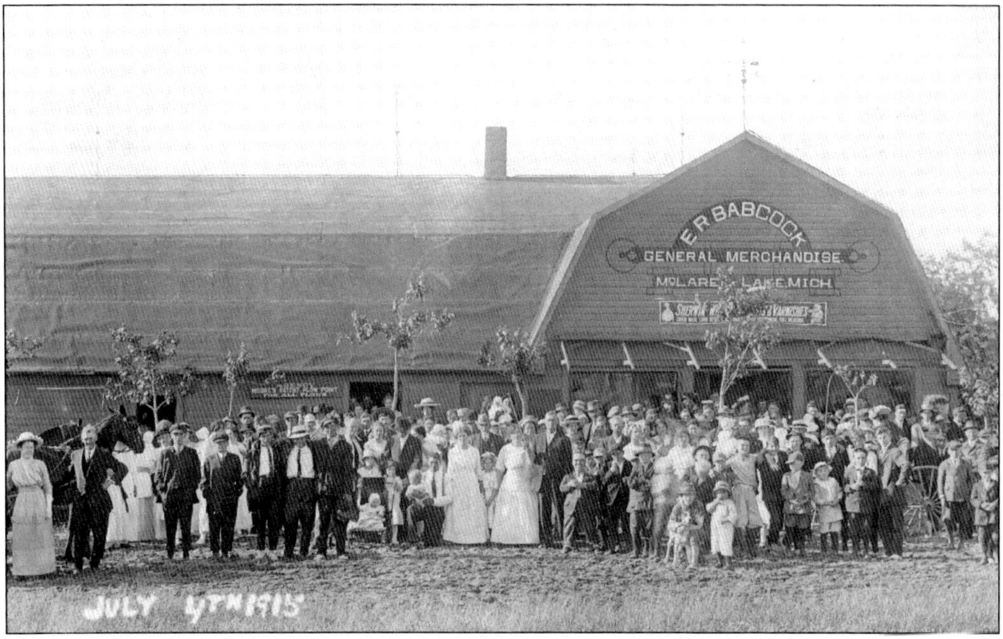

McClaren Lake Booster Club Celebration. McLaren Lake is located four miles northwest of Hesperia and was named after Alexander McLaren, a Scottish immigrant who came to Oceana County in 1858 to homestead in White River Country. This view shows residents and visitors of McClaren Lake on July 4, 1915, in front of the E.R. Babcock Store.

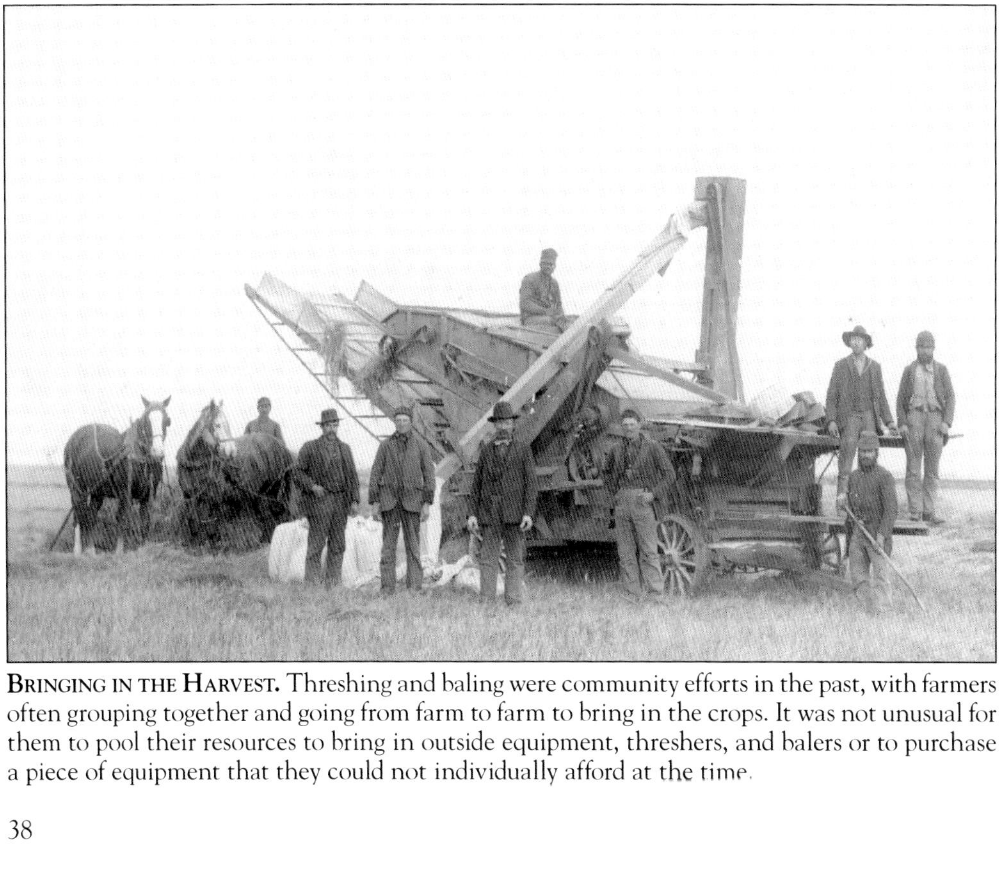

Bringing in the Harvest. Threshing and baling were community efforts in the past, with farmers often grouping together and going from farm to farm to bring in the crops. It was not unusual for them to pool their resources to bring in outside equipment, threshers, and balers or to purchase a piece of equipment that they could not individually afford at the time.

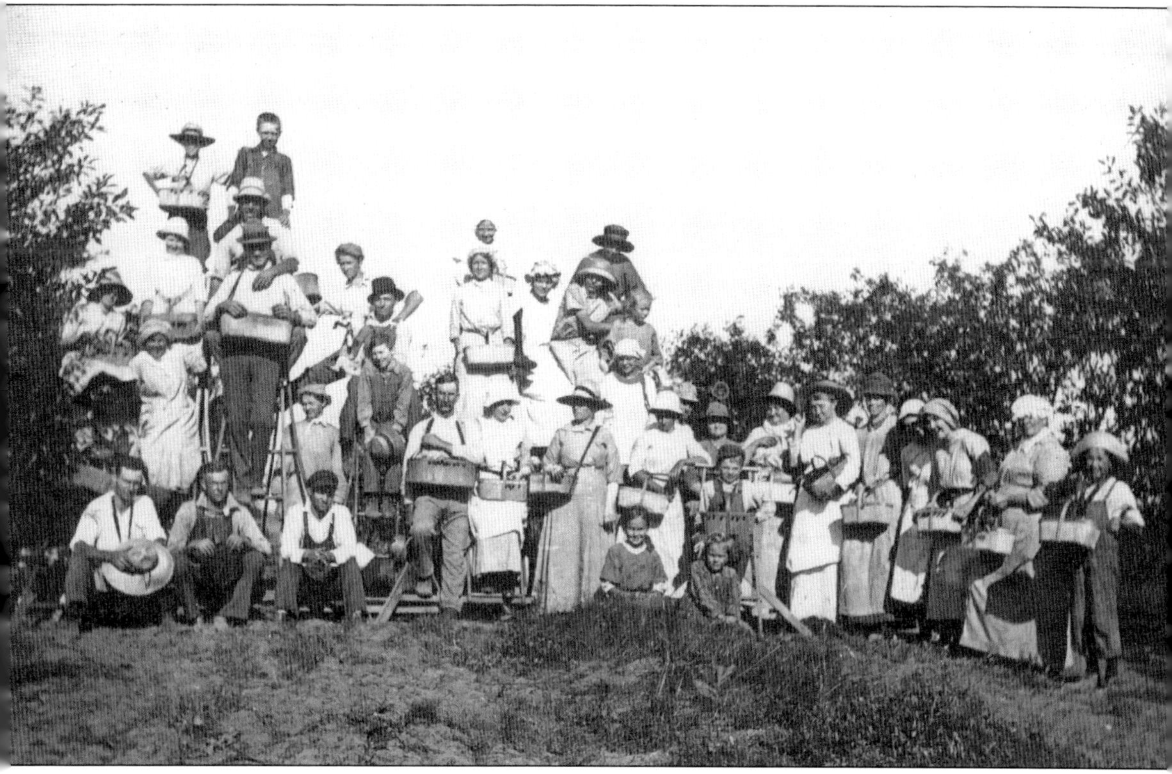

OTTO TOWNSHIP CHERRY PICKERS. Organized in 1860, Otto Township held its first election the same year. The township was named by the Germans who settled there in recognition of Otho from their homeland. In 1868, the size of Otto was reduced by half when Reed Township, which includes Ferry, was organized. After the township was lumbered off, the land was sold to farmers who found it difficult to maintain their farms and make a profit on lands that consisted of poor soil. Overall, orchards did well in the county, as cherries were plentiful. It was intensive work that required many hands during the short season. Initially, there were but eight families between both Otto and Ferry Townships, and wolves were so plentiful that children were afraid to venture to school in fear of them. In 1858, only $130 was paid out in wolf bounties (13 adult wolves). By 1869, the bounty had doubled to $20 per adult wolf. The abundance of wolves were not without their benefits, as settlers would watch a pack run a deer to the ground and then move in and confiscate the kill.

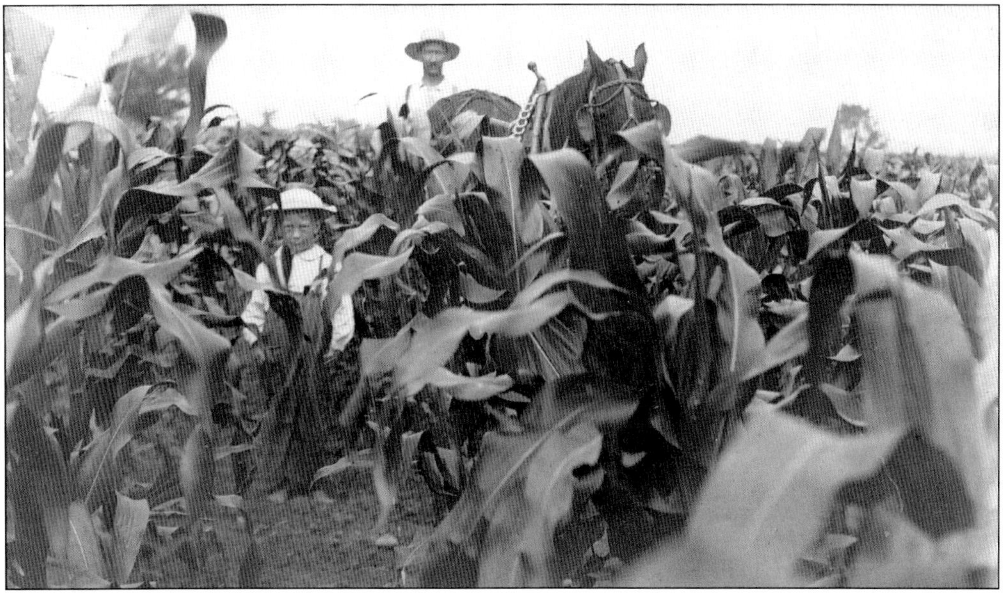

Knee High. An old farmer's adage is that corn must be knee high by the Fourth of July in order to provide a good crop yield. A good crop and a good horse were the trappings of success for any farmer. Many prided their barn and livestock more than their house, and when itinerant photographers came by, rest assured that the barn and all of the family horses would have their own portrait taken.

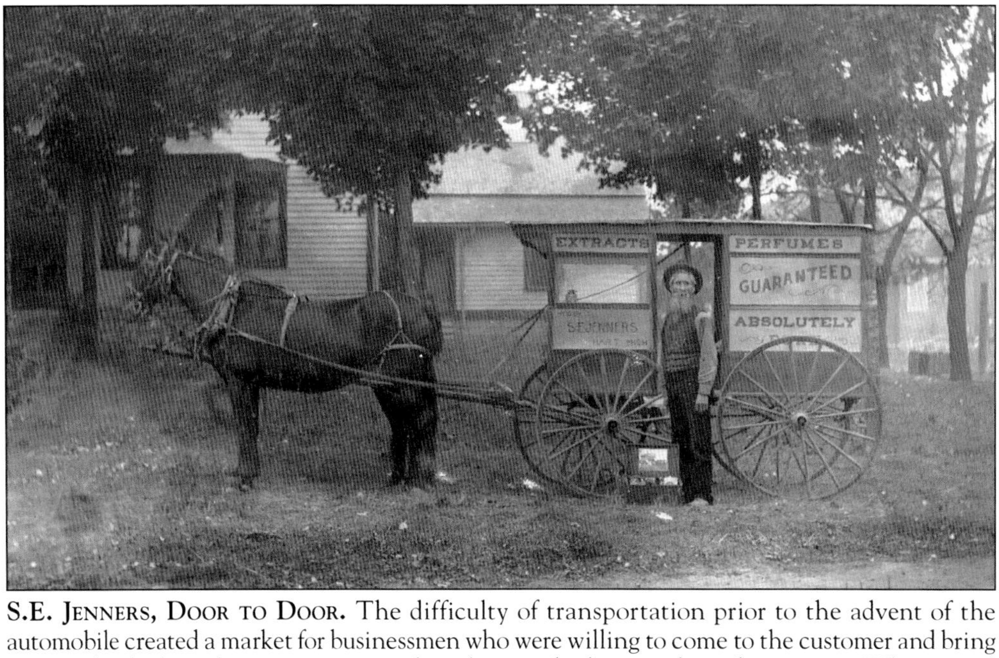

S.E. Jenners, Door to Door. The difficulty of transportation prior to the advent of the automobile created a market for businessmen who were willing to come to the customer and bring a wagonload of supplies, pots, pans, and trinkets to the housewife in the country. When travel to town might occur only once every week or two, the traveling salesman was often a welcome sight, bringing goods, as well as news, from the area.

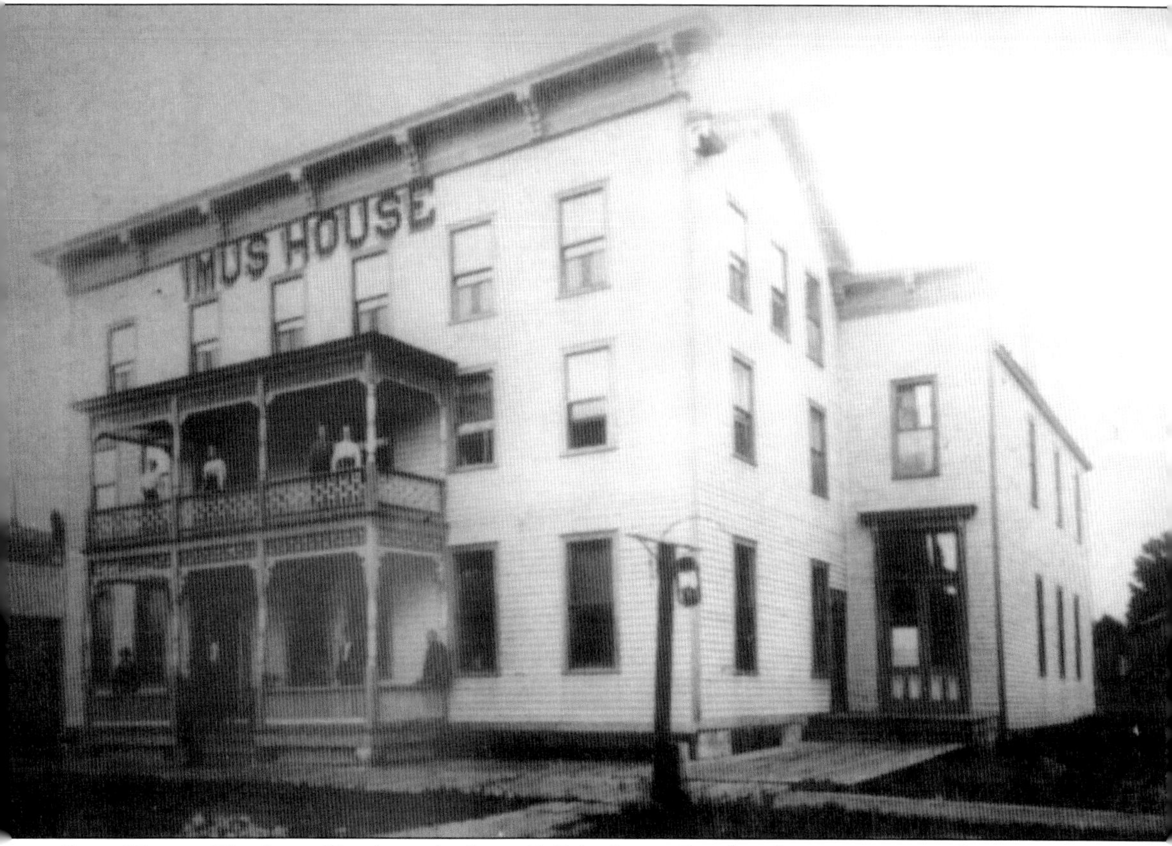

Imus Hotel. The Imus Hotel was built in 1863 by James Brooker, but it was E.W. Elliott who refitted the hotel and raised it to three stories in 1871. The hotel boasted 50 rooms and 42 beds and was purchased a few years later by George W. Imus and renamed. Prior to his arrival in Pentwater, Imus was engaged in teaching, farming, and owning a mercantile before purchasing the landmark hotel that bore his name. As written in *Oceana County Pioneers and Businessmen*, published by Louis Hartwick and William Tuller in 1880, "The first town meeting was held in the house of E. R. Cobb, April 7, 1856, when the township officers were elected, although in the 1855 meeting of the Hoard of Supervisors Edwin R. Cobb appeared and acted as Supervisor for Pentwater. At the township election above mentioned the following officers were elected: Supervisor, E. R. Cobb; Clerk, James Dexter; Treasurer, Norman Rogers: Highway Commissioners, A. Rector, J. D. Green and N. Rogers; Constables, J. G. Blowers, N. Codner; School Inspector, J. G. Blowers." Originally, Pentwater consisted of two villages: Middlesex, organized by Charles Mears, and Pentwater, organized by Rector and Cobb.

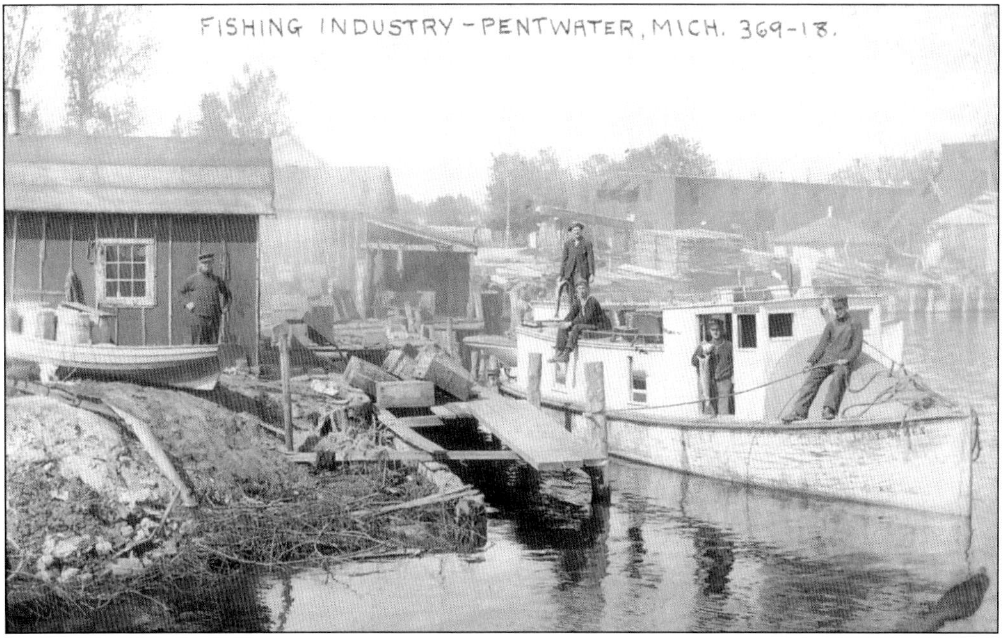

Early Fish Tugs. Commercial fishermen Frank and Tamler, identified only by their last names, were operating out of Pentwater as early as 1857. This is an early view of the fishing industry in the village of Pentwater. Like most lakeside villages and towns that had a good harbor, there were those who made their living from the waters of Lake Michigan either fishing or fashioning the vessels that sailed the lakes. Anton Edward Peterson was a boat builder in Pentwater whose operations were near this site on Pentwater Lake.

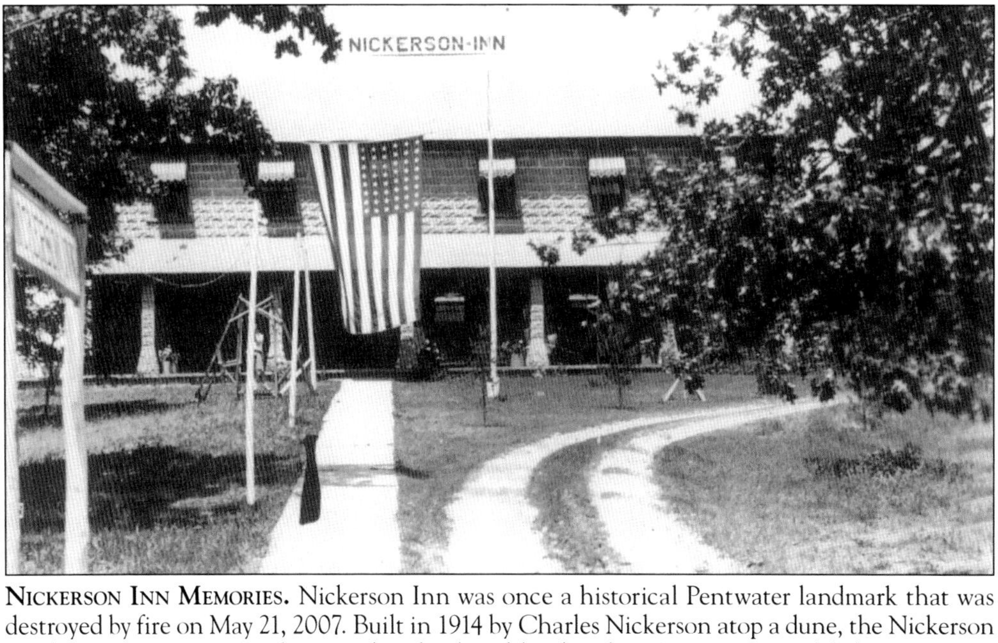

Nickerson Inn Memories. Nickerson Inn was once a historical Pentwater landmark that was destroyed by fire on May 21, 2007. Built in 1914 by Charles Nickerson atop a dune, the Nickerson Inn became an important historical and cultural landmark in Pentwater. Widely known for its charm, elegance, and meals, it was a popular stopping place for travelers in an earlier era when accommodations were sparse.

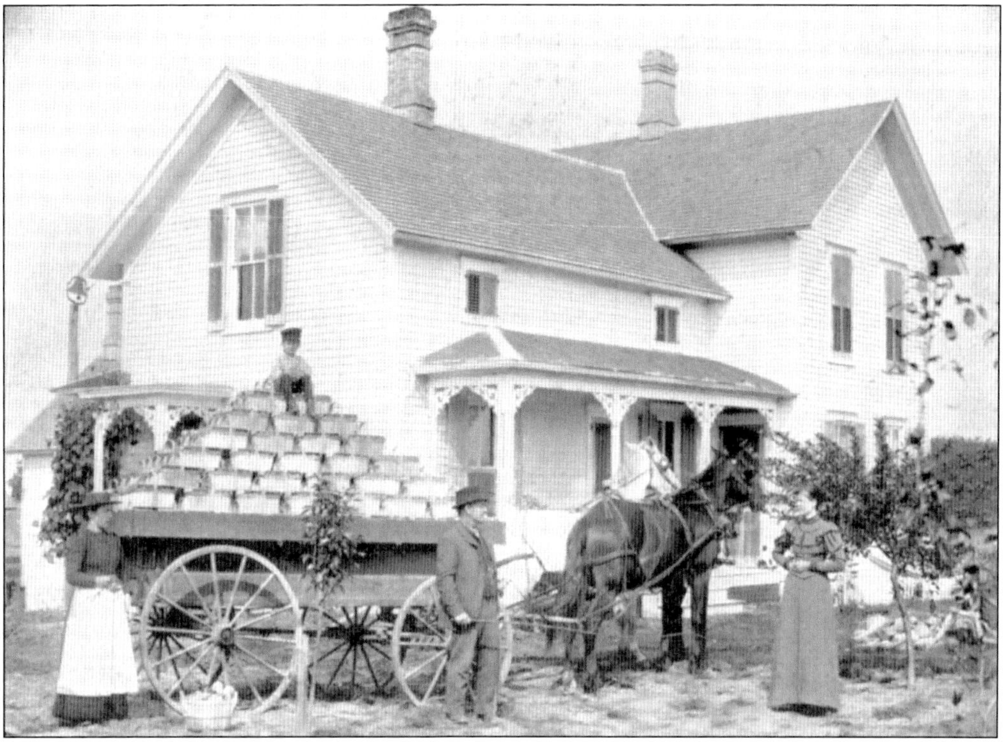

Shelby Township Plums and Peaches. H.S. Elliott is seen with 300 baskets of plums and peaches ready for market. The temperate climate in Oceana County made it perfect for farming, particularly for the planting of orchards and growing fruit. Fruit trees need to put down roots three or more feet, and the combination of climate and soils of Oceana County facilitated the rapid growth and prosperity of the farming communities there.

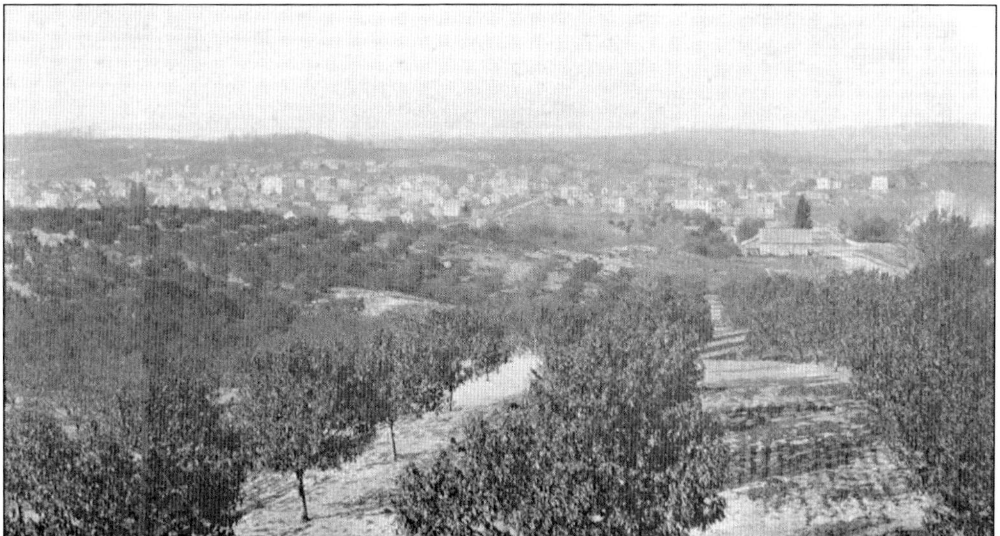

View from Cemetery Hill. Shelby can be seen in the distance in this early view taken from the top of Cemetery and Waterworks Hills. The hilly area surrounding Shelby was found to be perfect for growing fruit and had the extra advantage of protection against cold and frost.

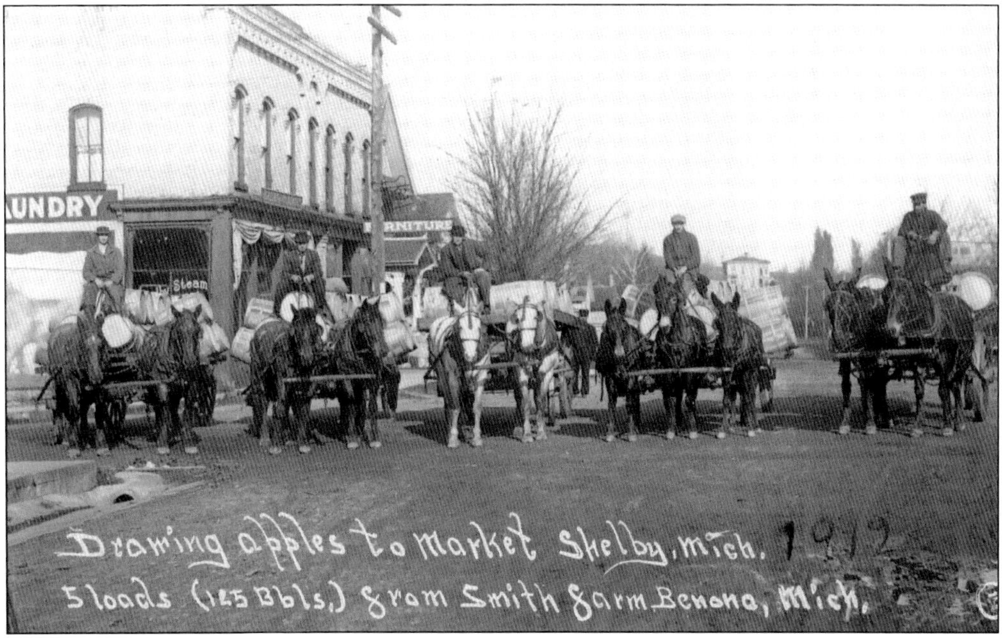

APPLES TO MARKET. Transportation of produce was slow, as the condition of the roads were not conducive to getting produce to market without bruising from being jostled about on the way into town. As a whole, Oceana County depended on the agricultural community to provide employment and a tax base after most logging came to an end in the late 19th century.

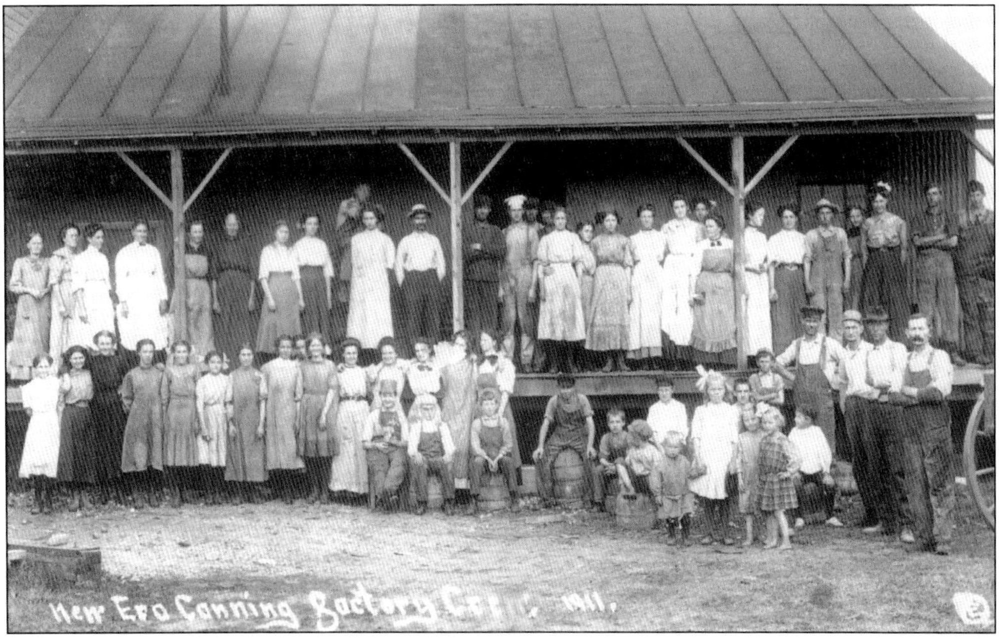

NEW ERA CANNING COMPANY. The New Era Canning Company began quite humbly as a response to the shipping time and costs of sending fresh berries to Chicago. Edward Ray decided it was better if he did it himself, and after a rough start, he convinced John and Peter Westing to each invest $2,000 in 1910 to form a canning company. World War I and the need for canned food to feed the troops bolstered the company significantly.

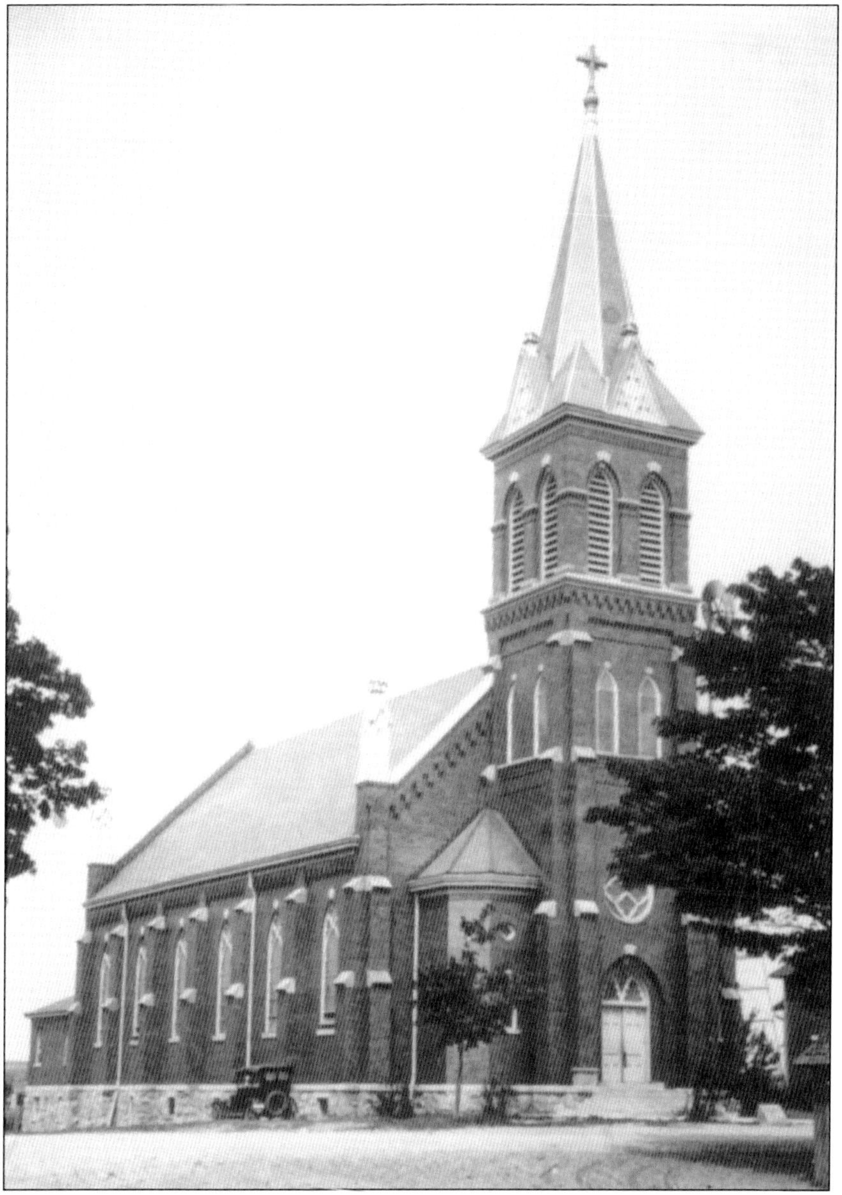

CATHOLIC CHURCH OF WEARE TOWNSHIP. In 1860, John Bean and others successfully petitioned the county board for the creation of a new township to be called Weare. The township of Weare was organized at the River House, which belonged to Charles Mears, on April 2, 1861. A total of 43 votes were cast in that first election. Weare was set off from Pentwater in 1860 and named for Dr. Benjamin Weare. Myrtle B. High was elected supervisor, A.D. Boomer as clerk, and William P. Harding as treasurer. Logging was the primary source of early employment and business and much of that was undertaken by Charles and Albert Mears. Charles had an important role in the development of the area from Grand Haven north to the villages of Pere Marquette, Lincoln (renamed Ludington in 1873), and Hamlin. The Catholic church in Weare was organized in 1884, but prior to that event, the community would have gone six months before a missionary riding the circuit arrived in the community. This was the location of the first Catholic church in the county, and the initial structure was built of local wood and constructed by the parishioners.

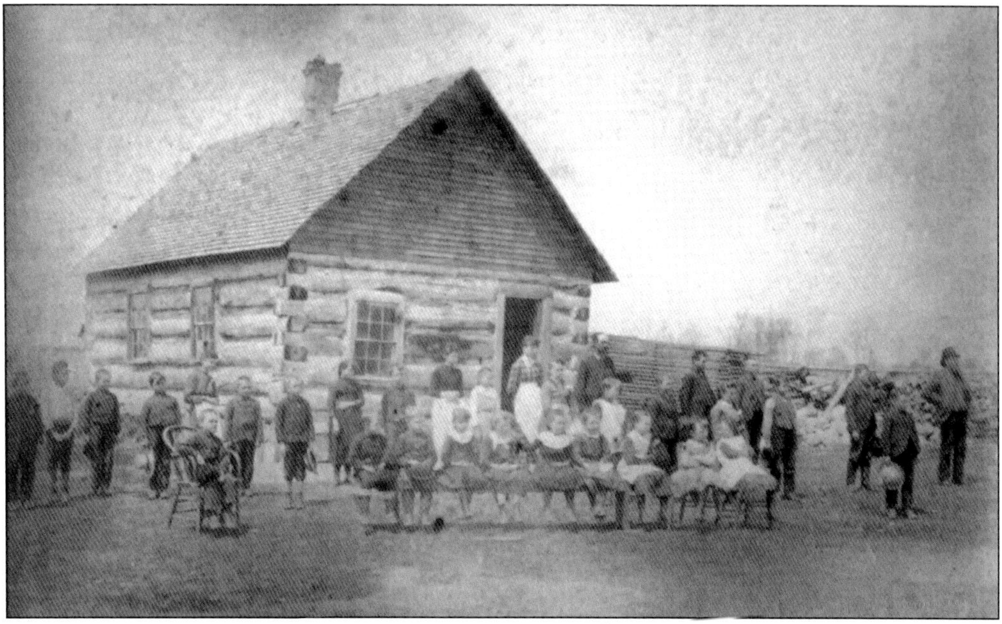

Cargill School. In 1890, there were a total of 86 school districts in Oceana County, and the county boasted a population of 17,000. Cargill School was located at 104th and Jackson Road sin Weare Township, about three miles from Weare. Teachers in one room school taught all ages up to about the eighth grade, with older students helping out with the younger ones under the teacher's watchful eye.

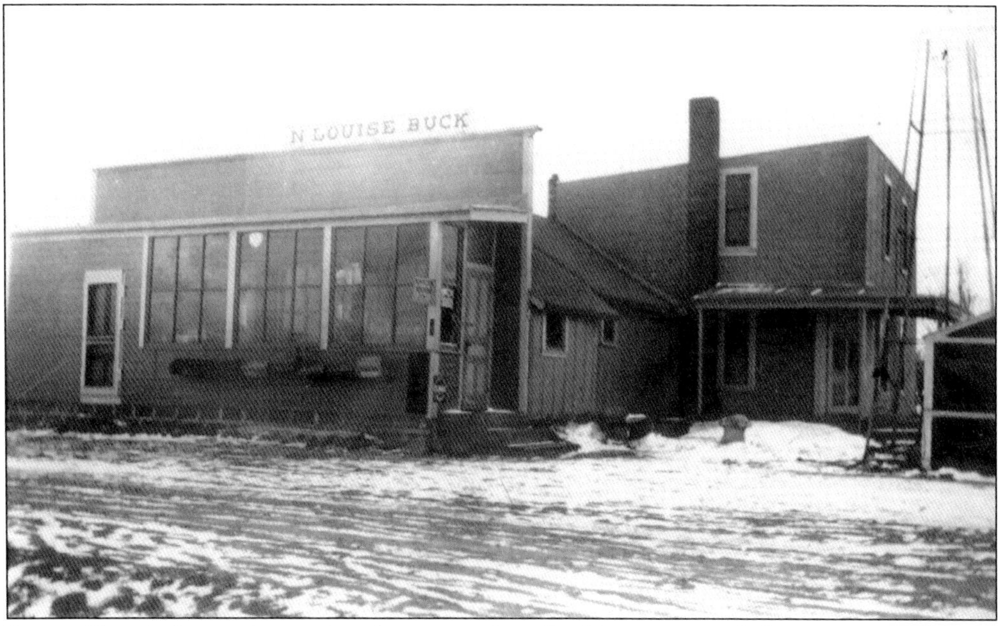

Louise Buck's Store. Located at the county line, Buck's store provided an important link in the community, as did the establishments in every rural area at that time. These stores provided staples, supplies, and a place to meet friends and neighbors and exchange news. The trip was within a reasonable wagon ride from each farm and reduced the time the farmer needed to be away from his work.

Three

Towns, Villages, and Place Names

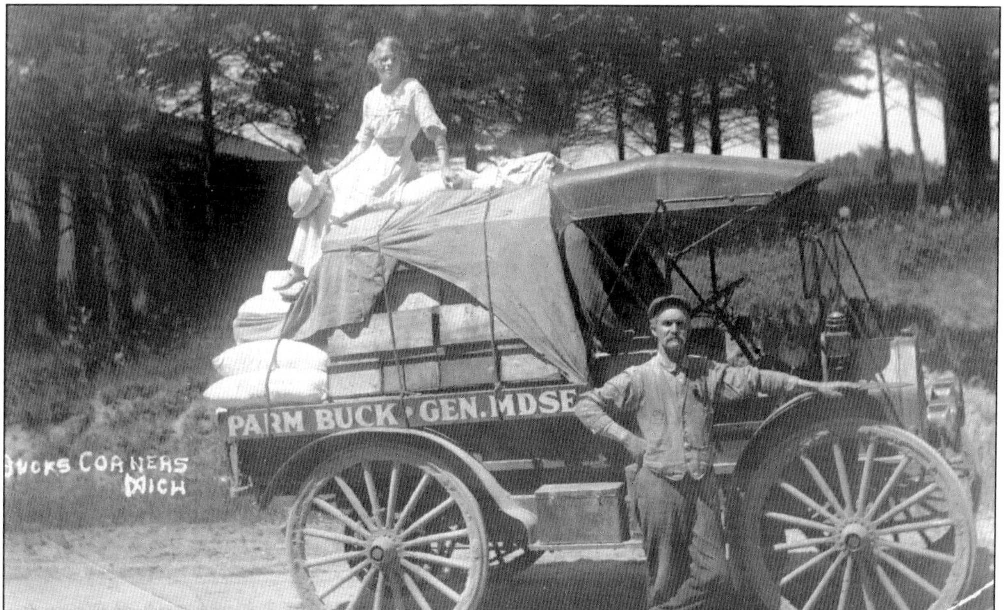

Everyone Came to Buck's Corners. Sylvanus Buck came to Oceana County from Ovid, Michigan. Originally, he was from Chemung County, New York. He arrived about 1861, around the time when the Richmond and Beans Sawmill were just being built. His son Frank Buck homesteaded in Weare Township, and the area that the families homesteaded and built their farms on was known as Buck's Corners, just to the south of the Mason and Oceana County lines. Other place names in Oceana County include Peachville on the Mason and Oceana County lines, Alice, Allen Creek, Forest City, Klondike, Spring Creek, and Stebbensville. Most of these communities had their own post office at one time, some lasting only a few years before being disbanded.

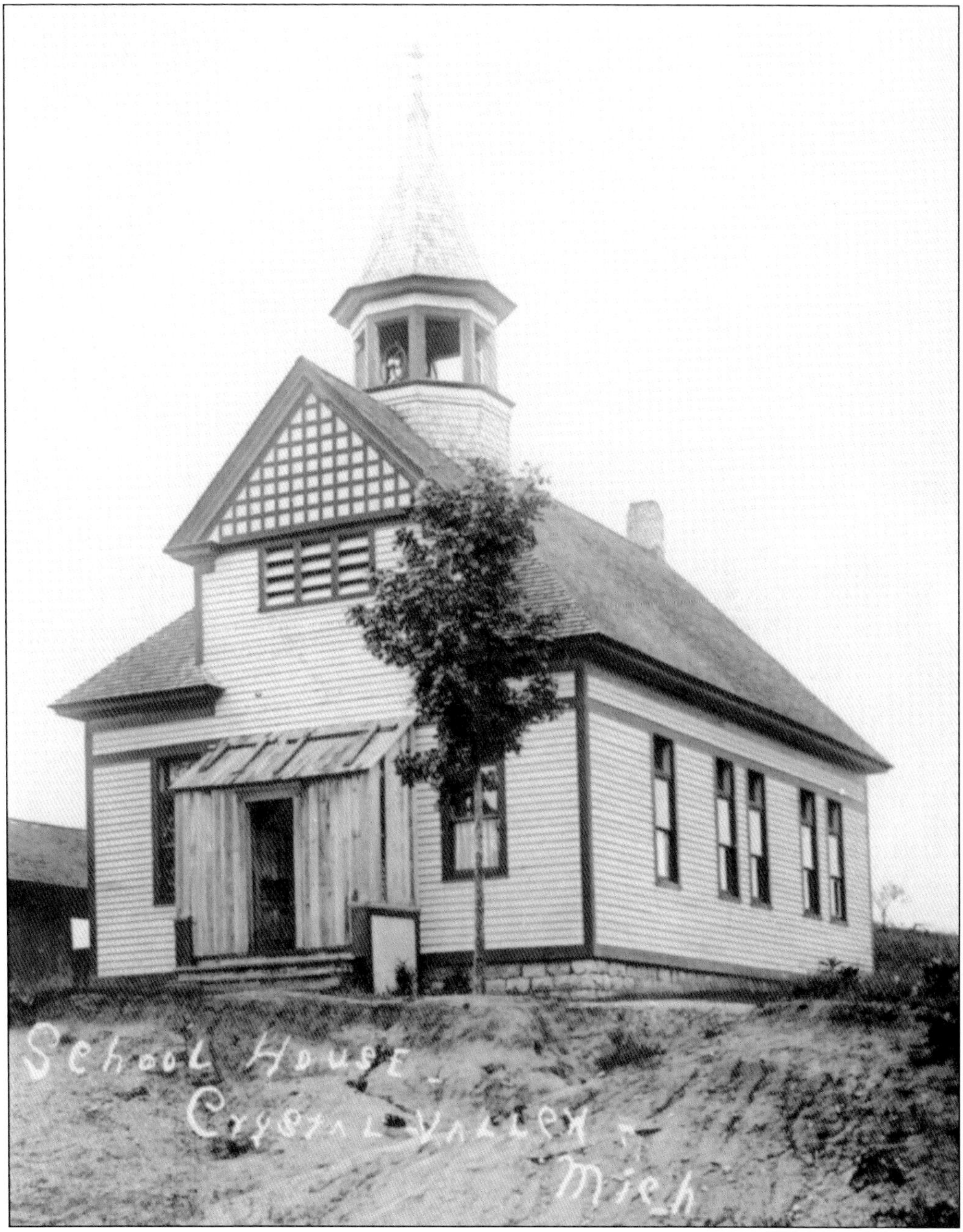

Crystal Valley Schoolhouse. This is a picture of the Crystal Valley Schoolhouse, located in Crystal Township. The township is situated in an area that was once part of the reservation originally set up in 1855 for the Grand River Ottawa tribe. The first permanent settlers of European descent in this area were Jared and Catherine Gay, who arrived in 1861. Jared was the blacksmith, and according to a treaty, he provided services for the natives living at the reservation. The township itself is comprised of 36 square miles and has no significant bodies of water, but even so, it is a picturesque wooded and farming area. After the logging panned out and transportation became easier, the population dwindled to fewer than 1,000 people. Crystal Valley is an unincorporated community on Crystal Creek, located directly south of the Mason County line.

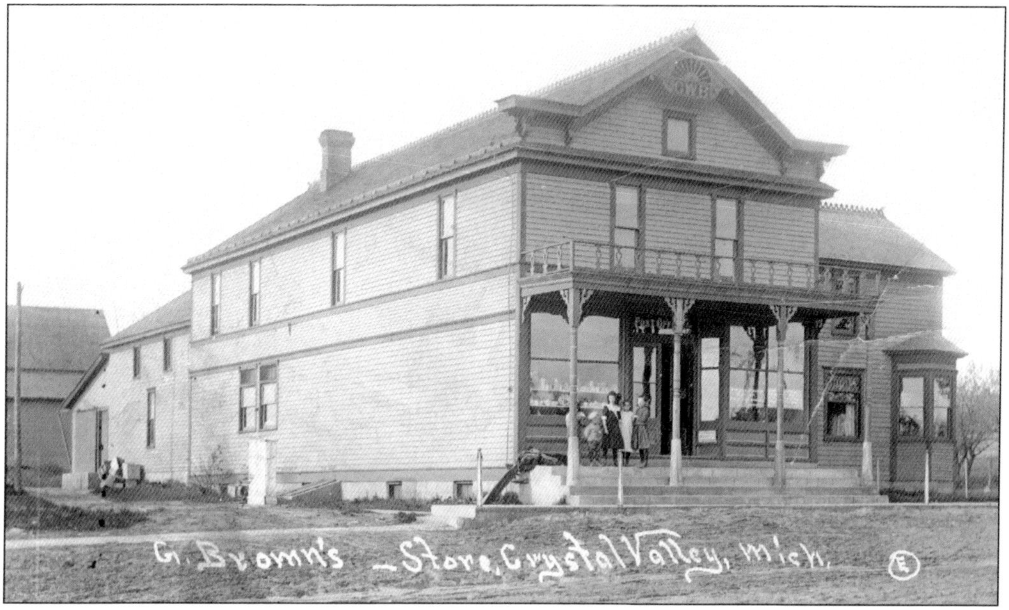

George Brown's Store. George Brown was born in Pentwater in 1873 and moved to the Crystal Valley area as a child; his father had a general store in Woodburn. When his father passed away in 1900, George took control of the store and made arrangements to move into Crystal Valley in 1894. He operated the store for about 50 years and served as postmaster for 43 years.

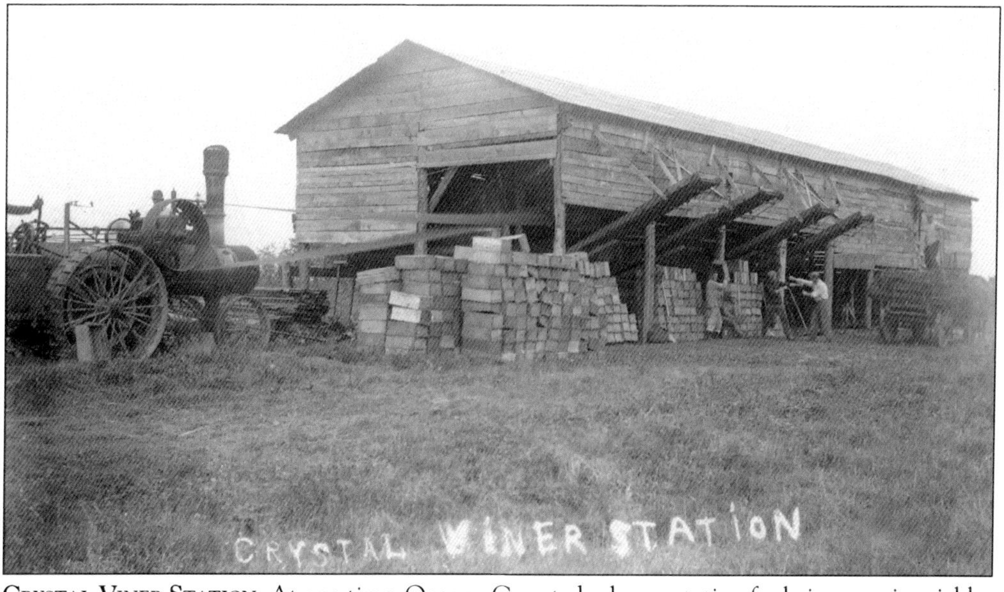

Crystal Viner Station. At one time, Oceana County had a reputation for being a major pickle-producing county in the United States, so much so that the Heinz Pickle Company had stations throughout the county in order to make it accessible and easy for the local farmers to bring their crops in to be salted in preparation of the pickling process.

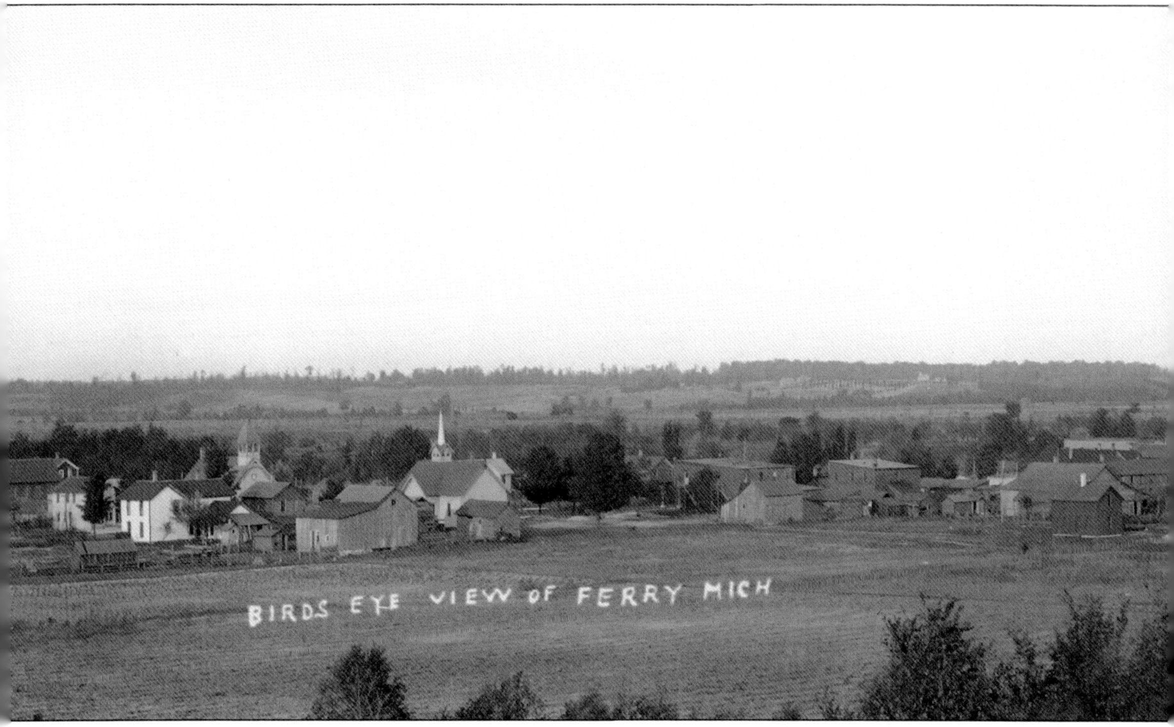

Bird's-eye View of Ferry. This is an early image of Ferry, showing the layout of the village. The north branch of the White River flows through the village. Of the four dams on that branch of the river, Peck and Ferry Dams are located in the township. With dams often came tragedy; the worst flood in the county occurred on July 23, 1883, in Ferry. John Helm built the first hotel and called it the Eagle. The Ferry House was a hotel that catered to the lumbermen. Ultimately, the village was named after Sen. Thomas White Ferry. His father was a Presbyterian pastor who, among other accomplishments, had platted the village of Ferrysburg near Spring Lake. Senator Ferry was president of the senate on March 4, 1877. Vice Pres. Henry Wilson had died, Ulysses S. Grant was no longer president, and Rutherford B. Hayes was not scheduled to take his oath until Monday, March 5, leaving Senator Ferry to believe that he was "president for a day." Unbeknownst to him and the rest of the country, Hayes had taken his oath on March 4 in a private ceremony.

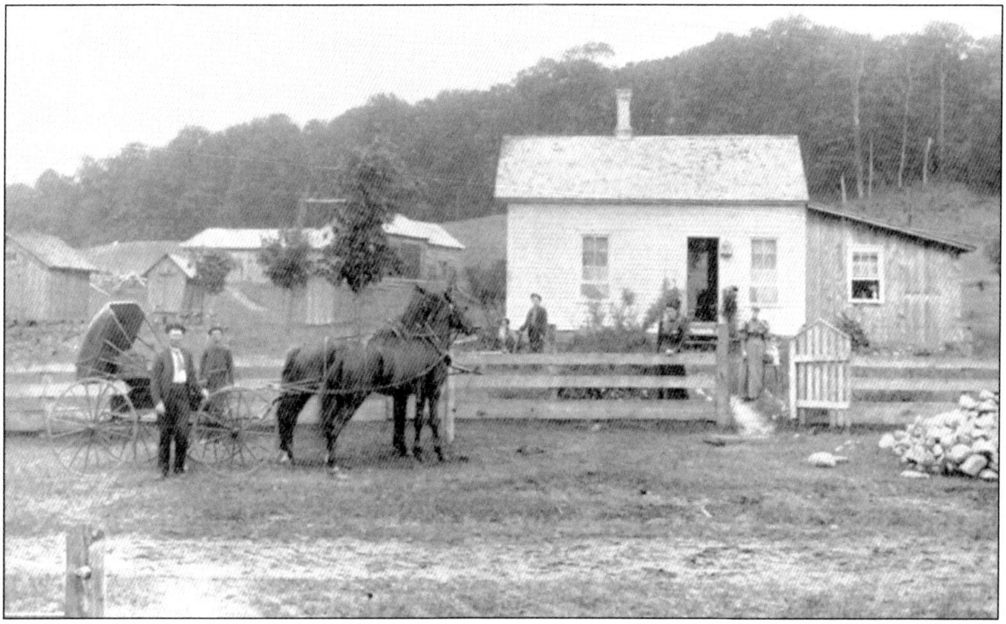

Home of Adelbert M. Prosser. Adelbert "Del" Prosser first came to Oceana County as a 17-year-old to work in the lumbering camps. Del returned to his home in Ohio for a time, and after his marriage to Floura Tourgee, he returned to the Ferry area, bought land for a farm, raised his family, and remained there until his death in 1926.

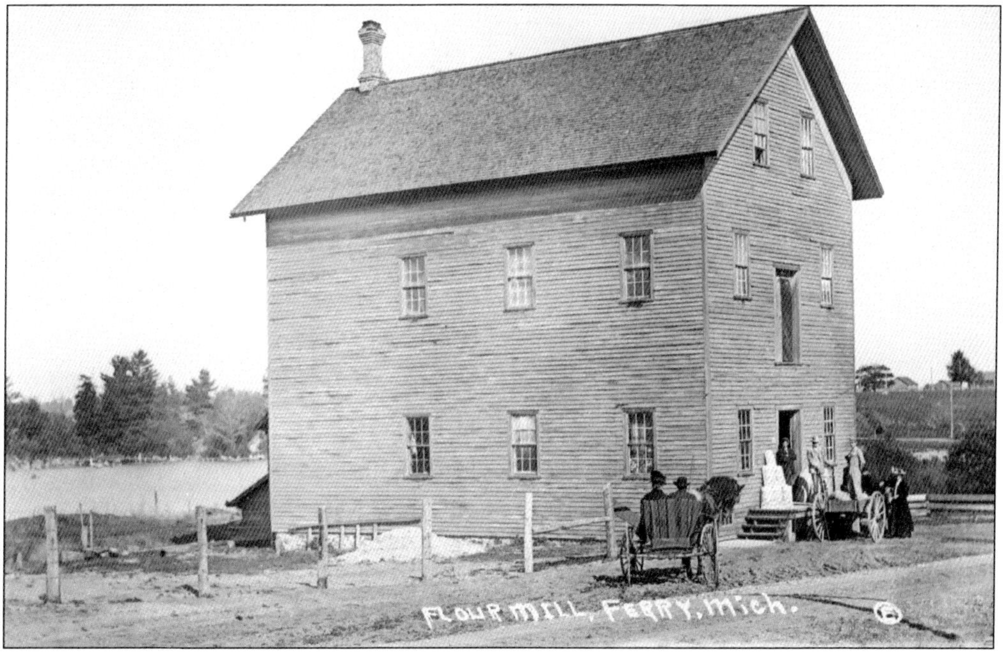

Flour Mill, a Community Anchor. The Flour Mill at Ferry, built in 1887 by William Powers and his brother Charles, boasted that its roller mill could turn out 50 barrels a day. The Ferry mill's most popular brands of flour were White Loaf No. 1 and Second Grade No. 2. In the 1800s, a flour mill would have been considered an anchor business, one heavily relied upon in the community.

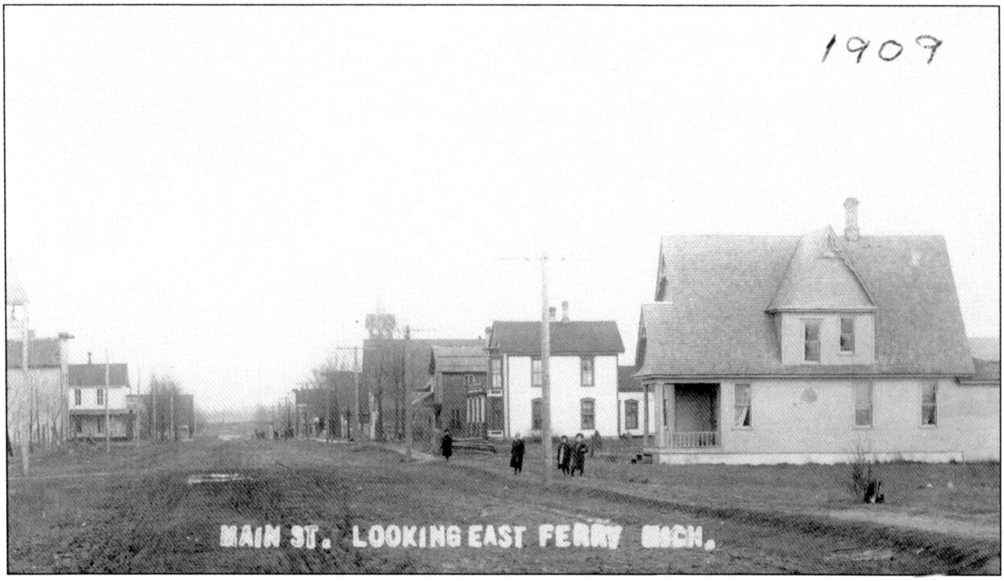

FERRY MAIN STREET EAST. In the past, transportation was an issue, and the lack of good transportation and roads contributed greatly to the opportunities for small businesses to flourish in these rural villages. It was difficult and time consuming to travel very far, and loading the wagon and coming to town once a week was all that many farmers had time for, as farming was very labor intensive. Improved roads and methods of transportation dealt a death blow to many small businesses in rural communities.

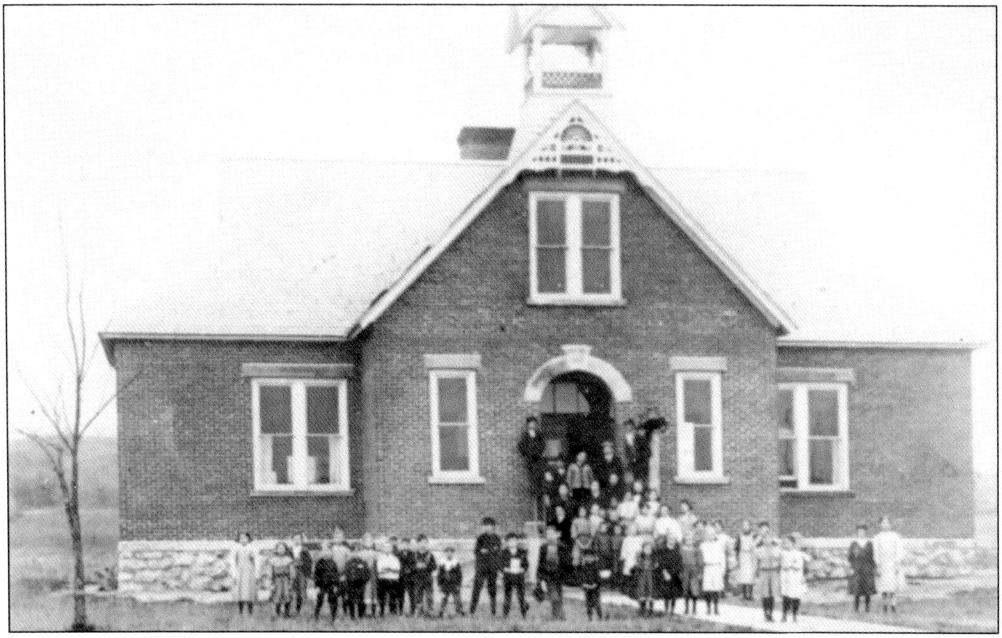

HIGH SCHOOL, 1915. The first school in the Ferry area was at the home of E.D. Smith. Later, Emma Powers held classes at her home and even had used the upstairs of the blacksmith shop for a time. Around 1905, a brick schoolhouse was built in the community and, to the dismay of the village, burned down shortly afterwards. After the fire, classes were held in Macabee Hall until other arrangements could be made.

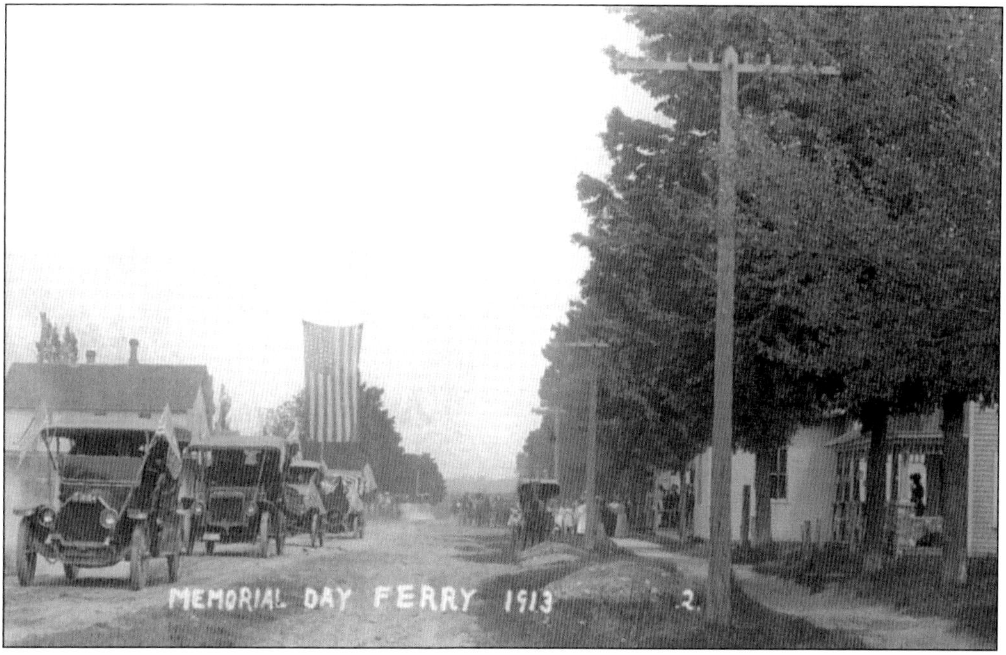

MEMORIAL DAY CELEBRATIONS, 1913. Probably every automobile in the village is seen taking part in this 1913 Memorial Day celebration. Celebrations of the past always seem to be larger than life, more of an event and an anchor in people's lives. Picnics and dinners, lemonade stands, games, contests, faux battles by veterans, and log riding through the dam were the day's events.

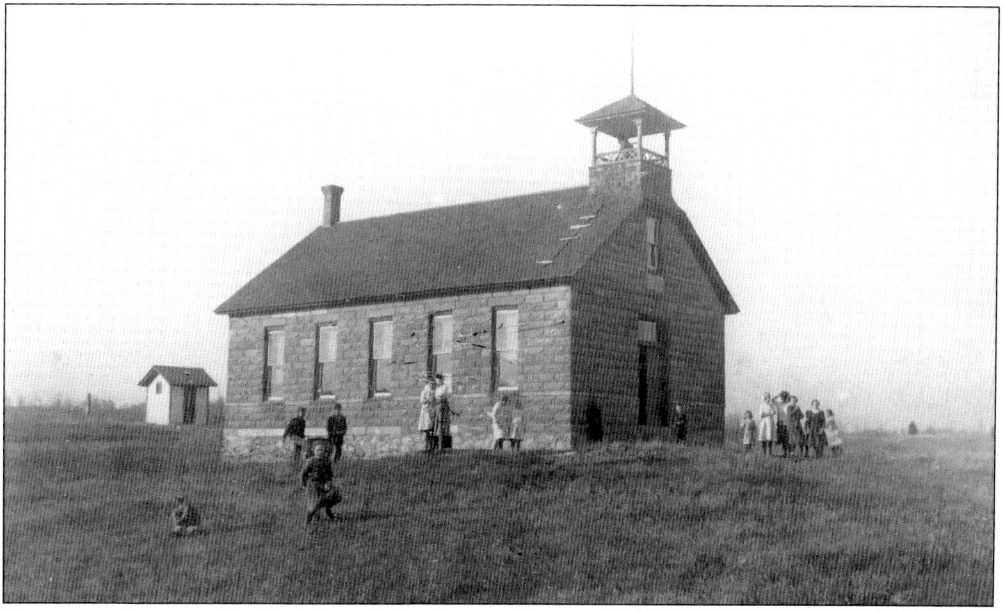

RATHBONE SCHOOL. The Rathbone School was in District No. 3. Located just north of Rathbone Corners, it was constructed of cement blocks. Some of the school districts in the Ferry area had unique names such as Lickskillet, Maples Range, Loop, Fish, and Condon Schools. All of them disappeared after the consolidation of the rural districts.

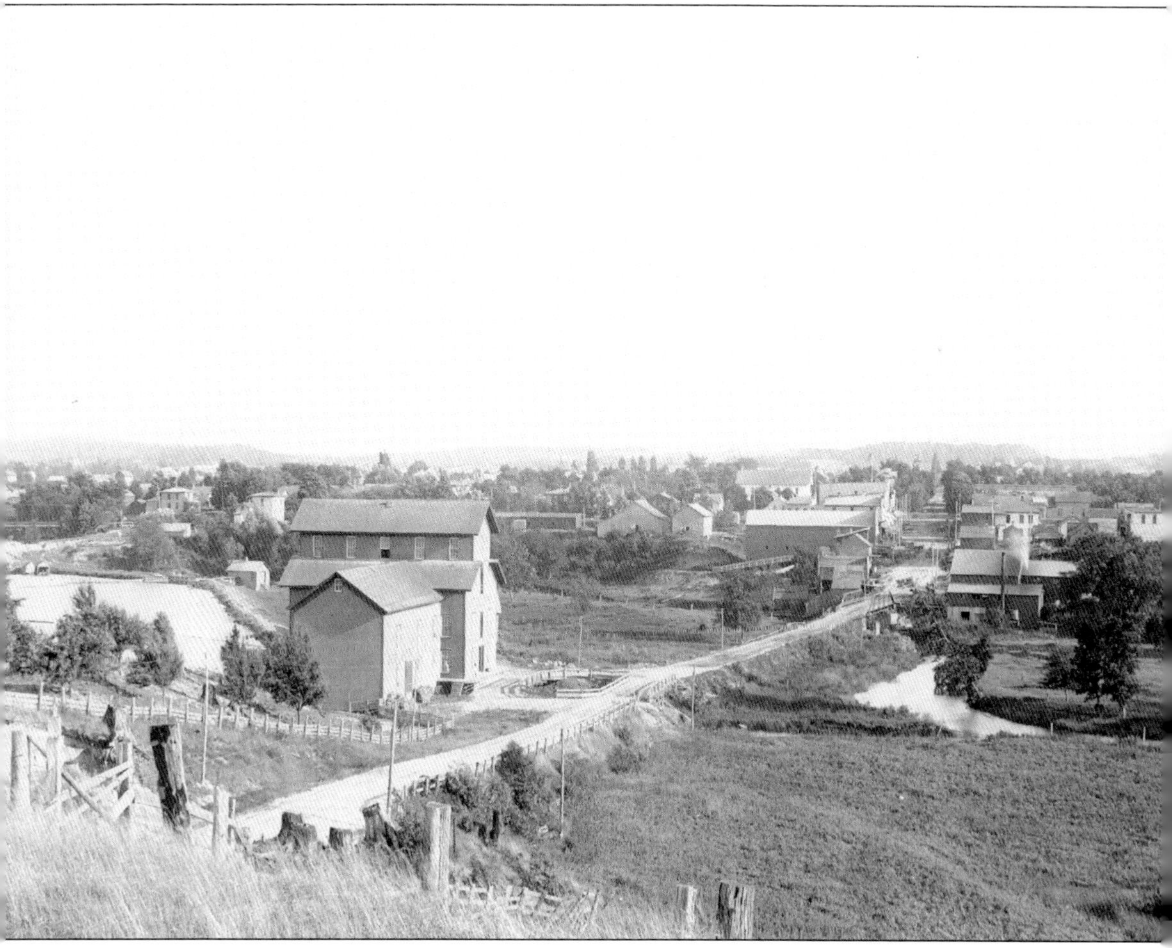

Hart Bird's-Eye View. This is an c. 1880 view of Hart, Michigan. Hart started as the site of a trading post on Russell Creek, established in 1857 by a man by the last name of Hart. J.R. Mooney arrived in Hart in 1858 and claimed to have built the first frame home there, as well as the first tavern in Pentwater in 1862. The first postmaster in 1861 was William Leach. In 1864, because of the shrewdness of Lyman Corbin in offering $1,000 to the county commissioners to build a new courthouse if the county seat were moved to Hart, the commission voted to make the move despite a lack of commerce and residents. A one-room courthouse was built shortly thereafter. In 1864, the *Oceana Times* was first published. The adage of "build it, and they will come" held true, and Hart began to grow. The first store was constructed in 1865 by two men with the last names of Cheny and Huff. In 1880, at the time this picture was taken, the population was 464. In 1885, Hart's petition to incorporate as a village was approved by the State of Michigan.

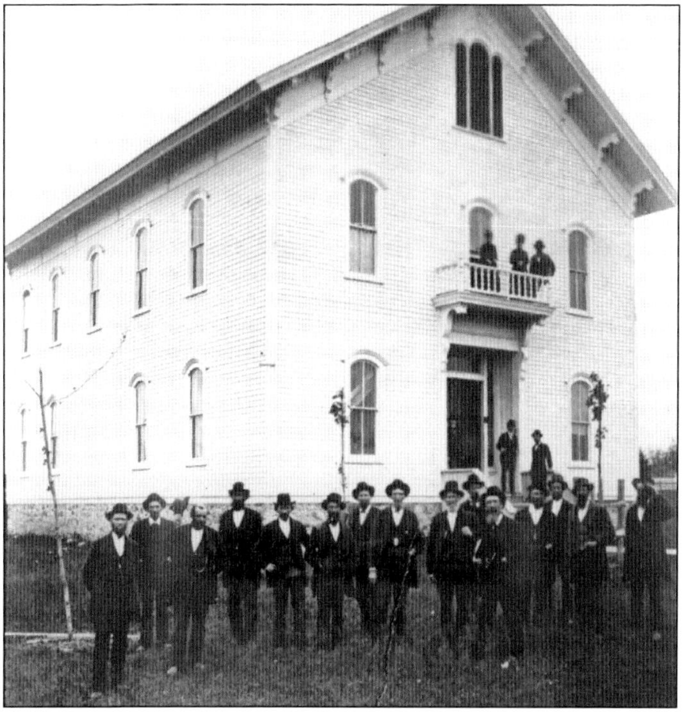

Hart Courthouse Remains. There were multiple attempts to move the county seat; Whiskey Creek wanted it returned, and efforts were made to move to Middlesex (later Pentwater). In 1873, Charles Mears offered to build a brick courthouse, complete with vaults, or donate $10,000 if the county seat was moved to Mears. Barnett (later Shelby) followed with its own offer, which failed, and it was finally decided that if the citizens of Hart could raise $2,500 for a new courthouse, it would remain in Hart.

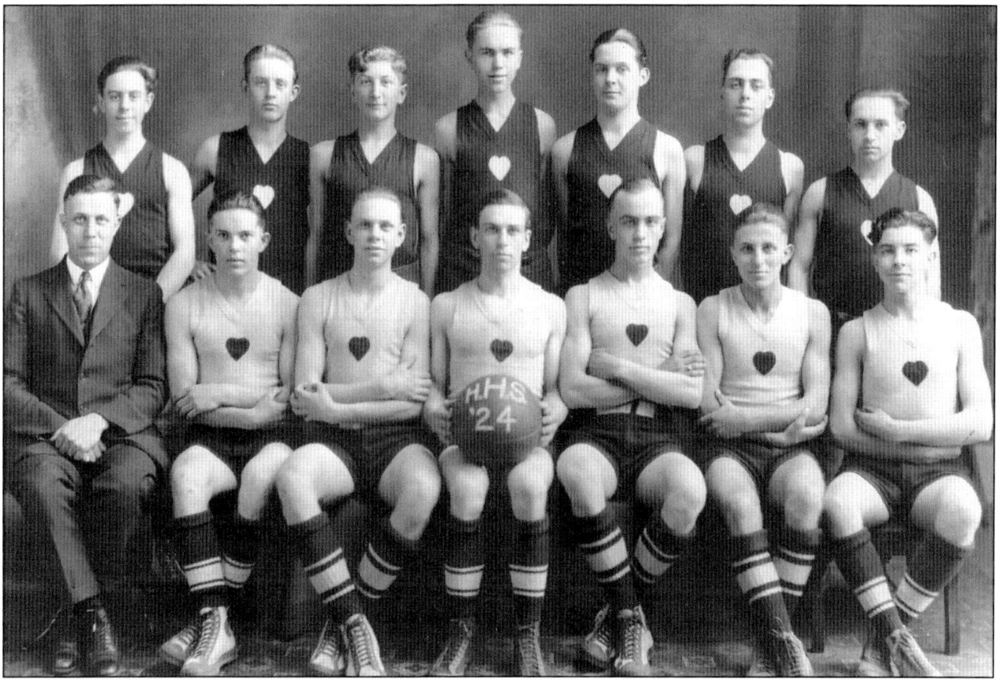

Hart Basketball Team. The game of basketball was invented in 1891 by Dr. James Naismith at a time when baseball had become entrenched as a national pastime and the nation was in the grips of a sports fever. Basketball provided an opportunity for athletic-minded individuals to continue playing sports in indoor arenas, and it quickly caught on in popularity, with schools of every size fielding teams.

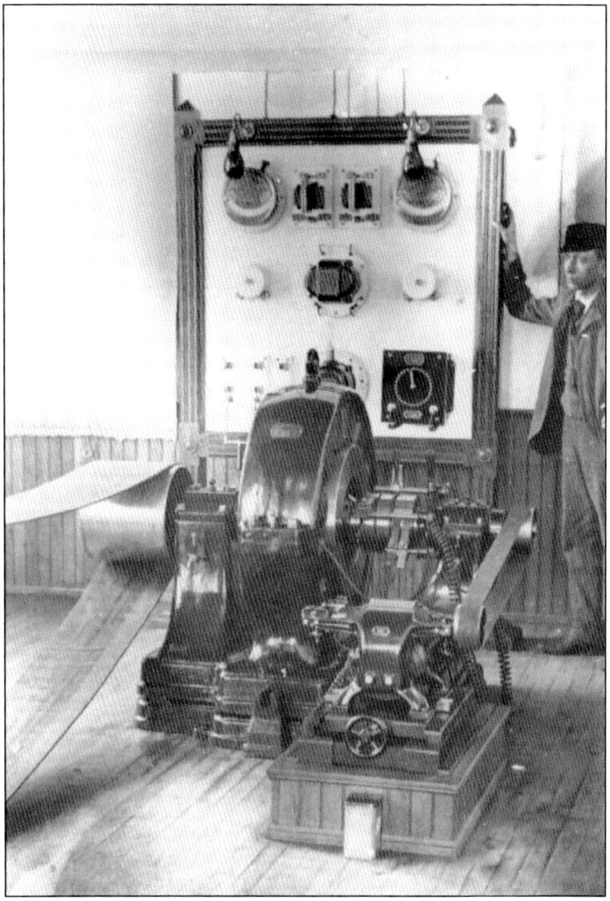

Hart Dam Brings Changes. Electrical power first came to Hart after two men with the last names of Theron and Carrie received their franchise to establish a power plant. In 1900, a steam generator was installed at the waterworks building and served the community until 1905, when Stearns Power and Light extended its lines to the village. In 1917, the Michigan Public Service Company took over the Stearns operations and provided energy until 1927. In 1894, a family would spend $1 a month to power five lights.

Hydroelectric Power Comes to Hart. Hydroelectric power was discussed as early as the mid-1890s, but plans for the Hart Dam and power plant were not developed until 1925. November 1, 1927, was the first day that the new hydroelectric system began providing power, and within a year, demands were so great, a diesel generator was purchased and installed to meet the growing needs.

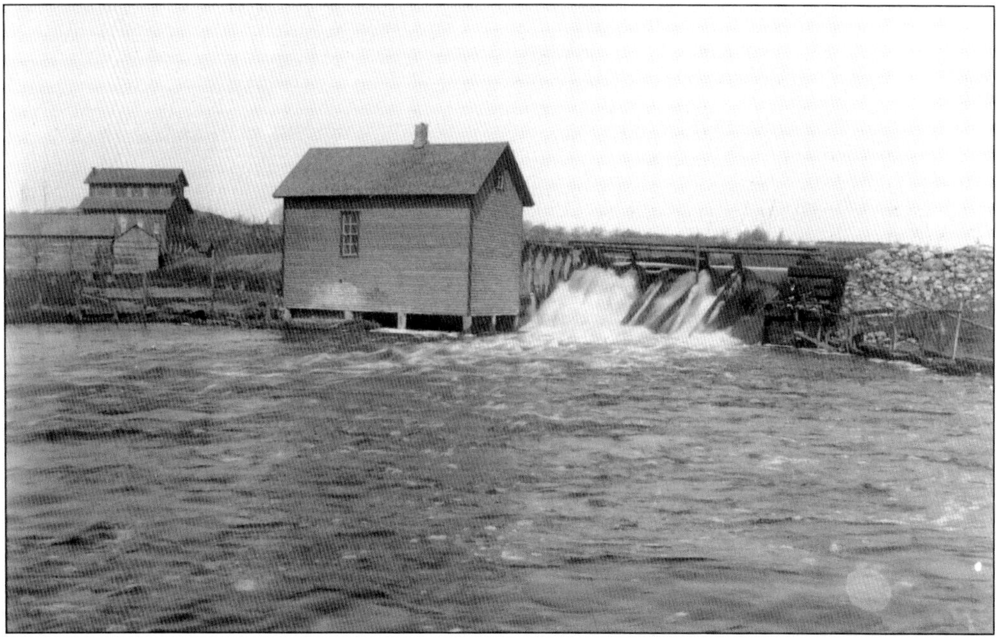

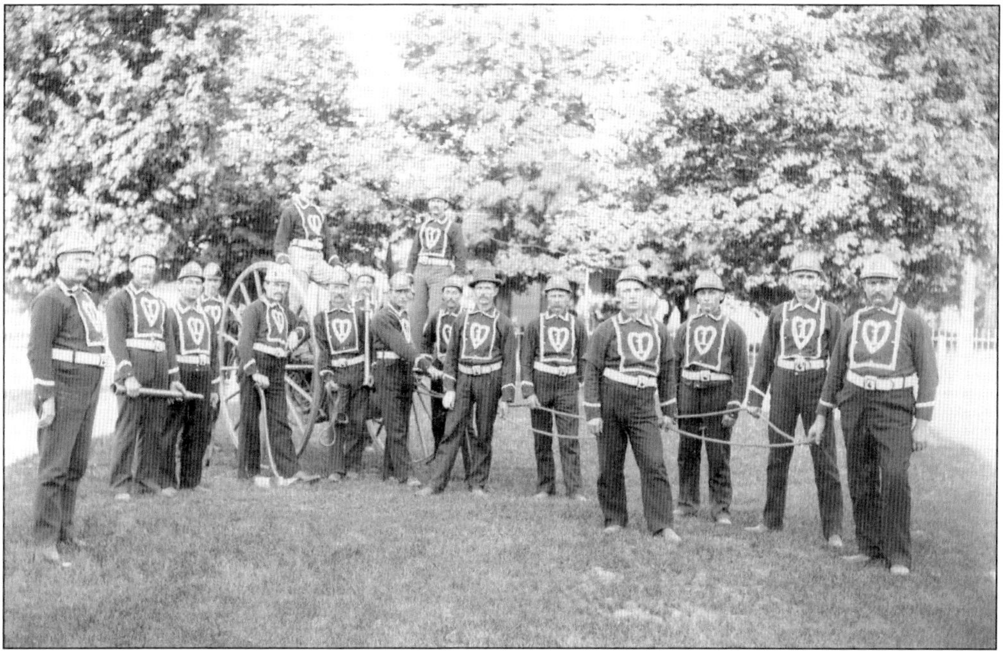

Fire Department Organized. Fire was a concern for every village and town, as structures were wood, and many times streets were used as dumping areas for sawdust. With just a spark, whole towns could disappear in a day. Organized in 1886, the first fire chief was John F. Widoe, and the fire barn was located next to the old city hall on Washington Street.

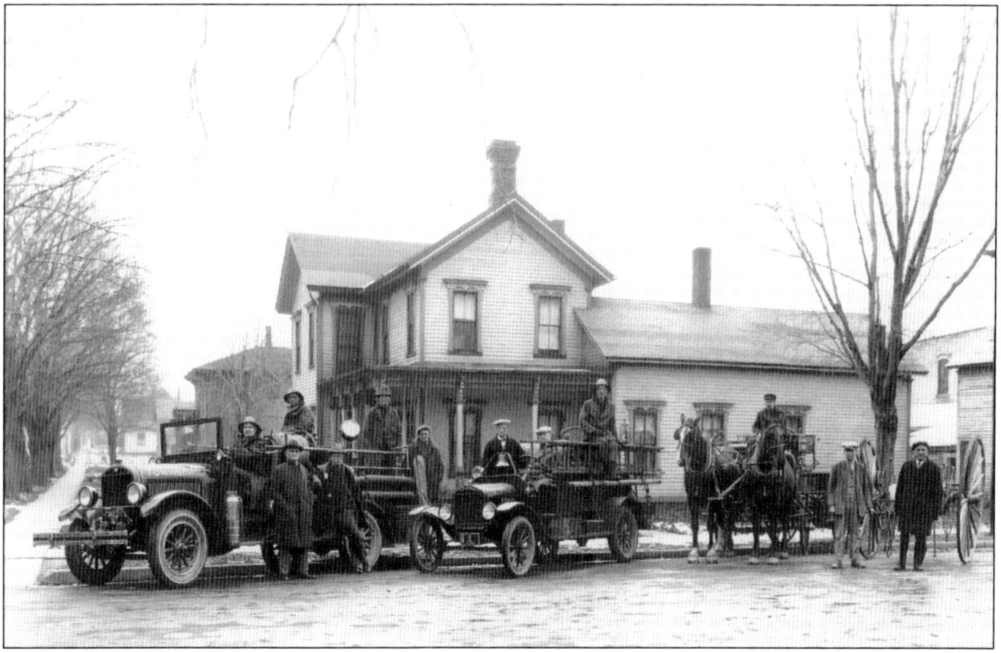

Fire Department Alarms. When a fire was discovered, a bell located at the northwest corner of the courthouse block was rung to alert volunteer responders. If no team of horses was available, the men would grab hold of the handles on the tongue of the wagon and pull the equipment to the fire themselves.

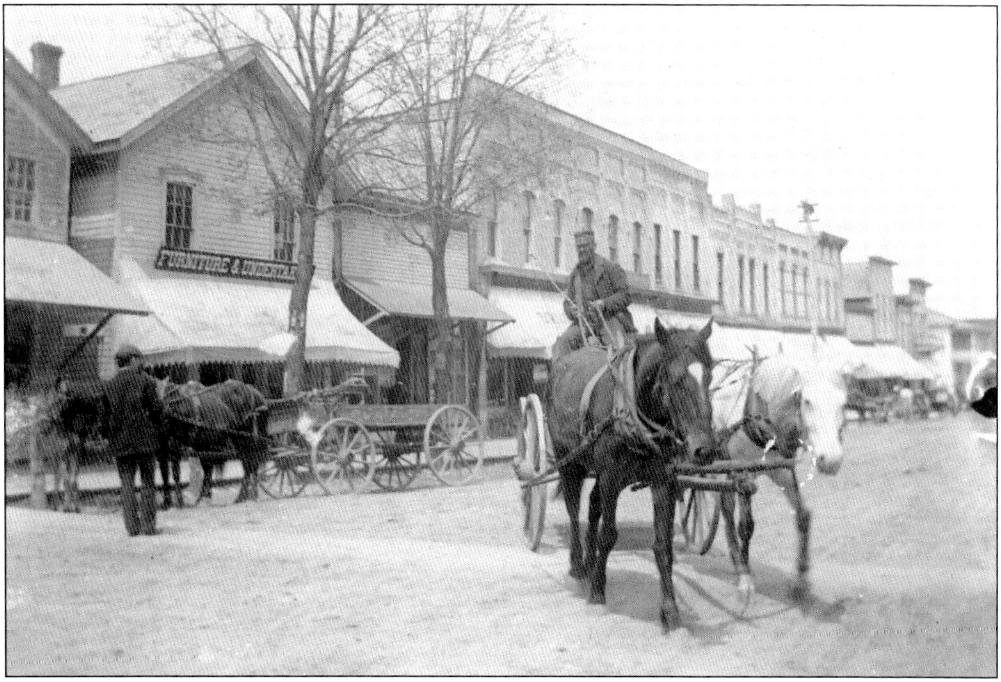

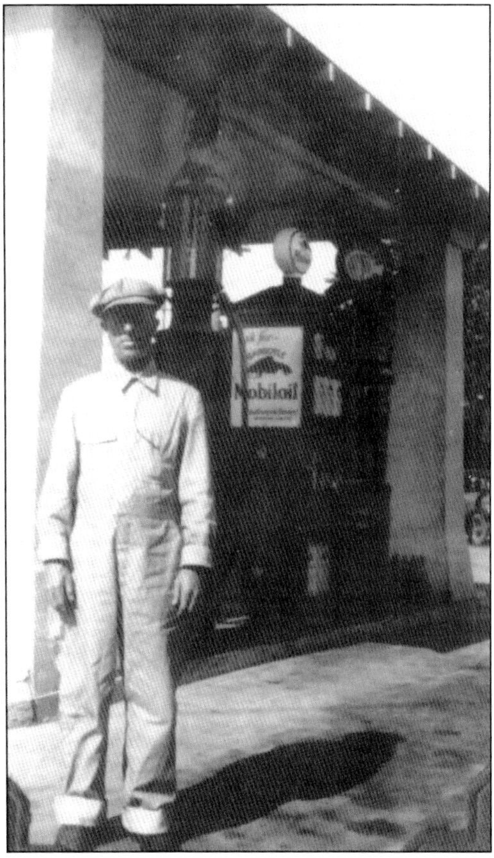

"FURNITURE & UNDERTAKER." Early pioneers and businessmen often wore many different hats, as seen in this combination of businesses. Formal funerals and services from an undertaker were growing in popularity but not yet fully established. Embalming was not yet mandatory; one must remember that it was not uncommon for a family to have a plot on the family farm, and viewings were often held in the bay window prior to a funeral service at church.

STANDARD GAS STATION. The Standard gas station was built in 1922 and has been reconstructed several times over the ensuing years, eventually becoming an Amoco station that was owned and operated by the Hodges family for over 50 years, beginning in the mid-1930s. H.H. Purdy, seen here, came up to Oceana from Hillsdale County as a child in the 1880s.

M. Earl Shaw Feed Store. The timing was not right for the establishment of a business of any kind, as the Great Depression was looming on the horizon, and its impact was devastating on families and businesses of every description. After the feed store failed, Earl went to work for the road commission for 30¢ an hour. After receiving a nickel, he wrote in his journal, "We're on easy street now."

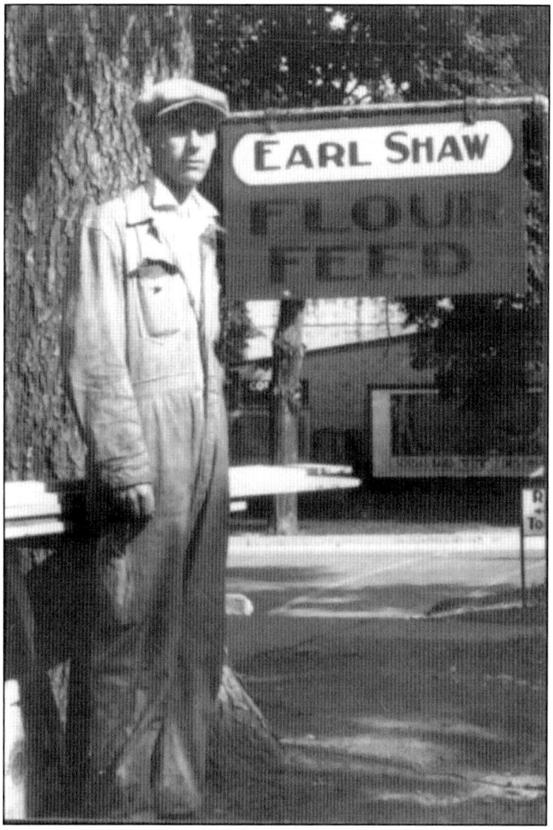

"Take Our Goods." M. Earl Shaw came from Indiana to Hart in 1920 and married Laura Fern Purdy. By 1929, he had two young sons and was opening a feed store. This vintage advertisement is the cover page of a calendar promoting the new business that operated for only a couple years before being sold to M. Earl's father-in-law, H.H. Purdy.

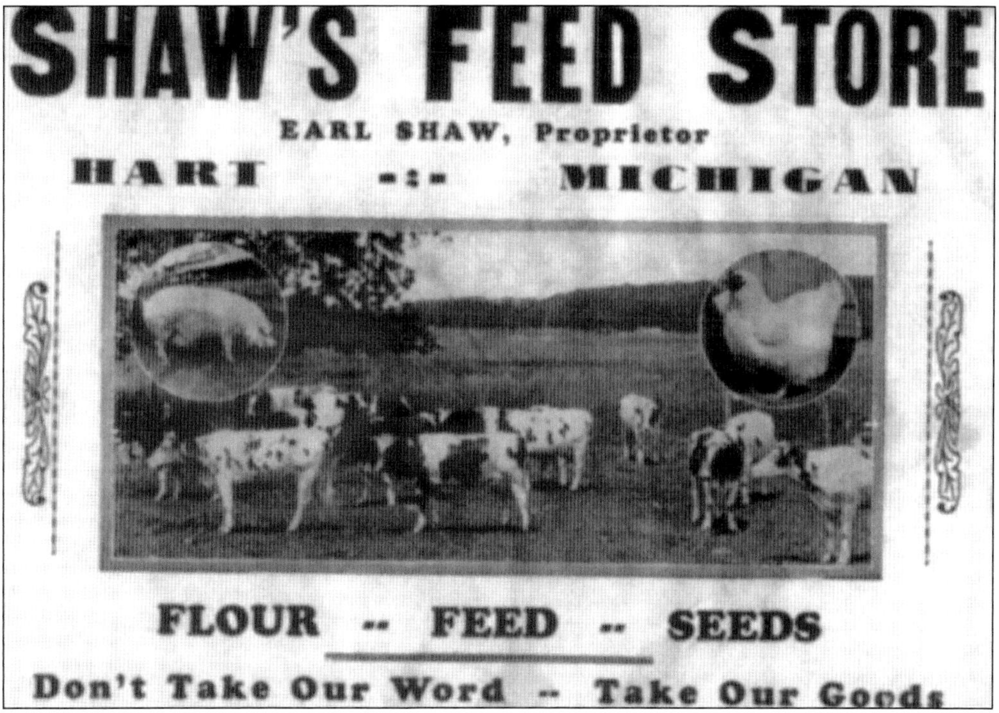

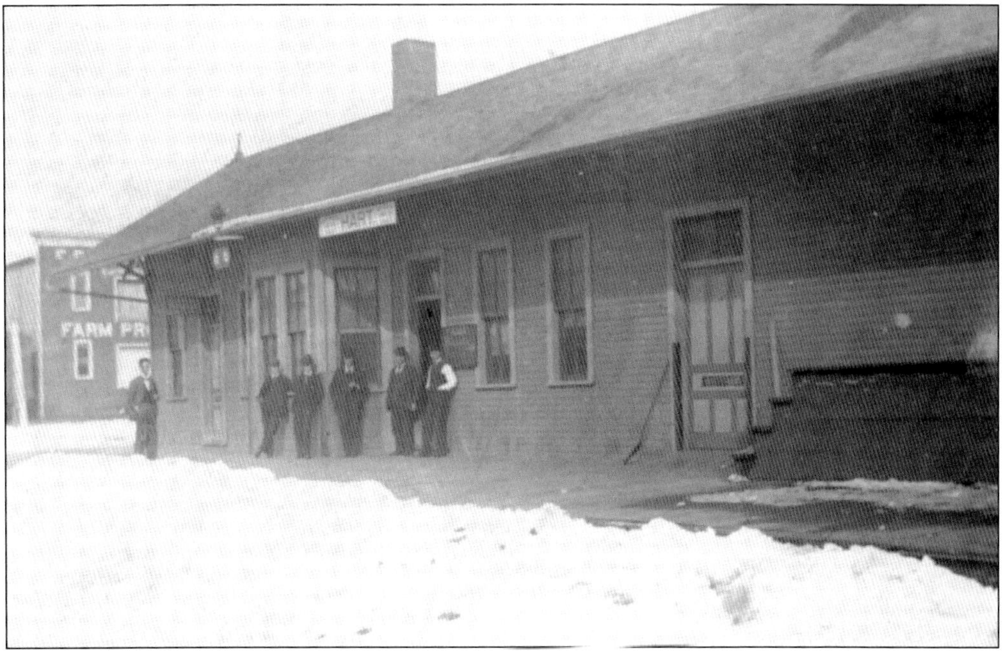

Hart Train Depot. In 1872, the Grand Rapids & Lakeshore Railroad passed right by Hart and went to Pentwater. The railway did not want to deal with the hills surrounding Hart and the additional expense to run track there. In 1881, a spur was built from Mears to Hart, and in 1882 the depot, which still stands, was constructed on Water Street.

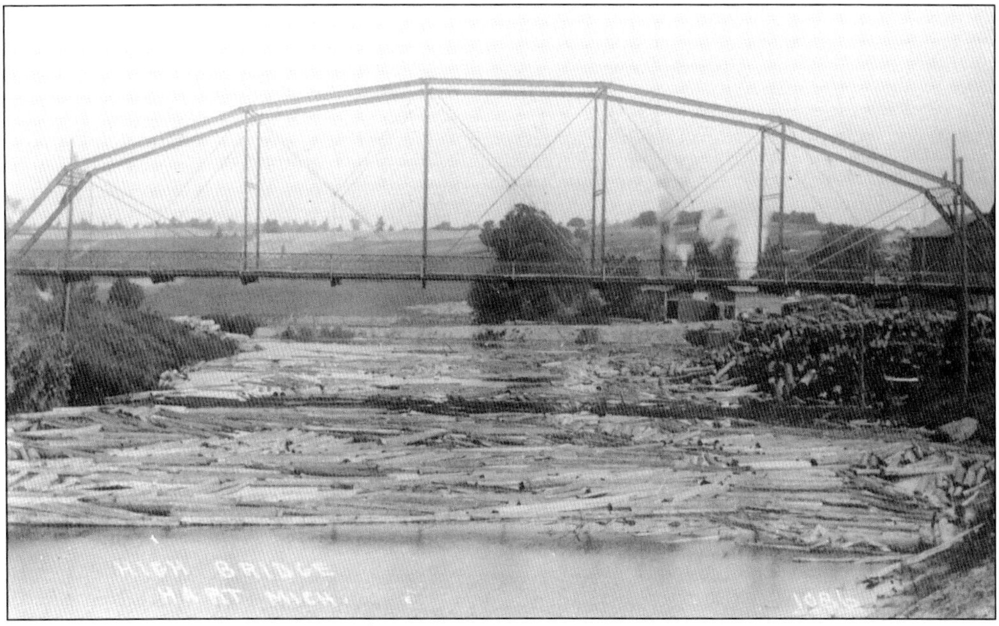

Hart Bridge. In 1881, a sum of $383 was authorized for the construction of an iron bridge across Chippewa Creek. The metal truss bridge replaced the wooden bridges in the latter part of the 19th century, but by the 1890s the bridges themselves were replaced by steel and, eventually, reinforced concrete. Metal truss bridges, such as the one pictured here, are American icons that are quickly vanishing.

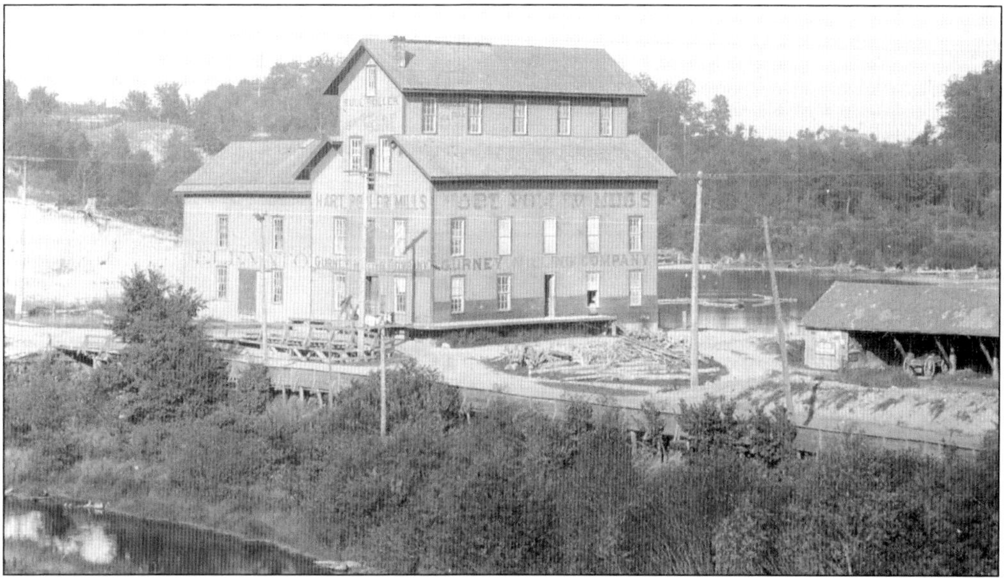

Hart Roller Mill. The Oceana County Mill was built in 1863 near the hydroelectric plant. The Hart Roller Mill was built around 1875 on top of the then new dam. The site of this old mill is currently under the waters of Hart Lake. Mills branded their flours, and as such, Sea Foam, Nickel Plate, and Perfection were popular local brands.

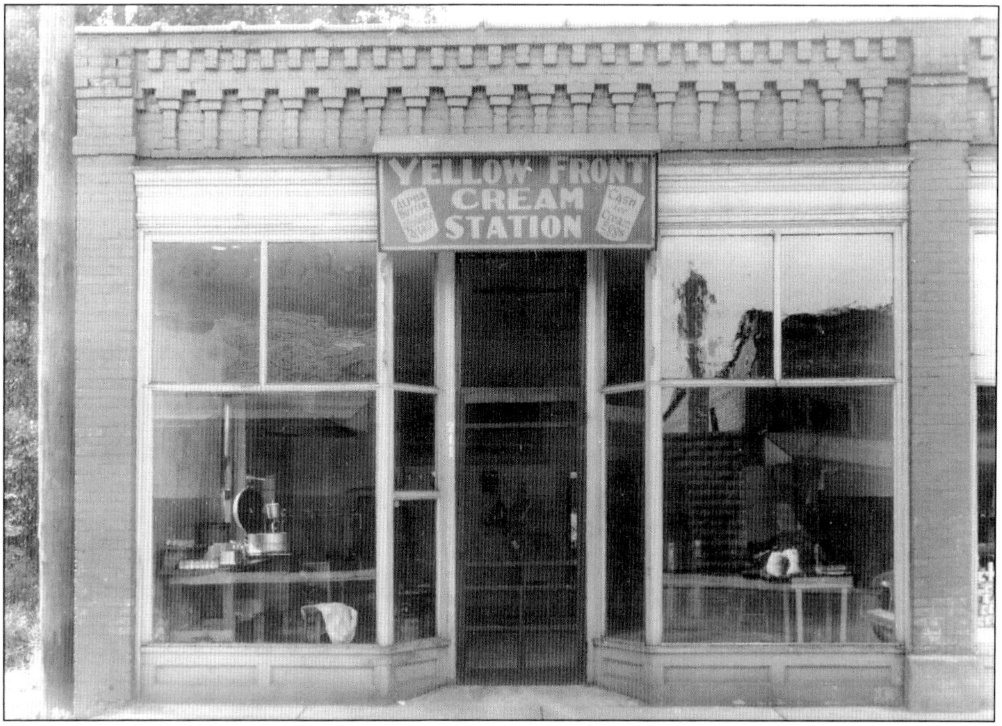

Yellow Front Cream Station. In 1916, a person coming to the cream station could not park an automobile in front of a hitching post. The Yellow Front Cream Station became Edson's Ice Cream Parlor, which was owned by Edson and Doris Billington in 1934. The business was subsequently purchased by the Alpha Creamery in Hesperia, Michigan.

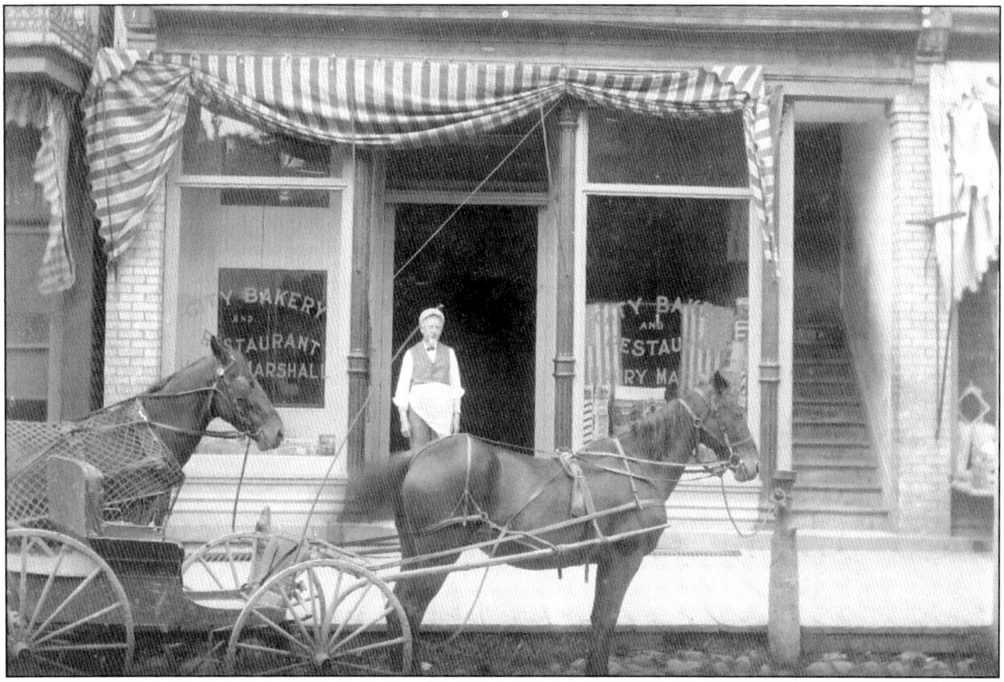

Henry Marshall City Bakery. Henry Marshall immigrated to America in 1876 from Canada. He was born in 1835 in Berkshire, England, and was working in a bakery there by the time he was 16 years old. He settled first in Eaton, Michigan, before coming to Hart and opening the city bakery, a livelihood and trade that he continued into his 80s.

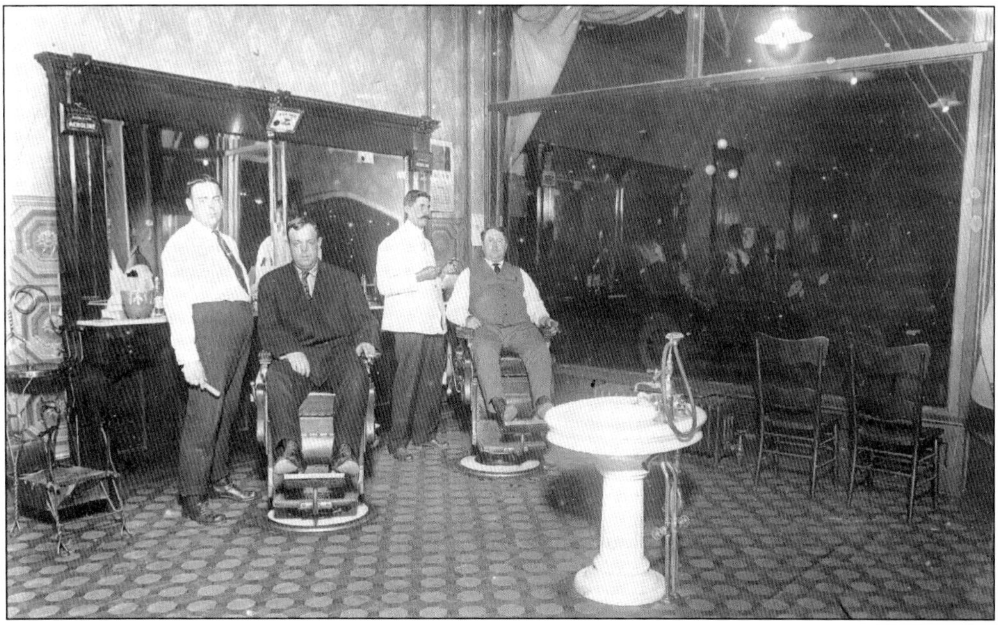

Henry Moon's Barbershop. A shave and a haircut was two bits. Henry Moon, born in Grand Haven, Michigan, opened a barbershop soon after his arrival to Oceana County. Moon was tragically killed in an automobile accident when he misjudged his turn, drove his Model T off the Hart Bridge, and subsequently drowned.

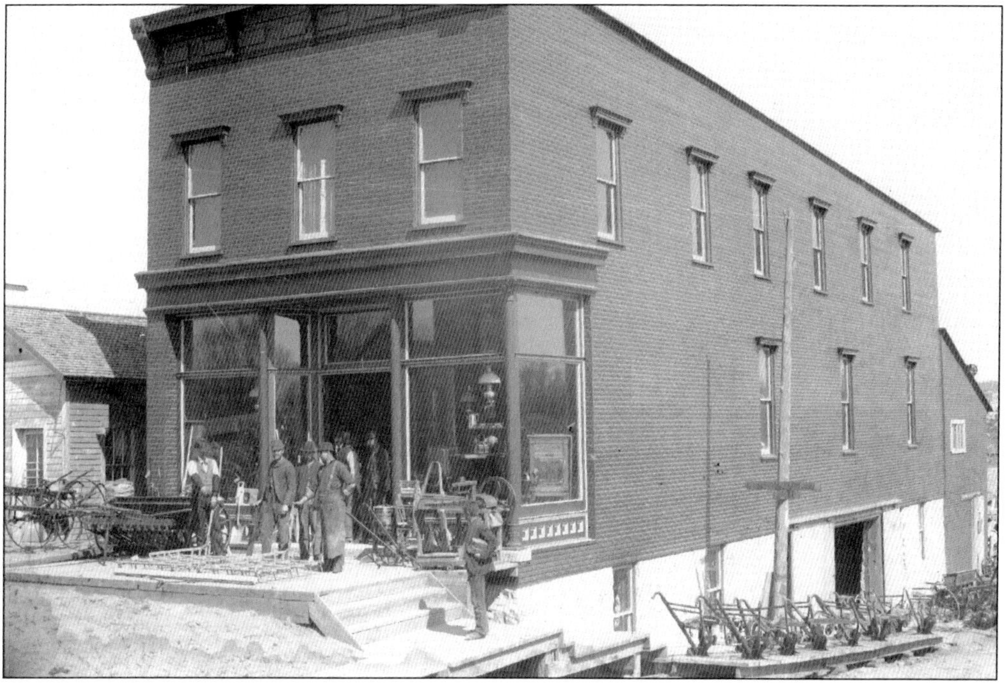

Spitler Building, 1892. By the time Spitler Hardware was constructed in 1892, Hart had become a modern village. Just a few short years earlier, in 1864, Hart residents were still leaving their mail in a fence corner, as there was still no post office, and in 1867 Hart established its first baseball team, the Pioneer Baseball Club. By 1893, a new brick-constructed high school was built on Main Street in the location where the present city hall is now located.

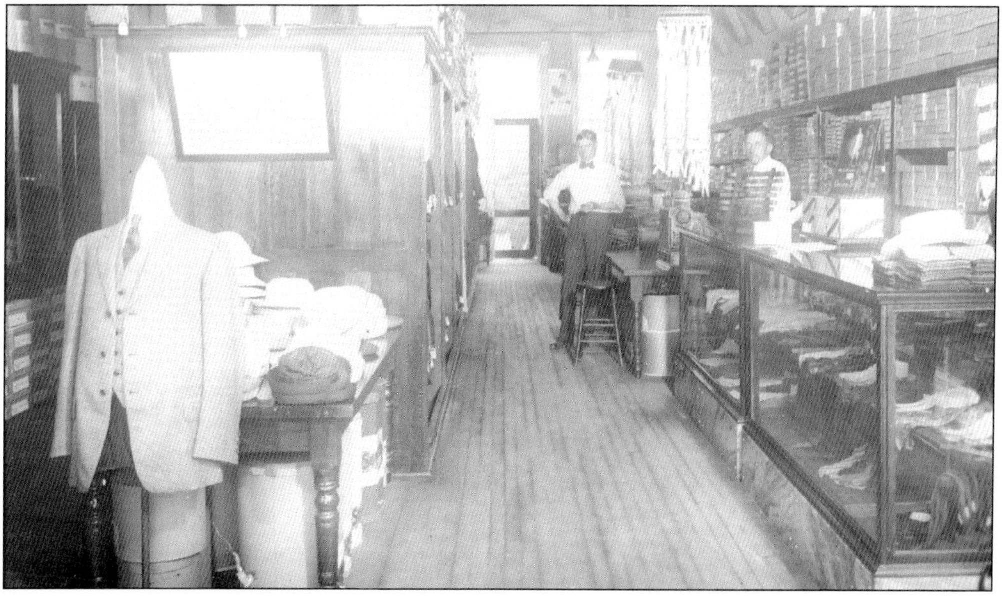

Powers's Clothing Store. George Powers is on the right in this c. 1920 image of Powers's Clothing Store. George worked for James Collins for 10 years prior to purchasing the business. Often called a haberdashery, a gentleman could come in and be fitted for his suit, which was tailored, and purchase a wide assortment of other accessories befitting of the Victorian age.

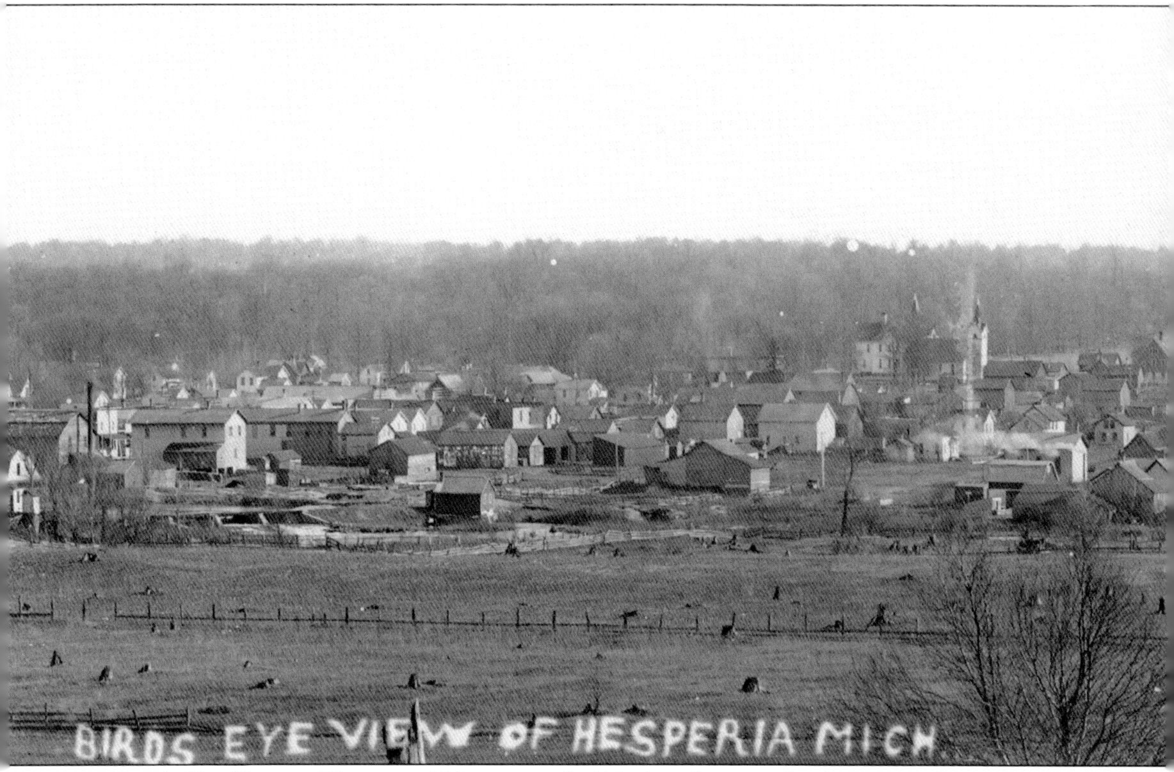

BIRD'S-EYE VIEW OF HESPERIA. Taken around 1910, this photograph of Hesperia shows a neat, tidy community of wood-framed structures in a space that once was covered by a primeval forest. One of Hesperia's natural resources was the position of the village in relationship to the White River, which gave it the advantage of a ready supply of waterpower at a time when it had an advantage over other communities. The mill at Hesperia was capable of providing 25 barrels of flour and 100 barrels of feed per day. A number of dams had been built on the White River to aid in lumbering operations there. On McLaren Lake, lumberjacks would move logs cut in Newfield Township onto the ice during the winter, and when the ice melted, the logs slipped into the water and were transported down the river to the mills in Montague and Whitehall.

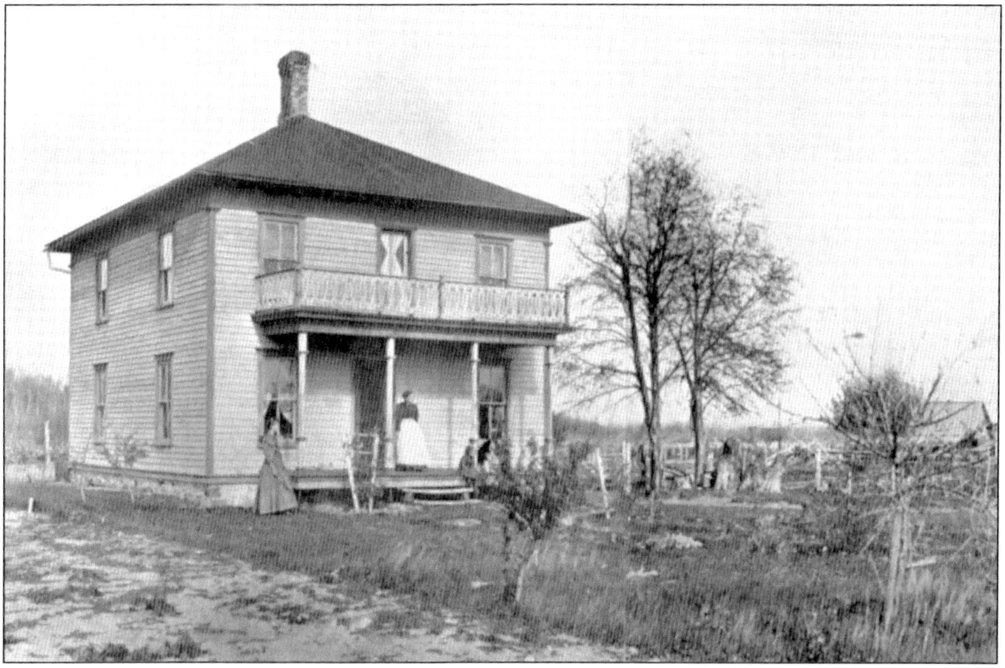

HOME OF MONROE STURTEVANT. Monroe Sturtevant was born in 1830 in New York and enjoyed a life of sailing before marrying in 1861. He came to Oceana County to build a life and a farm for himself and his family. He was also well known as a local logger. Early settlers often found themselves wearing more than one hat as they cleared the land of trees and stumps in preparation for planting. Clearing the land could be a slow and tedious process, and often only a few acres could be cleared each year. Clearing was done either by felling and burning the trees or by girding them, which left the stumps and posed a danger to livestock. Often these early settlers only had enough supplies to get them through the first year, and their possessions were often meager.

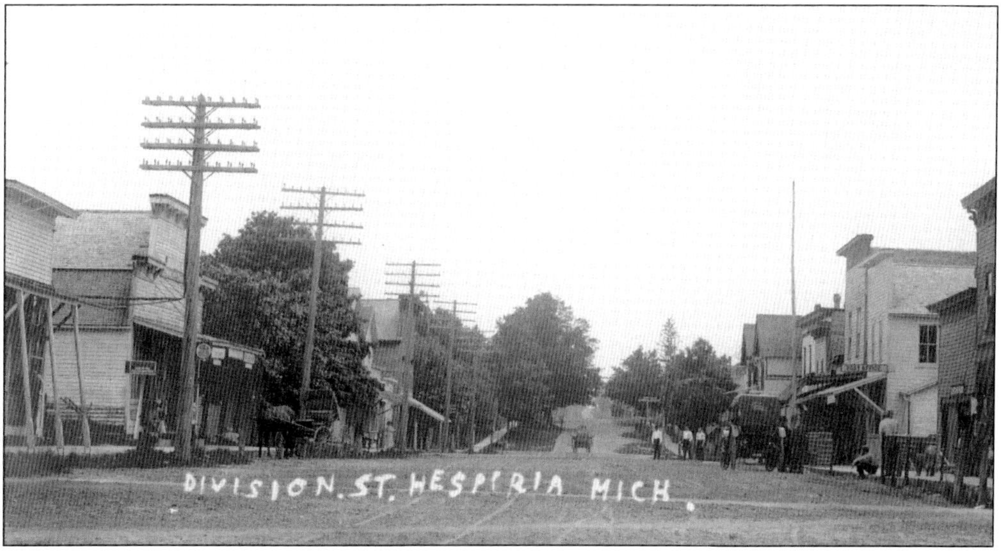

HESPERIA MAIN STREET. Local residents and farmers have come to town to shop along Division Street and to view the wares offered by local merchants. Hesperia is divided between Oceana and Newaygo Counties along this street.

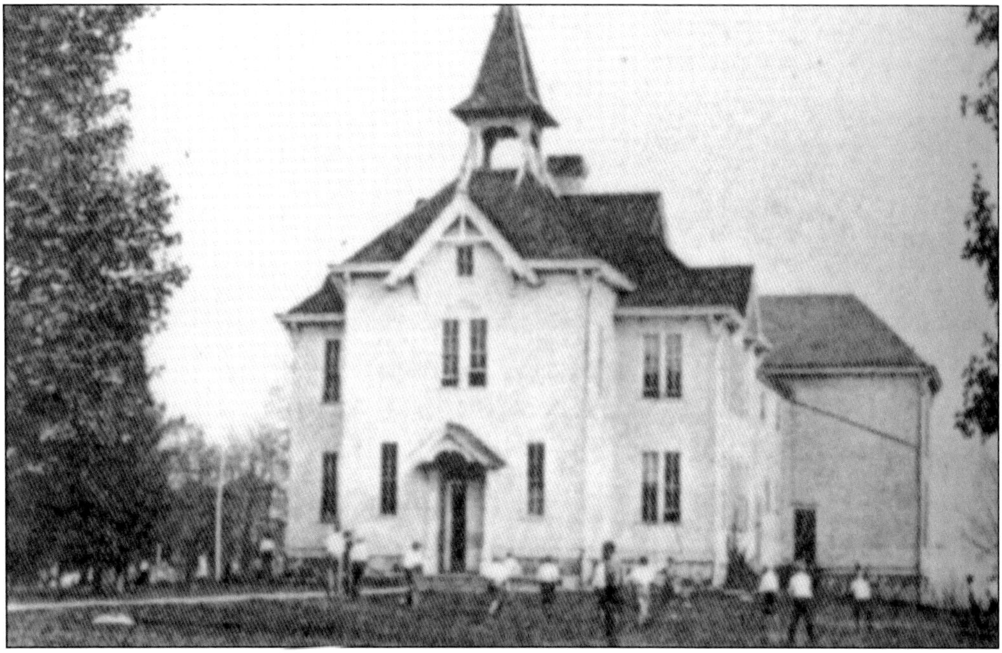

Hesperia High School. The Hesperia School, built around 1880, was located on the Newaygo County side of the line dividing Hesperia. Initially, about 20 students attended, and that number had increased significantly at the time the building burned to the ground in 1932. Students were required to use temporary quarters in the community center building until a new school was completed in 1939.

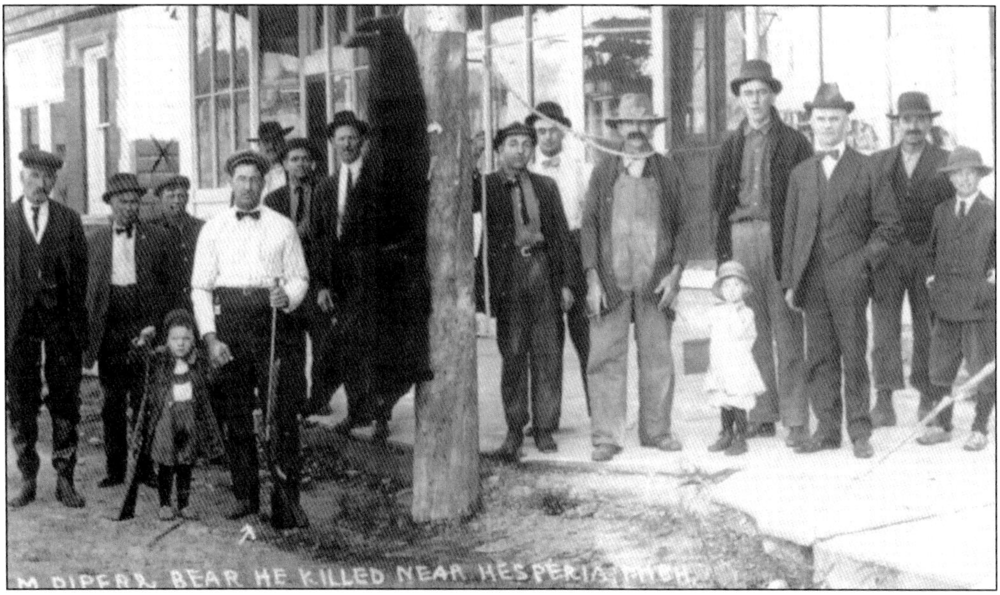

A Successful Hunt. Half of the village appears to have turned out to get their picture taken with the black bear that M. Piper shot near Hesperia in about 1915. Located in Newfield Township, the Hesperia area is blessed with more than a dozen lakes and an abundance of game. Hunting played an important role in the ability to provide meat for the dinner table, and a successful hunter was a good provider.

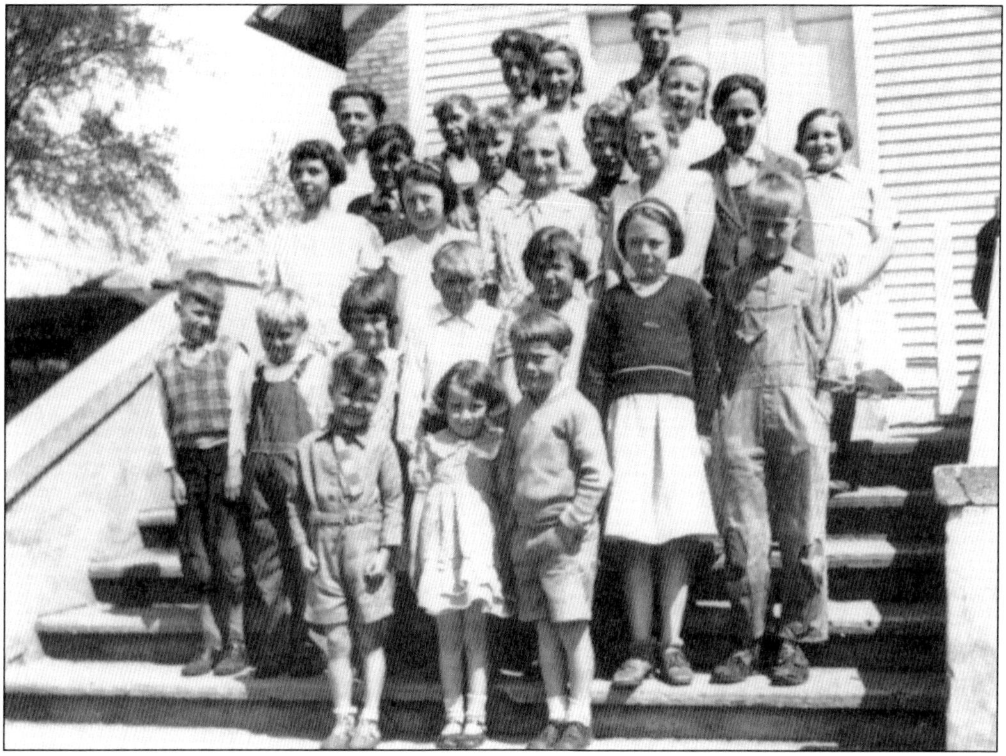

Marshville School. In 1859, George Marsh came from Vermont to Oceana County and began construction of a gristmill, sawmill, and a dam to power the operation. The gristmill was completed in 1863. The Marshville School, located at Fifty-sixth and Marshville Roads in Benona Township, was in District No. 4. It had been named for George and Henry Marsh. The school operated until consolidation in 1956. Shown here are the students of Marshville School in 1932.

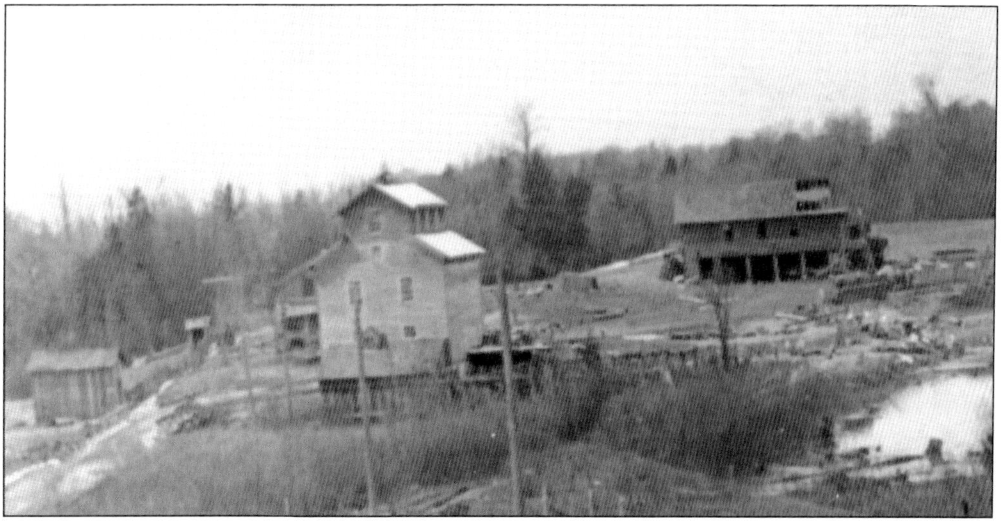

Marshville Mill Uses Old Process. The mill at Marshville was located on Stony Creek. While under the management of I. Lutz, the mill continued to use the old process of milling with a stone long after its competitors had changed over to the roller-process system. The process breaks the grain down in a series of steps using different types of grinding rolls.

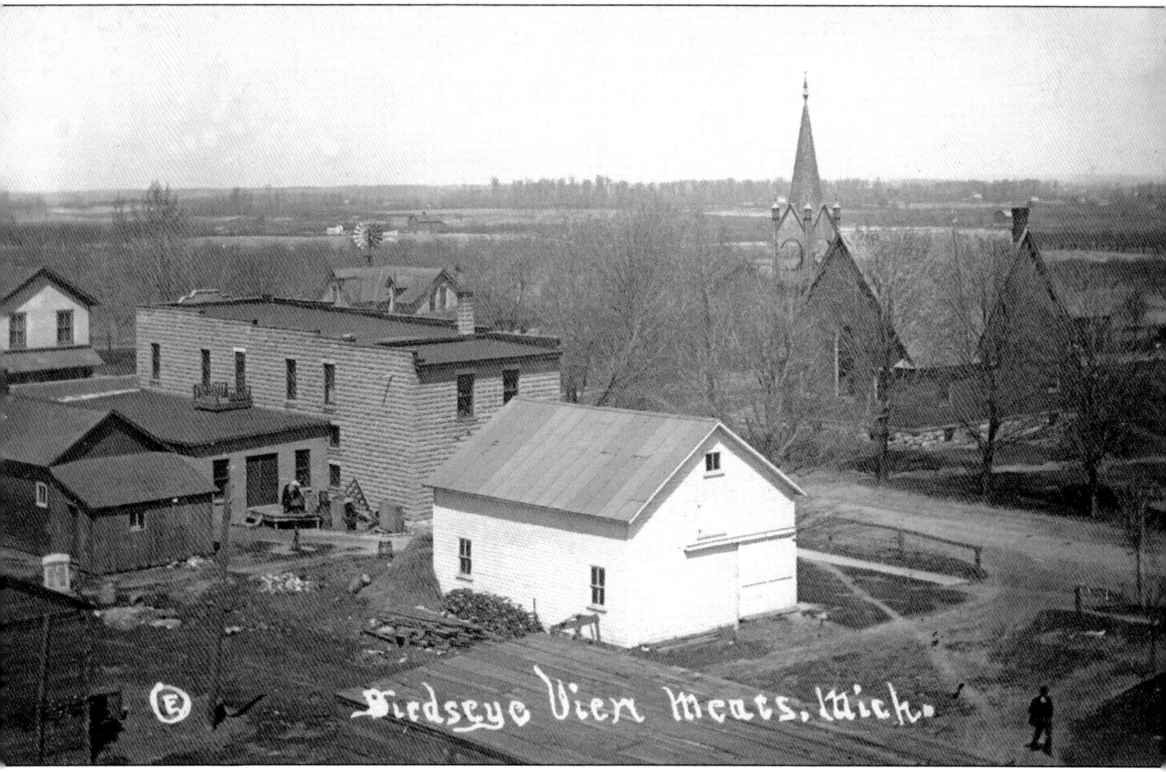

BIRD'S-EYE VIEW OF MEARS. The village of Mears came into being in 1873 when Charles Mears, along with Samuel Odell, bought a piece of land from a local physician. The village grew rapidly, fueled by the influx of loggers and the sawmills that began operation in the village. Mears was in control of the logging villages of Lincoln and Hamlin in Mason County and, in 1873, saw the removal of the county seat from Lincoln to the newly incorporated city of Ludington. Mears attempted to regain dominance and control in Oceana County, and in 1873, he petitioned to have the county seat moved to the village of Mears; however, that petition was denied. Over the next decade, Mears sold his holdings to the north, consolidating his operations in Oceana County. By 1890, both Lincoln and Hamlin had become ghost towns. As Mears's influence waned there, it grew in Oceana County, leaving his indelible mark on the development of this section of western Michigan.

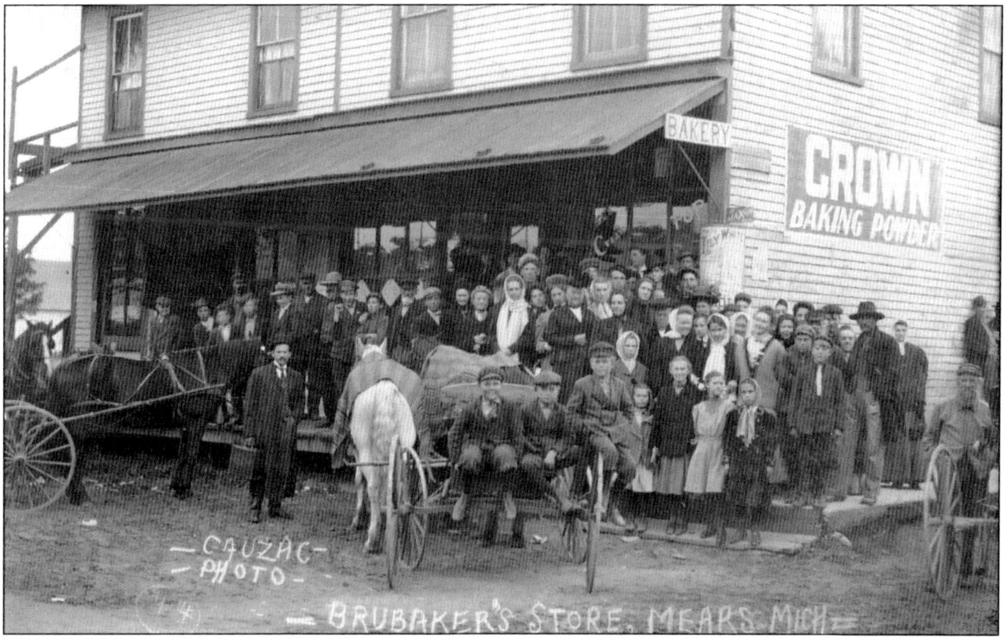

Lofty Goals. Mears attempted to gain political control in every community he had operations in. When the store was built in the village of Mears, the second story had a vault and rooms that could be used as offices, as well as a larger room that easily could have been used as a courtroom. The county seat in Oceana County, however, eluded his grasp and remained in Hart.

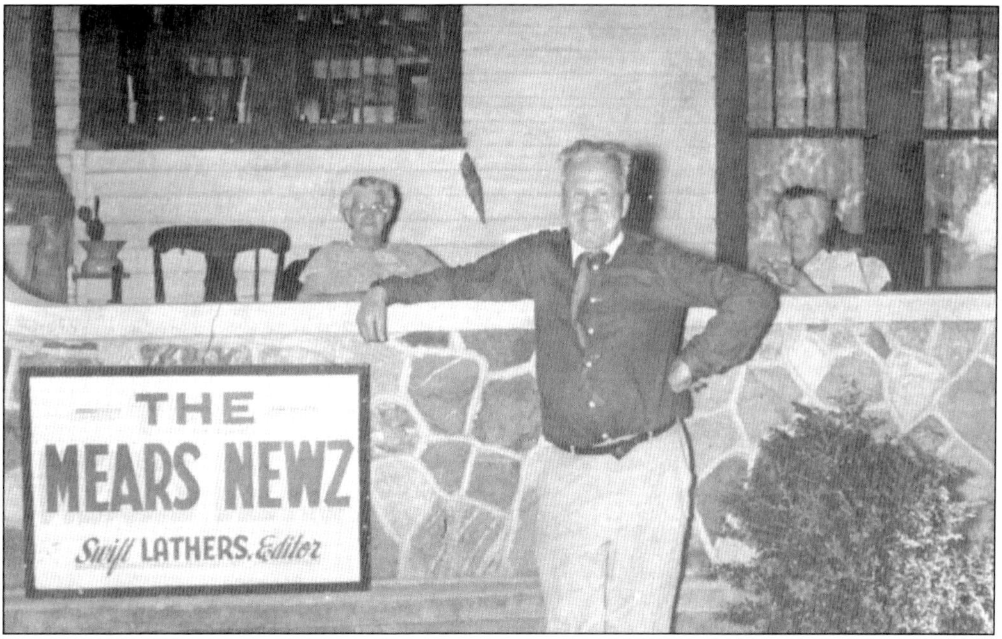

Swift Lathers Makes Waves. It is difficult to talk about Oceana County without making reference to Swift Lathers, who was known worldwide as the controversial editor of the *Mears Newz*. The world's smallest newspaper was published out of his home starting in 1914 (currently a museum) in what Lathers referred to as the "Land of Mears." He was inducted into the Michigan Journalism Hall of fame in 1986, sixteen years after his death.

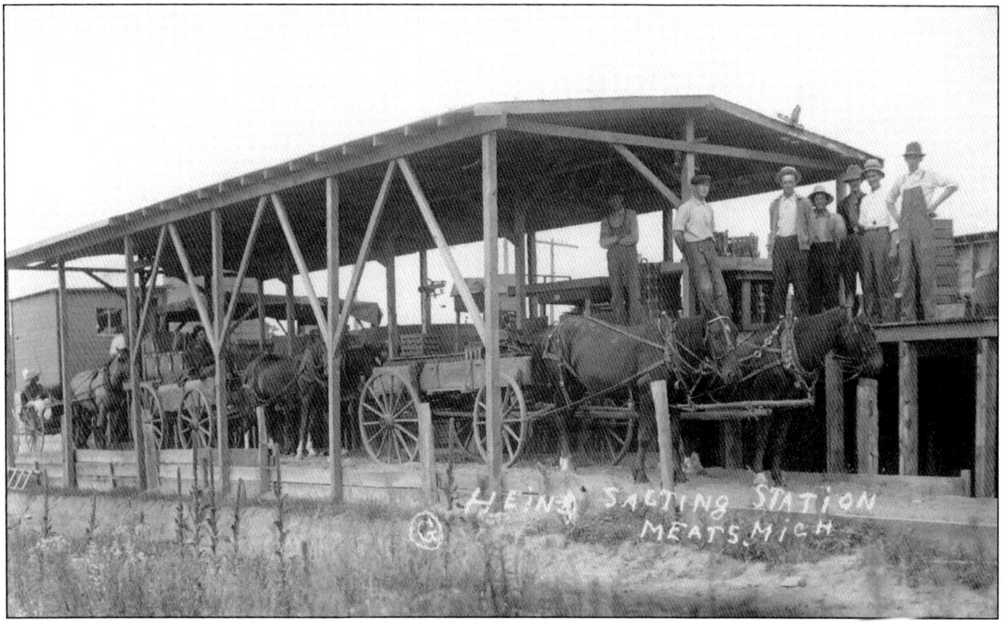

THE SALTING STATION. Another of the H.J. Heinz Company salting stations is seen here. Cucumbers were placed in large vats of salt brine before being packed in barrels. The barrels were then shipped out by train and eventually found themselves in the corner grocery, where a person could reach into the barrel and grab a fresh pickle.

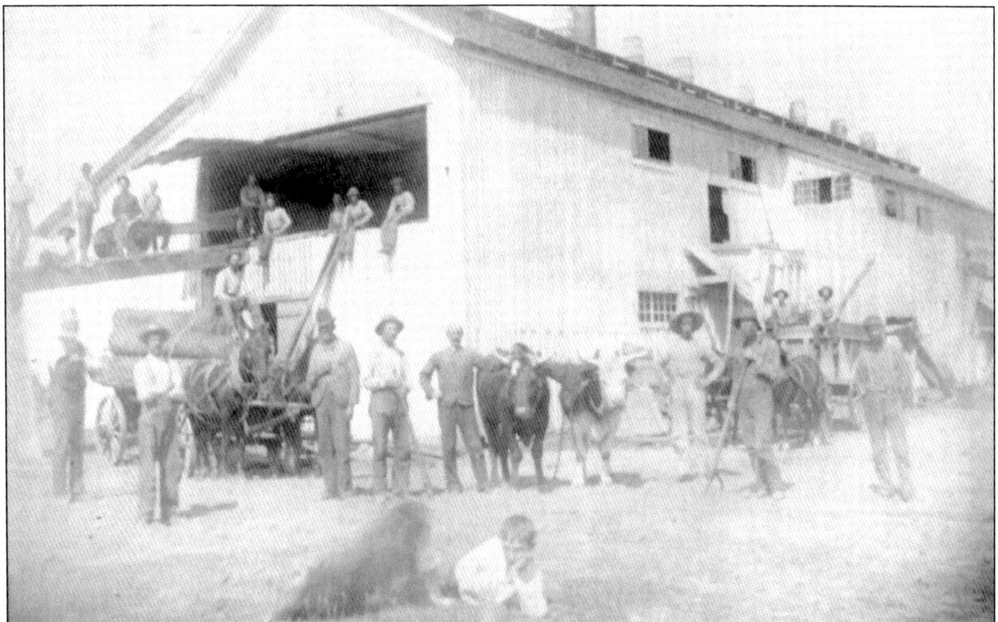

CHARLES MEARS SAWMILL. Charles Mears established a number of mills and camps along western Michigan's shoreline, starting in 1838 at White Lake. Next, he built at Duck Lake in 1844 and also had mills in Lincoln in 1851, Pentwater in 1856, and Hamlin in 1861. He operated the mill at Pere Marquette, as well as a mill for James Ludington from 1859 to 1861. The second sawmill built by Charles Mears burned prior to completion.

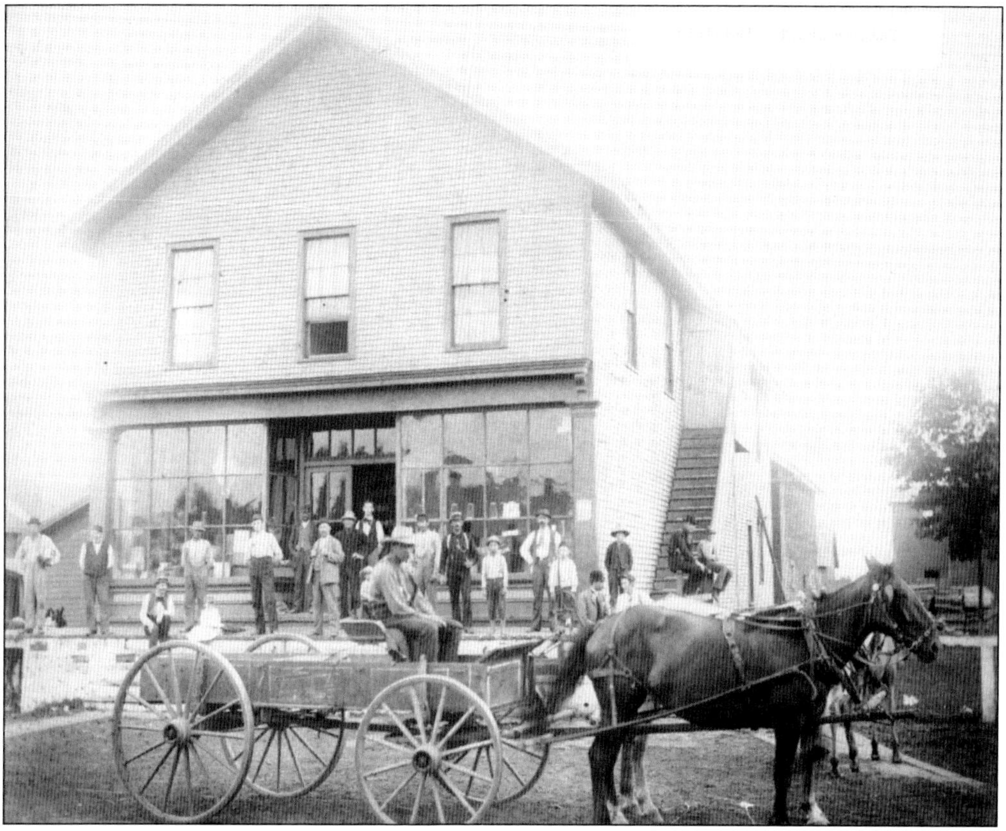

BRUBAKER'S STORE GIVES PIANO AWAY. Andrew Brubaker came to Oceana County and settled in Mears after purchasing a farm there. Andrew had owned a store in Illinois, and he worked towards that goal in Mears by traveling home to home selling patent medicines and other goods until he earned enough money to be in business there. Andrew operated his store in Mears for more than 30 years and promoted his business in novel ways, such as a ticket drawing for a piano.

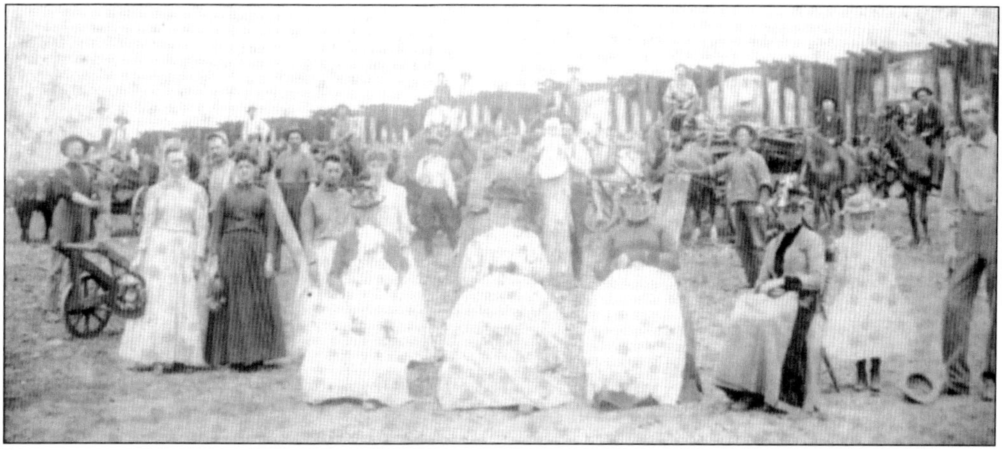

SPRING LAKE IRON COMPANY COAL KILNS. In 1879, the Iron Company of Spring Lake built ten 75-cord charcoal kilns just north of the village of Mears. The company also constructed a charcoal hot-blast furnace in Spring Lake the same year to produce pig iron. Three kilns operated in Oceana County, producing charcoal from wood, with no other commercial purpose.

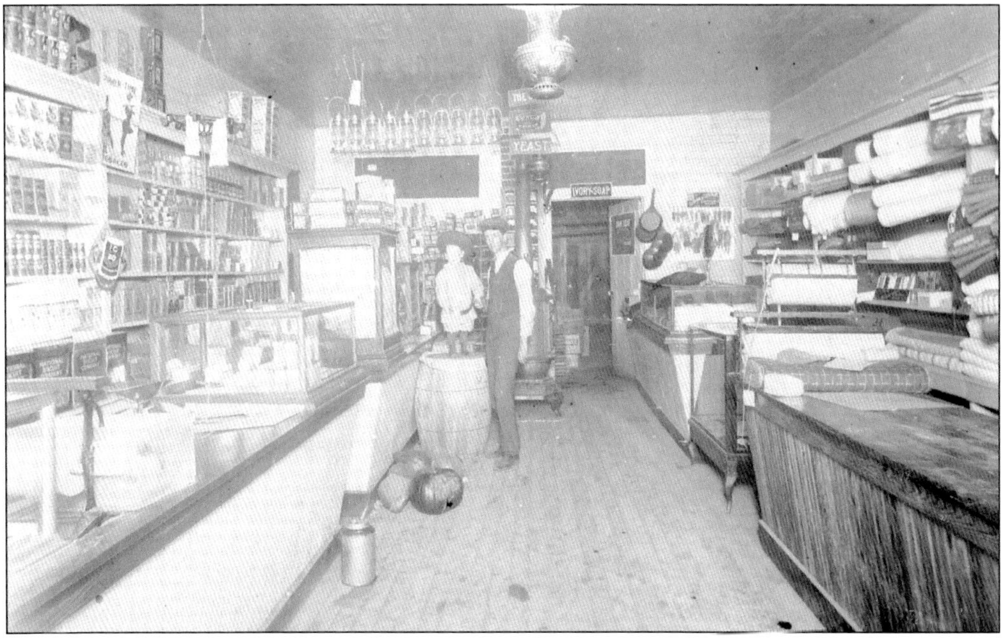

West Half of Dunlop Bakery. The west side of the Dunlop Bakery was outfitted as a general store where one could purchase materials, goods, and groceries. The shelves in this c. 1910 image are loaded; even a fresh pumpkin is available for purchase. Note the kerosene lamps hanging from the rafter in the back of the store.

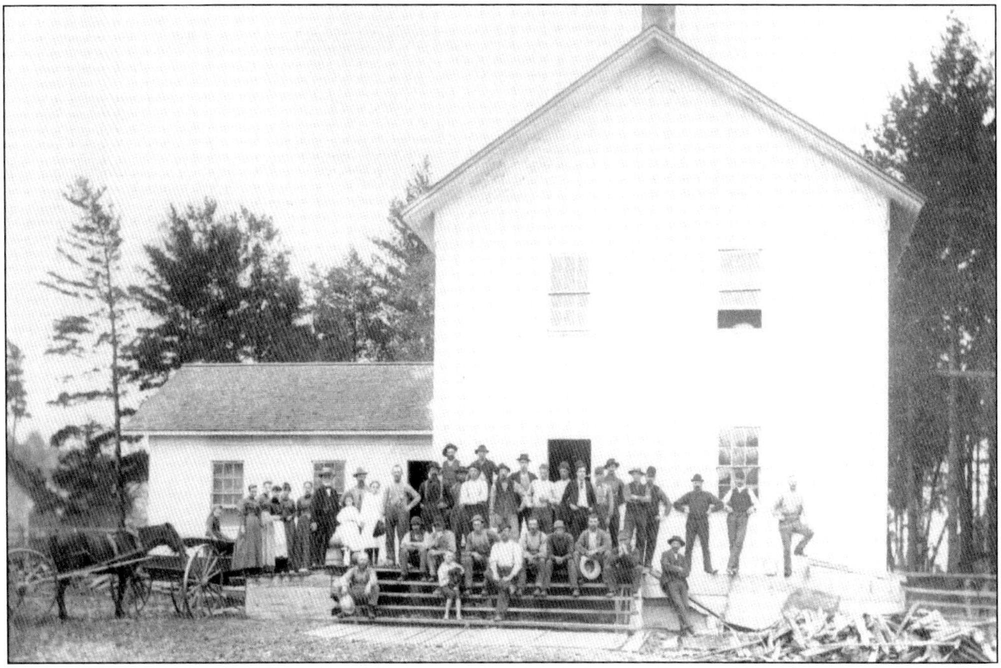

Charles Mears Boardinghouse. Built about 140 years ago for the lumber crews of Charles Mears, the old boardinghouse was a crucial piece of the lumbering operations because it provided not only a base of operations when needed, but also a stable place for the lumberjacks to enjoy a hot meal and a warm bed after a hard day's work in the woods.

A Lumberman's Legacy. Charles Mears was a lumberman whose legacy lives on. He was an important, if not critical, element in the development of the western Michigan area taken in by Mason and Oceana Counties. His name lives on in the village of Mears and in the Charles Mears State Park in Pentwater as a result of lands donated by his daughter Carrie.

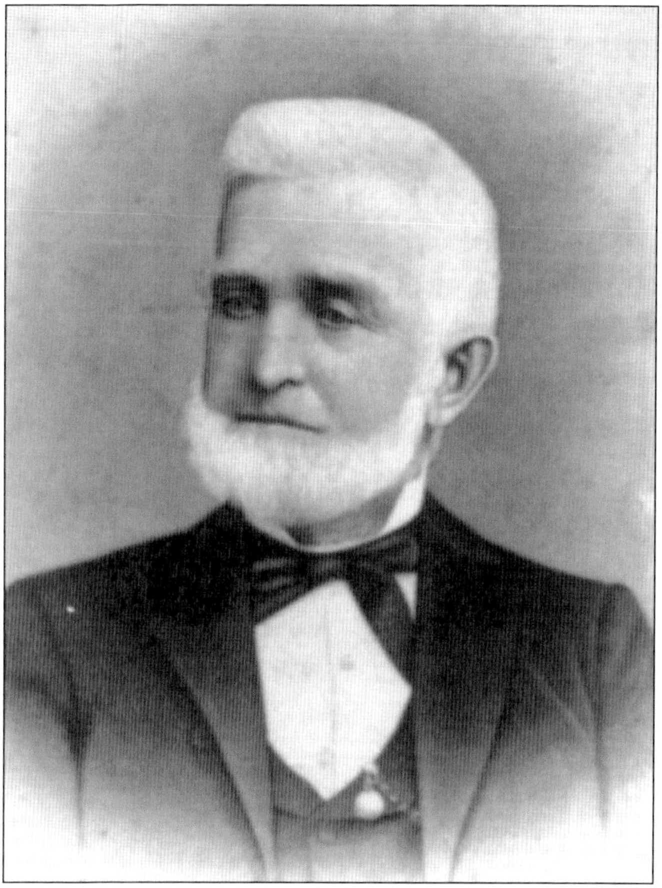

Mears Schoolhouse. The building pictured offered classes for kindergarten through third grade, an intermediate that housed fourth through seventh grades, and a high school room that held classes for eighth through tenth grades. The building stood at the site of the baseball diamond at Golden School.

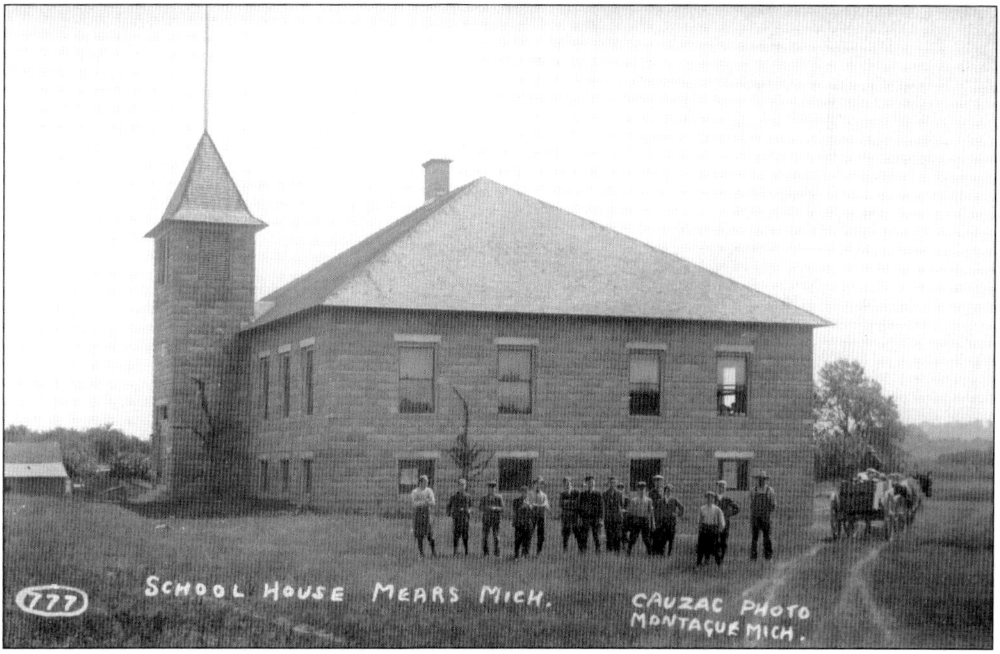

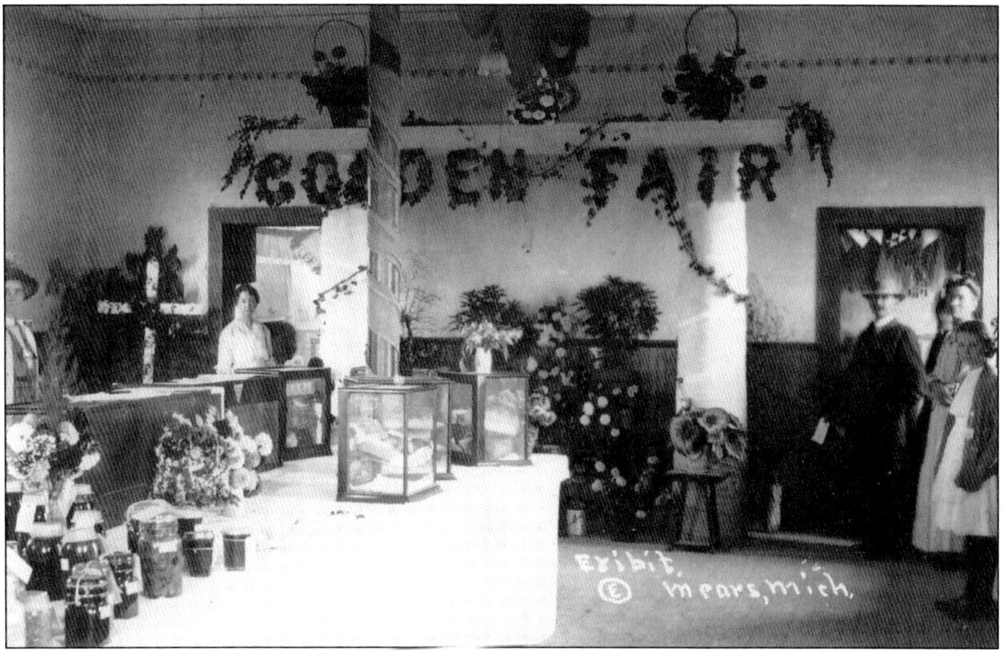

Golden Fair at Mears. There were a lot of competitions between school districts within the tight-knit community for the fair each year, as each attempted to outdo one other. Bragging rights over which school had the best displays was a good-natured, if not a coveted, achievement.

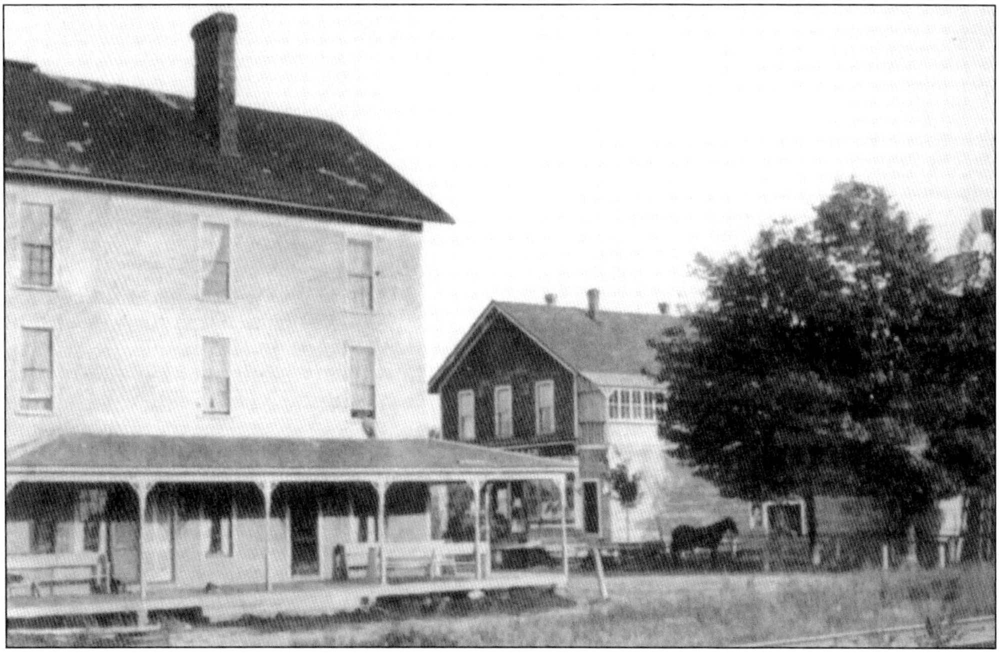

Mears Hotel and Boardinghouse. Pictured here are the Mears Hotel and boardinghouse around 1910. By 1877, the village had laid claim to three sawmills, a shingle mill, a broom-handle factory, three general stores, and a bowl factory. Mears was a hub of activity and commerce. After the lumbering era ended, Mears became a center of activity for the resort and tourism industry that developed after 1930.

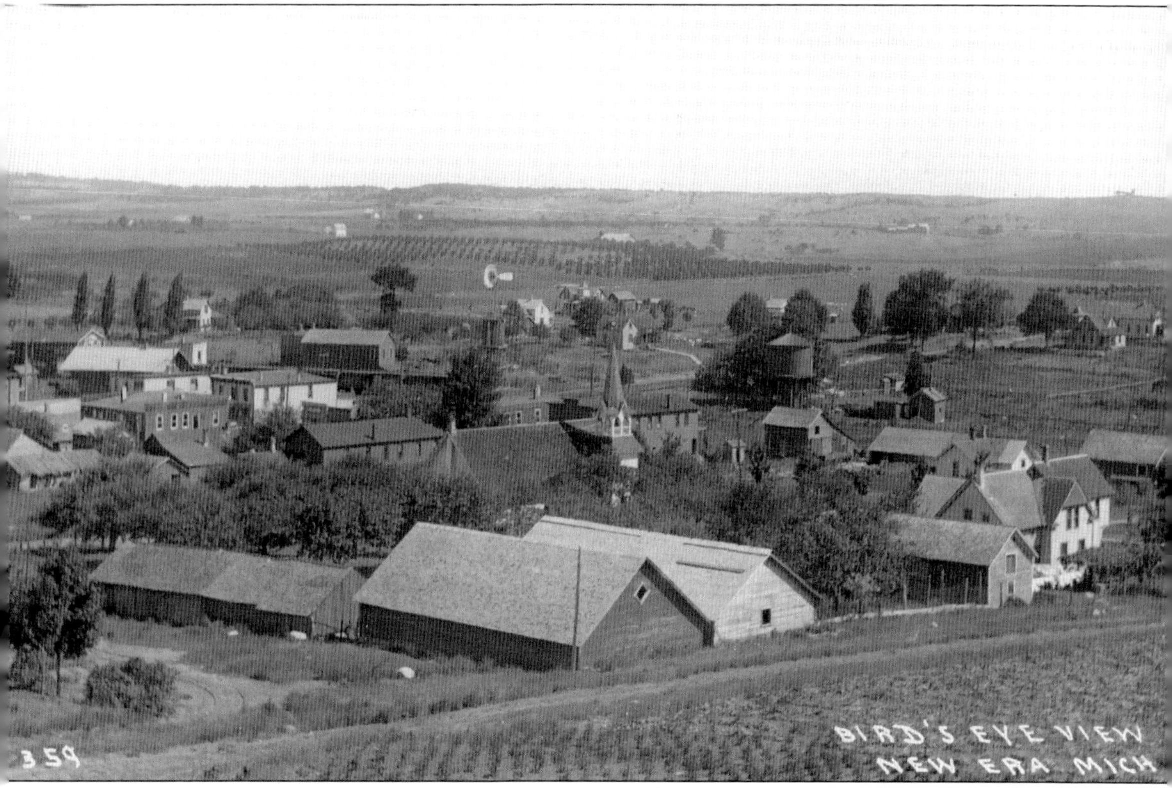

Bird's-Eye View of New Era. New Erie was the original suggestion for the name of this village when it was founded in 1872. It was intended to be named after Erie, Pennsylvania, the hometown of Dr. A. Spaulding. The name was instead designated as New Era, and the village flourished in the early logging years. When New Era was founded, a statement was made in 1872 that this is a "new era" the community is living in, and the idea stuck as a name for the village itself. The railroad came to New Era first on May 15, 1872, and then the post office was established, which was housed in the hotel for a period. The first postmaster was Gilbert Gobles. Rural free delivery (RFD) began on October 1, 1915. Another milestone in the communities, John Runner is listed as the first rural carrier. The village boasted a train station and a post office but never sustained a large number of residents despite its location and quality of life.

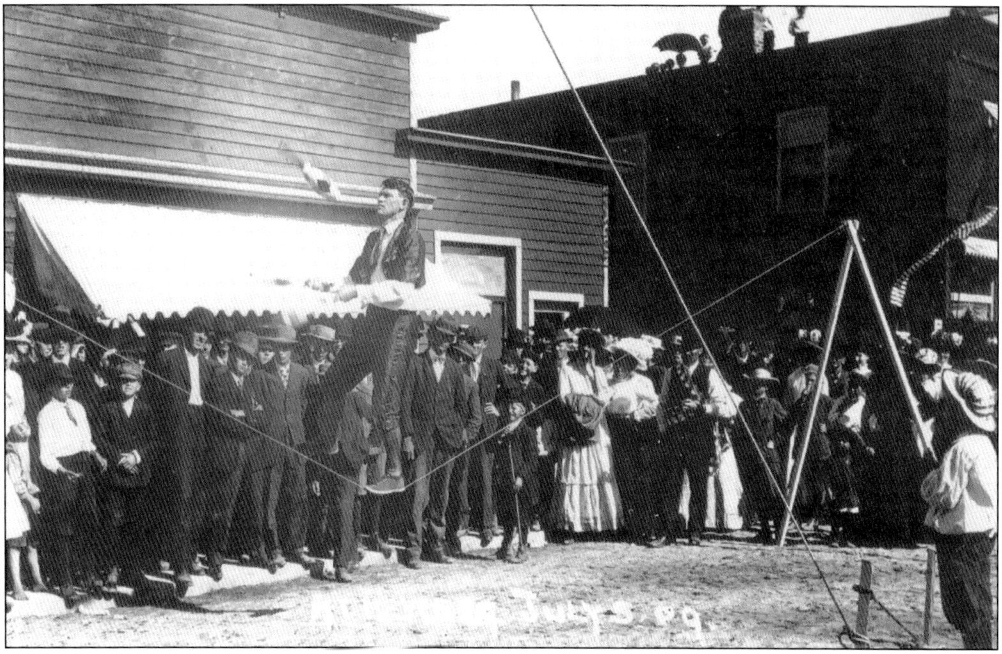

New Era Slackwire Artist. A slackwire artist demonstrates his skill to a crowd of interested visitors at a local celebration around 1910. A slackwire is a different form of balancing act than a tightwire. In slackwire, the only tension on the wire comes from the performer and whatever props are carried along during the performance.

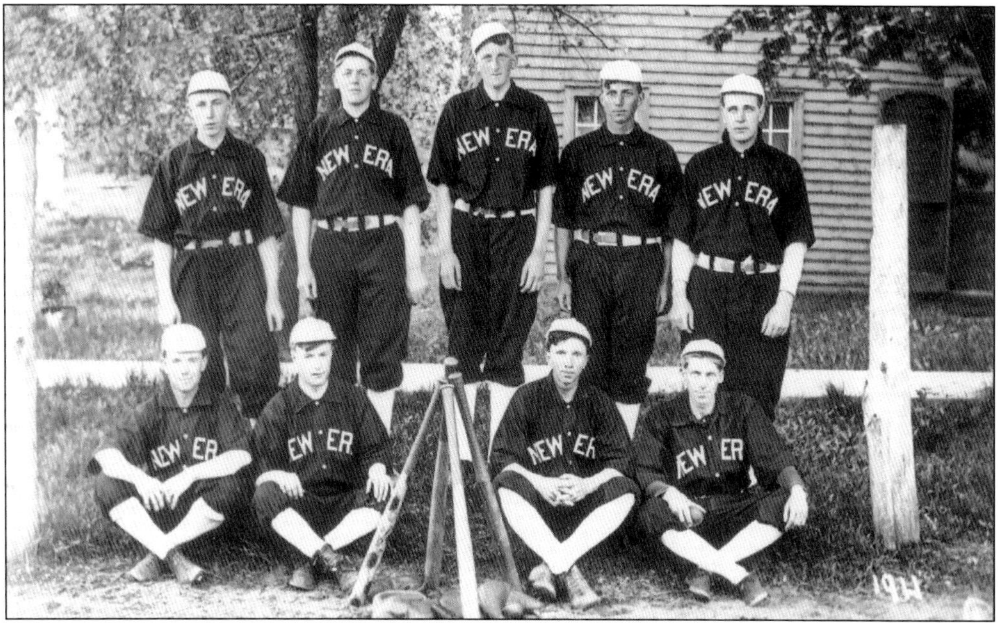

New Era Baseball Team. Hart's baseball team formed in 1867 with other communities following suit. Baseball became popular in small towns and villages several decades before the creation of the first national league in 1876. By the mid-1880s, every town, village, and community of any merit or size had at least one team. Communities played each other for local fame, bragging rights, and notoriety, as well as cash purses and prizes.

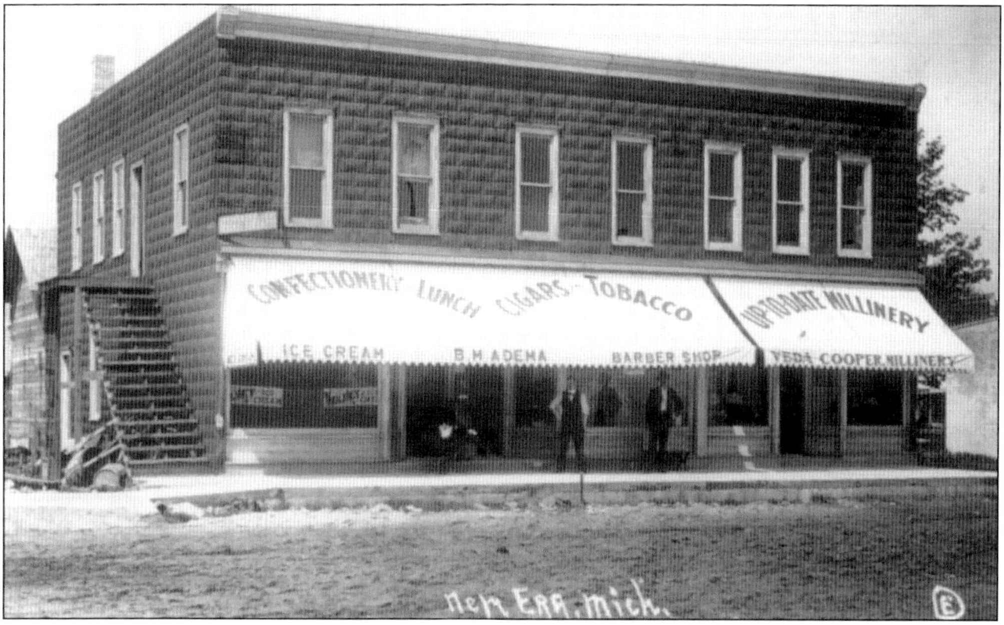

New Era Storefronts. There have been many small businesses in New Era. Reeds Variety was built in 1911 and burned in 1918. Reconstructed in 1919, it was named the same as before. The Curiosity Shop was housed in a building that was constructed after 1904 and used as a potato warehouse and for bean sorting before housing an ice cream parlor called Norberg's. After 1953, the building was occupied by an antique store.

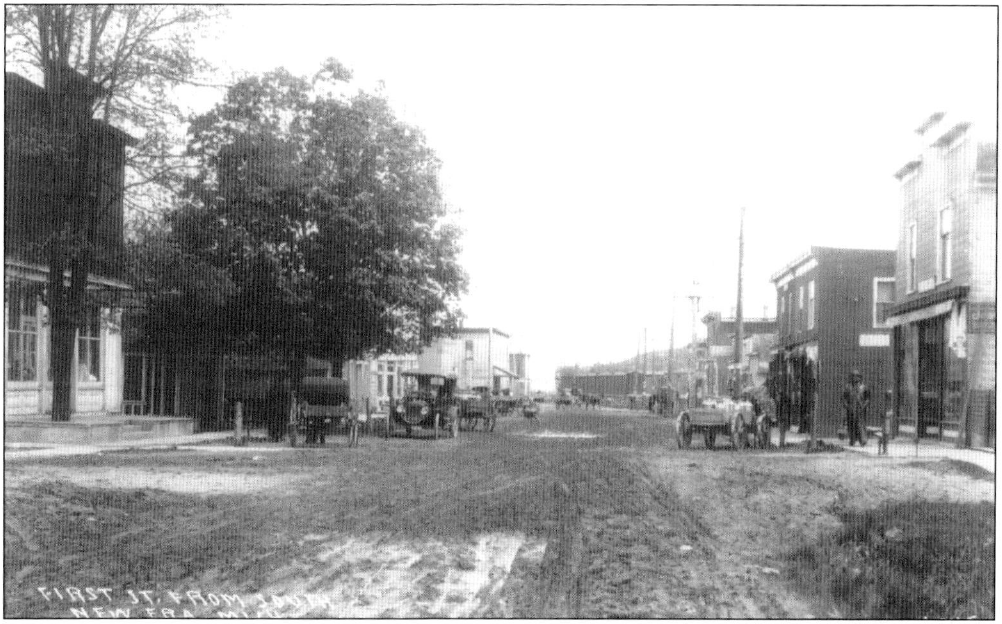

Newfangled Contraptions. By about 1915, the horseless carriage had made inroads, even to the smallest community. The vehicles shared the roads with the horse and buggy, which was still utilized by many rural residents. The roads, as seen here, were still undeveloped, and as the road system improved and automobiles became more common, the horse and its supporting businesses vanished from Main Street.

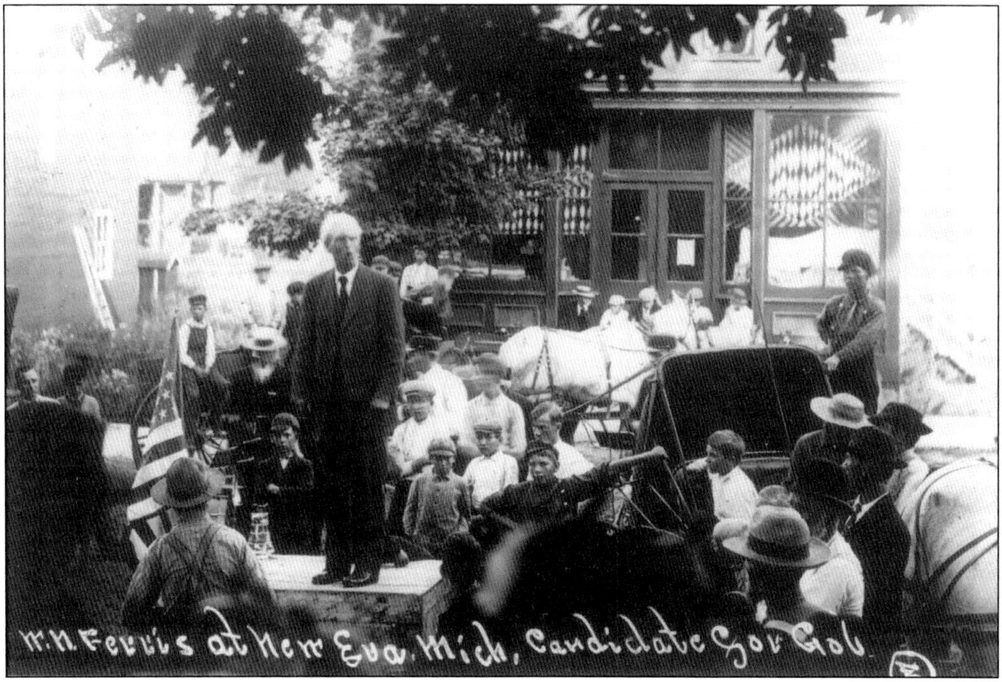

FERRIS STUMPS AT NEW ERA. In the early years of political campaigning, politicians really had to press the flesh in order to get out the vote. Woodbridge Ferris is standing on his soapbox meeting with a group of potential voters in the village of New Era during the governor's race of 1912. After winning the race, he served as Michigan's 28th governor from 1913 to 1917.

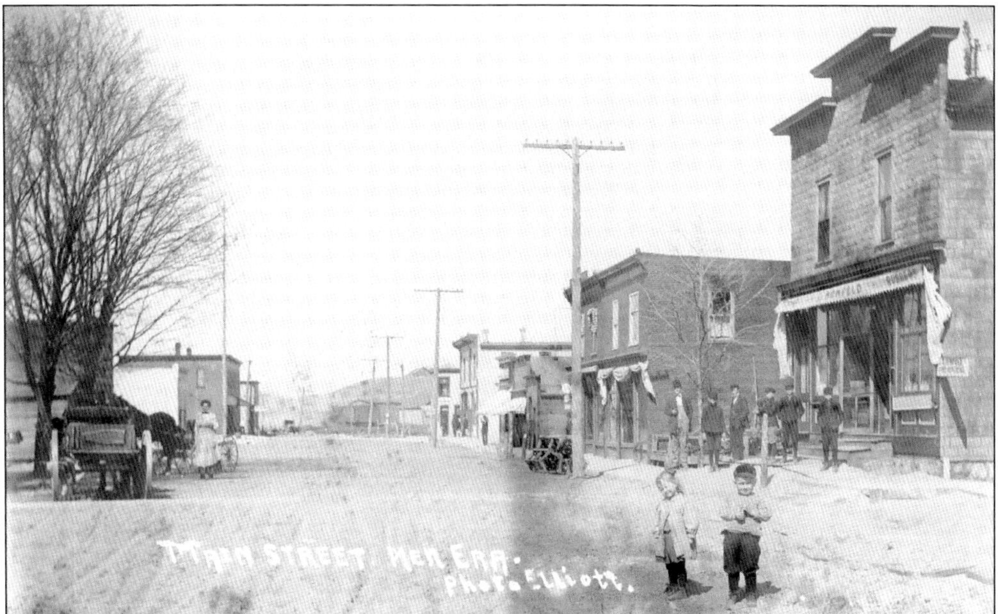

MAIN STREET BY ELLIOTT. These two youngsters seem preoccupied with photographer Harlo Elliott in this c. 1910 view of New Era's Main Street. The street is noticeably devoid of automobiles, with only posts for hitching wagons to in view. New Era was incorporated as a village on June 28, 1948.

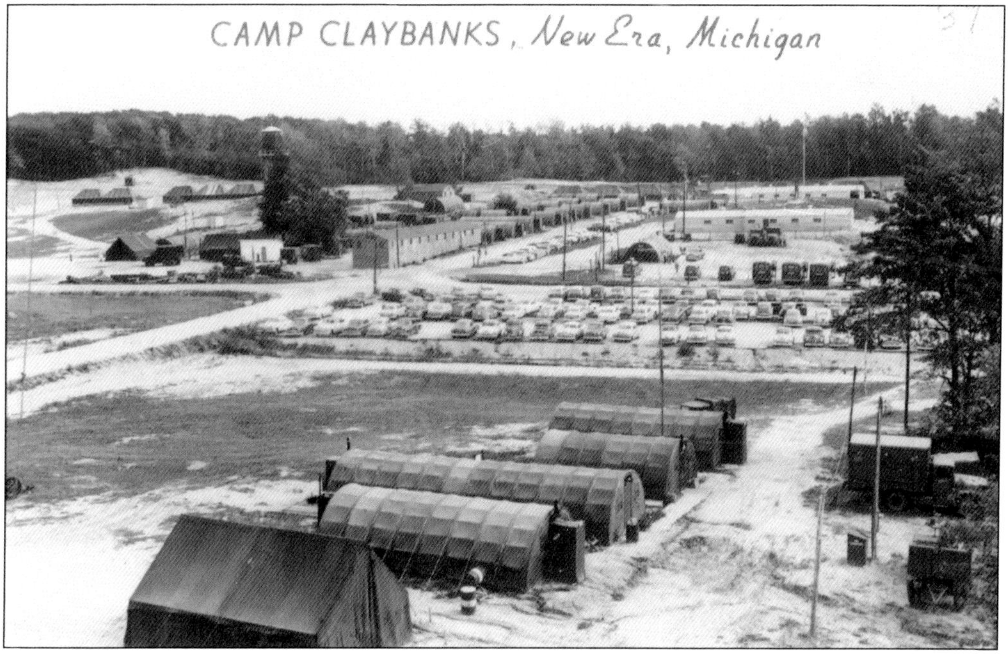

CAMP CLAYBANKS PROVIDED TRAINING. Established in 1953 on land leased for the purpose of creating an Army training base near Rothbury, the camp operated for about five years. The camp provided training for National Guardsmen from Michigan and surrounding states to learn anti-aircraft techniques. The personnel and the guardsmen who attended provided a short-lived economic boom for the region.

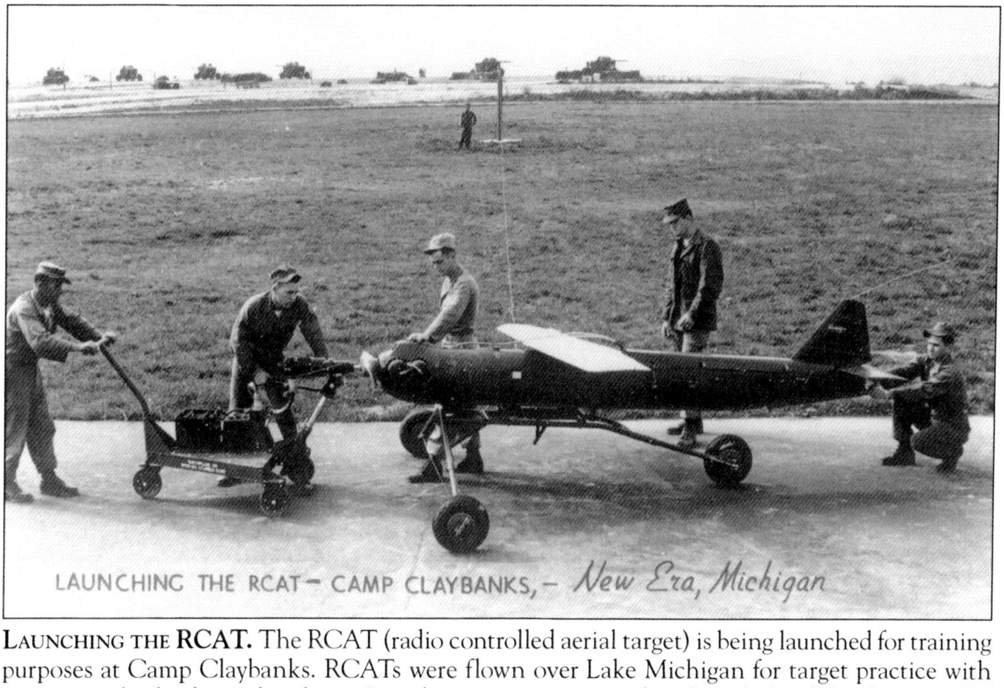

LAUNCHING THE RCAT. The RCAT (radio controlled aerial target) is being launched for training purposes at Camp Claybanks. RCATs were flown over Lake Michigan for target practice with one unusual rule: do not hit them. Guardsmen were instructed to shoot behind the drone, as the cost of replacement was excessive, and the Army wanted to conserve resources.

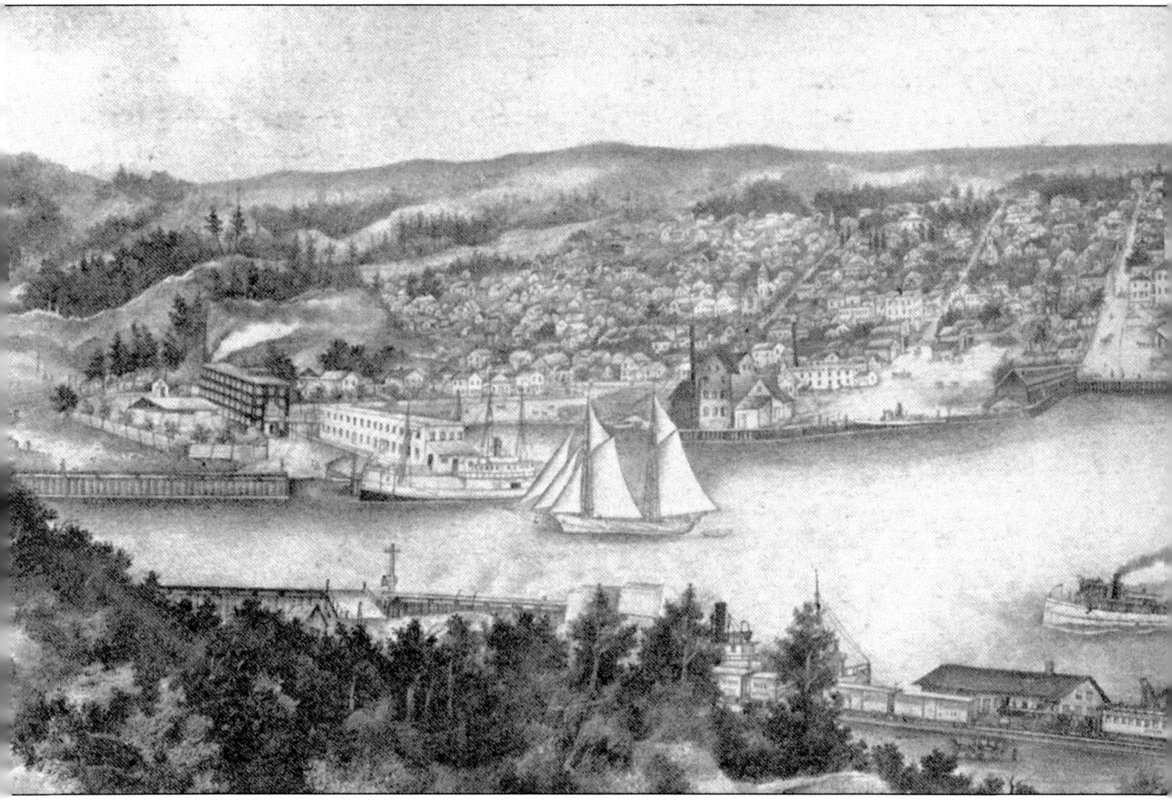

PENTWATER BIRD'S-EYE VIEW. Originally called Middlesex, Pentwater was the first community in the county to incorporate as a village on March 16, 1867. In 1871, Gray Brothers and Company opened the first bank in the county there. This is an early view of Main Street in the village, founded in the early 1850s by Rector and Cobb. The name *Pentwater* is attributed to the local Native Americans and is thought to mean "penned-up waters." The channel was so shallow, one could wade across it, and some accounts claim that only a few years earlier, there was no channel there at all. Early occupations centered around lumbering and farming and the trades that supported them. Originally, land in the area could be purchased for 75¢ to $1 an acre. The village was a center of activity, thanks to the natural harbor, but it lost the bid for the county seat to Hart. In the first meeting, $150 was decided on for town expenses. Pentwater benefited by much of the early growth and settlement in the county.

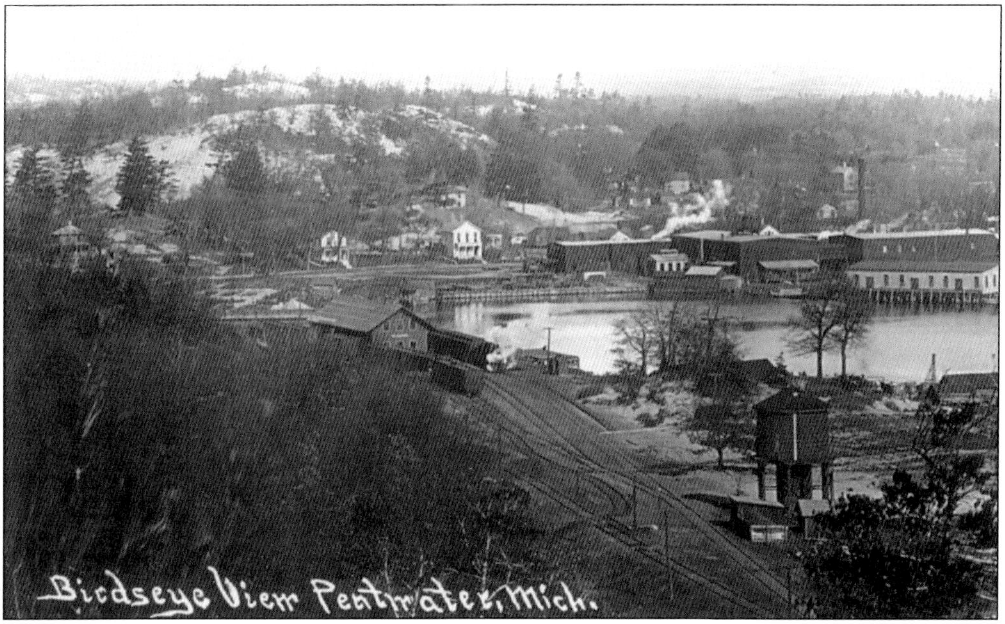

LONG VIEW OF PENTWATER, 1910. Having the channel and harbor meant that many people landed at Pentwater first and then moved out into the interior of the county to settle in the townships. Roads were nonexistent; deer trails and logging trails were passable for foot traffic and followed the paths of least resistance. It was not until many years later that the roads were surveyed, platted, and built.

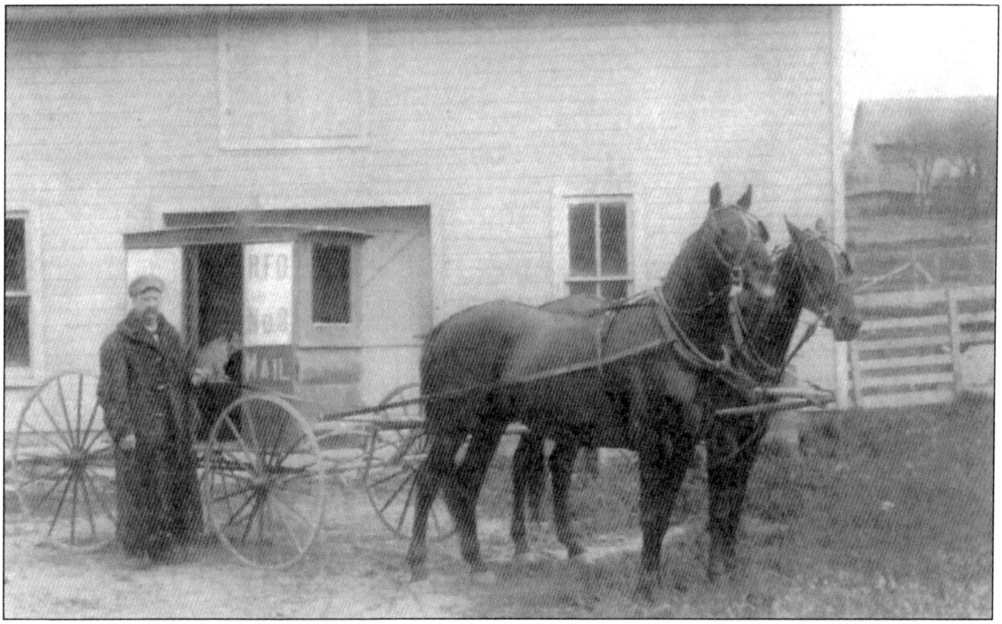

RURAL FREE DELIVERY. The Pentwater Post Office opened in 1856 with Edwin Cobb appointed as postmaster. The village is located on the north side of the Pentwater Lake. In 1882, the population was about 1,500 people, and the current year-round population is about 1,000. The village population swells many times during the summer tourist season. Pentwater embraced the summer resort trade very early and built upon that success to carry it past the end of the logging boom.

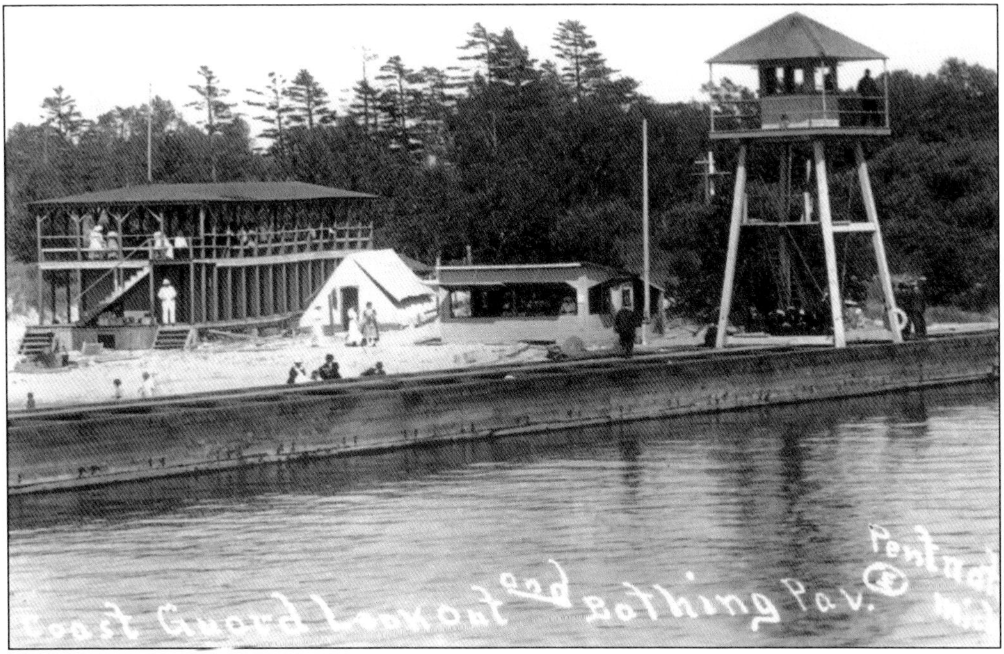

Coast Guard Tower and Bathing Station. The tower was an important aspect of the early lifesaving efforts, overseeing the destruction of over 40 sailing ships off the Pentwater coast. None were so tragic though as the Armistice Day storm of 1940, when three freighters were lost. The *Anna C Minch* and *Wm. B. Davoc* were lost with all hands, and the *Novadoc*, which foundered within sight of the shore, lost two crewmen; however, the *Novadoc*'s remaining crew was rescued by the *Three Brothers* fish tug.

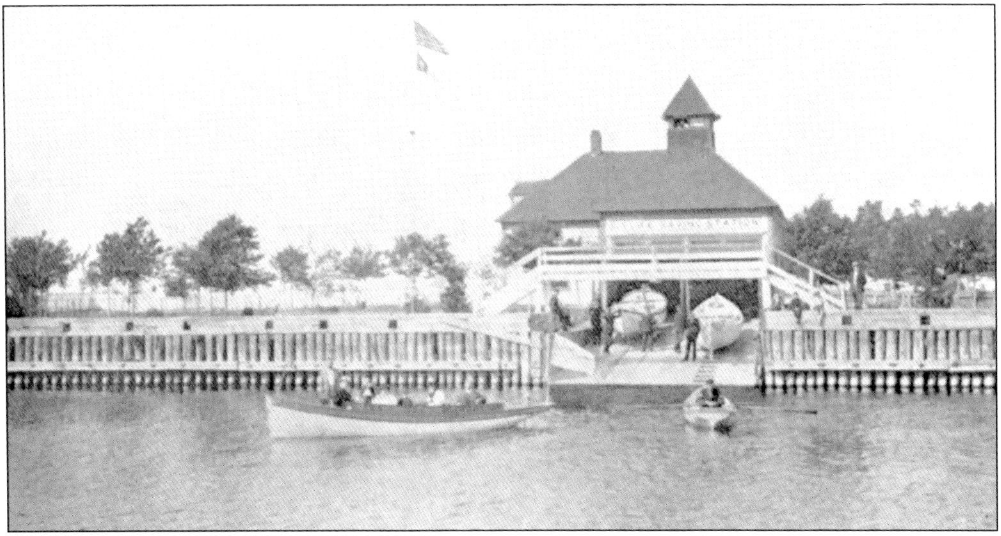

Pentwater Lifesaving Station. The lifesaving service was the predecessor of the Coast Guard, and the men who served were at the ready to risk their lives in the service of others. The station was built in 1886 and 1887 along the Pentwater Channel. Prior to 1916, most lakeside communities had lifesaving stations that were established to aid in the rescue of mariners caught in storms. Often, the winds would catch a schooner's sails and drive the ship toward shore despite the best efforts of the crew.

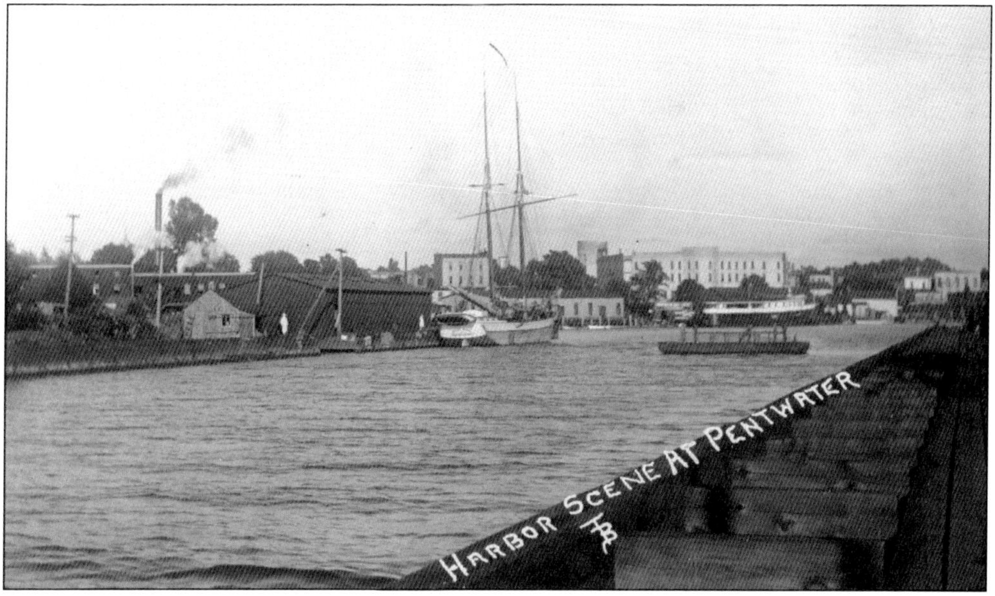

Channel and Harbor Scene. The establishment of a channel with a depth great enough to allow commercial ships into the harbor insured the community a degree of prosperity and growth. Originally excavated by Charles Mears in the 1850s, the channel was improved by the federal government in later years. The lake was the superhighway of the 19th and early 20th centuries, and being bypassed carried the same negative economic impact communities felt when the freeways passed them by.

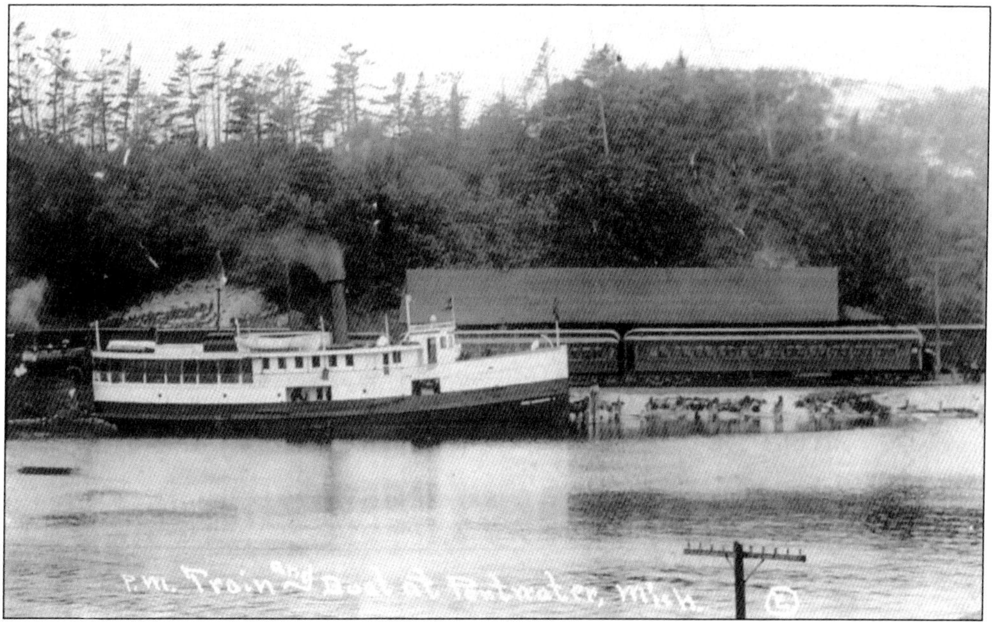

Night Train and Boat at Pentwater. The Pere Marquette Line, owned by Gus Kitzinger, serviced small towns in the vicinity of Ludington. There were a succession of local excursions, charters, and other lake passenger vessels that serviced every small town and village with a harbor and dock. They would pick up mail, packages, and passengers along their routes. The improvement of roads and increased ownership of automobiles brought this service to an end.

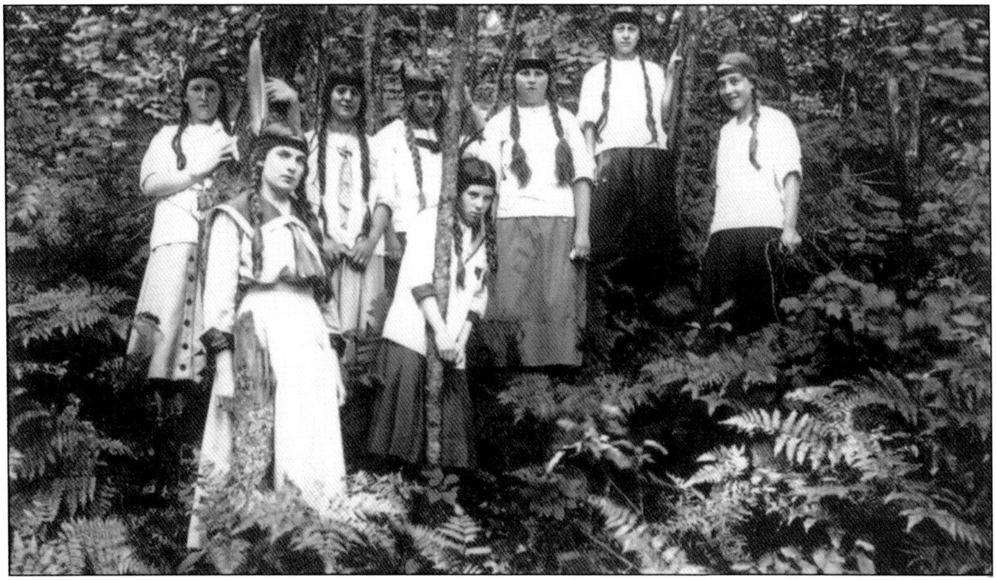

Pentwater Camp Fire Girls. The Camp Fire Girls were organized in response the Boy Scouts of America and the desire to create an organization to provide leadership opportunities for girls as well. During 1910 and 1911, three groups formed for girls, and for a time, all three operated under the moniker of Girl Pioneers of America.

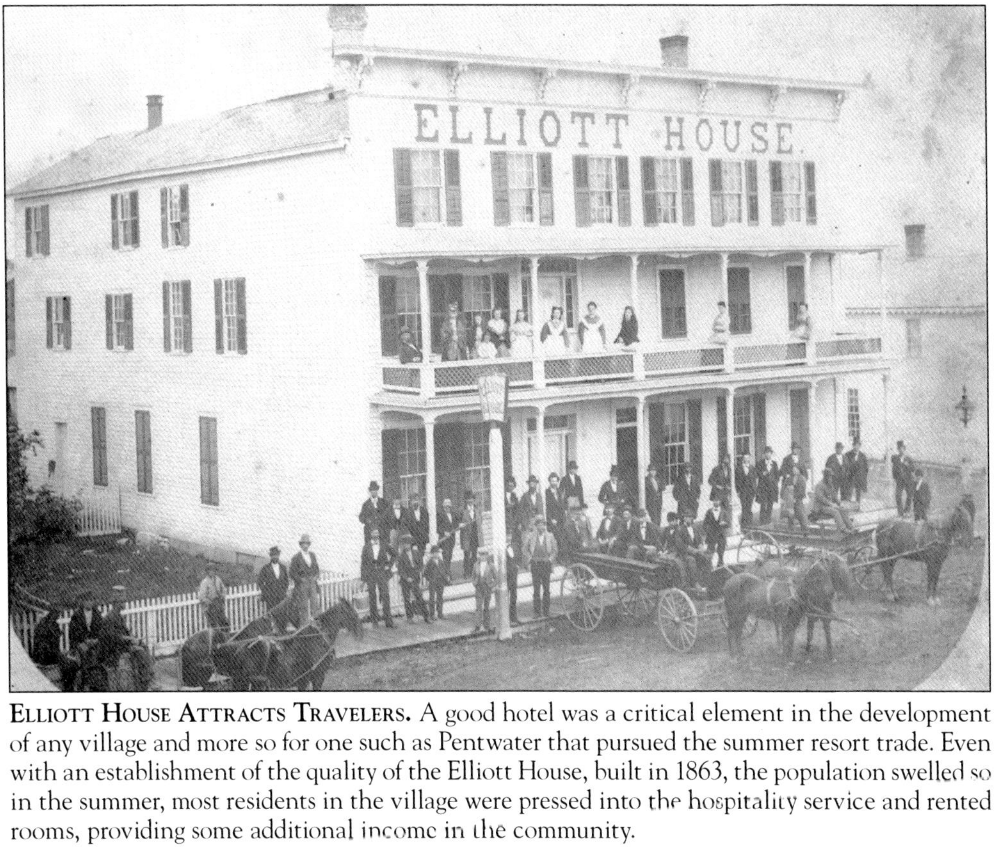

Elliott House Attracts Travelers. A good hotel was a critical element in the development of any village and more so for one such as Pentwater that pursued the summer resort trade. Even with an establishment of the quality of the Elliott House, built in 1863, the population swelled so in the summer, most residents in the village were pressed into the hospitality service and rented rooms, providing some additional income in the community.

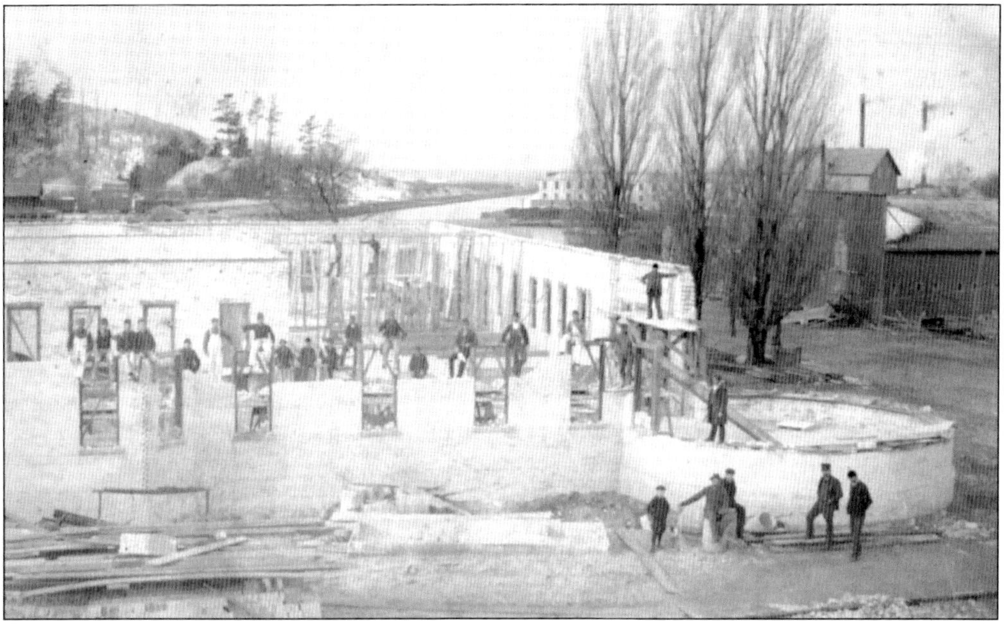

Fruit Evaporator, 1890s. The evaporator was constructed near the channel in Pentwater for the drying of fruits. The Alden Steam Evaporator was invented in 1870, and it was a few years after that before it was discovered by accident that fruits could be bleached and the discoloration arrested. The preservation of foods before refrigeration and home freezers was an important business, particularly in areas where fruit was raised and in need of immediate preservation.

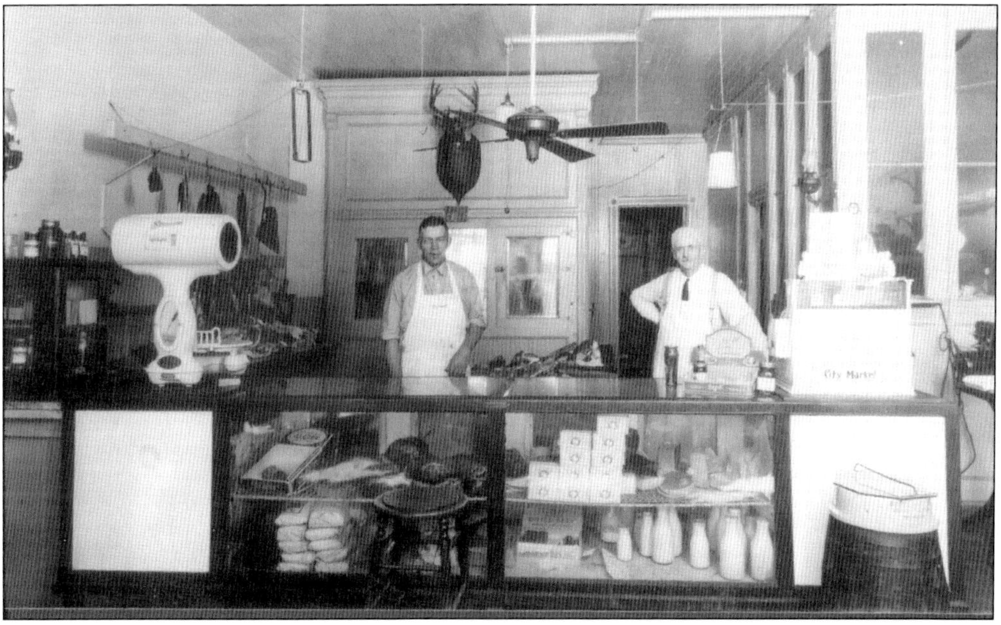

Daggett's Meat Market. Daggett's Meat Market is shown here in this c. 1915 photograph. In the days before commercial refrigeration, meat was butchered daily to insure its freshness. The same year Pentwater was organized, the mill owned by Cobb and Rector burned and was purchased and rebuilt by Charles Mears. Mears was always watchful for ways that he might expand his influence and holdings in the area. (Author's collection.)

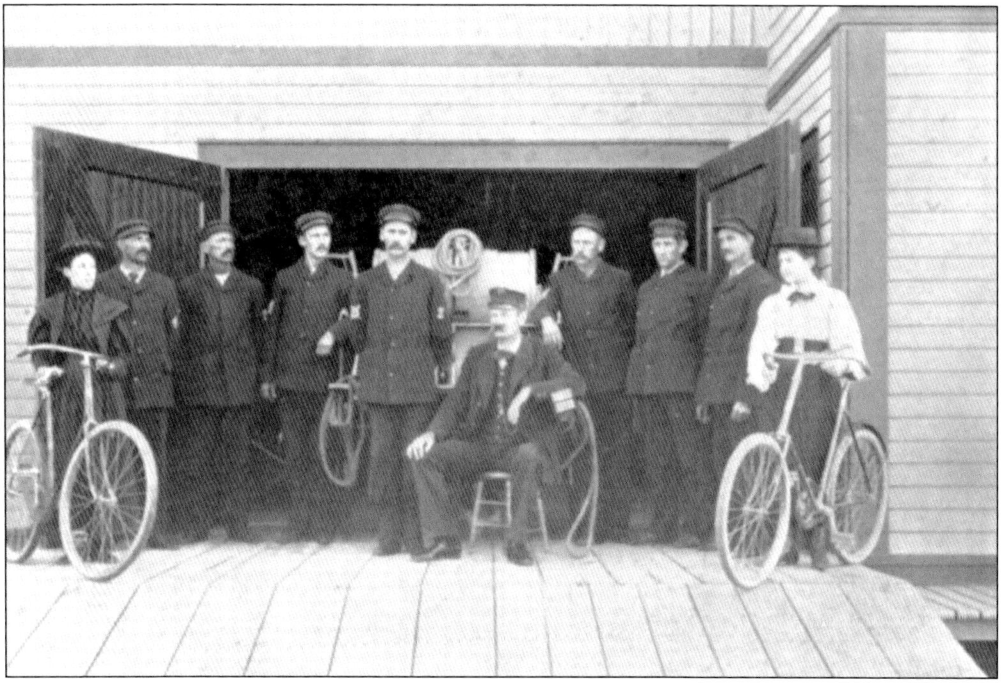

Lifesaving Station. The lifesaving station at Pentwater was put into service in the spring of 1887 under the command of Martin Ewald. Lifesaving stations operated during the shipping season, which ran from April to about December 1 each year. In 1916, the lifesaving service was integrated into the Coast Guard service.

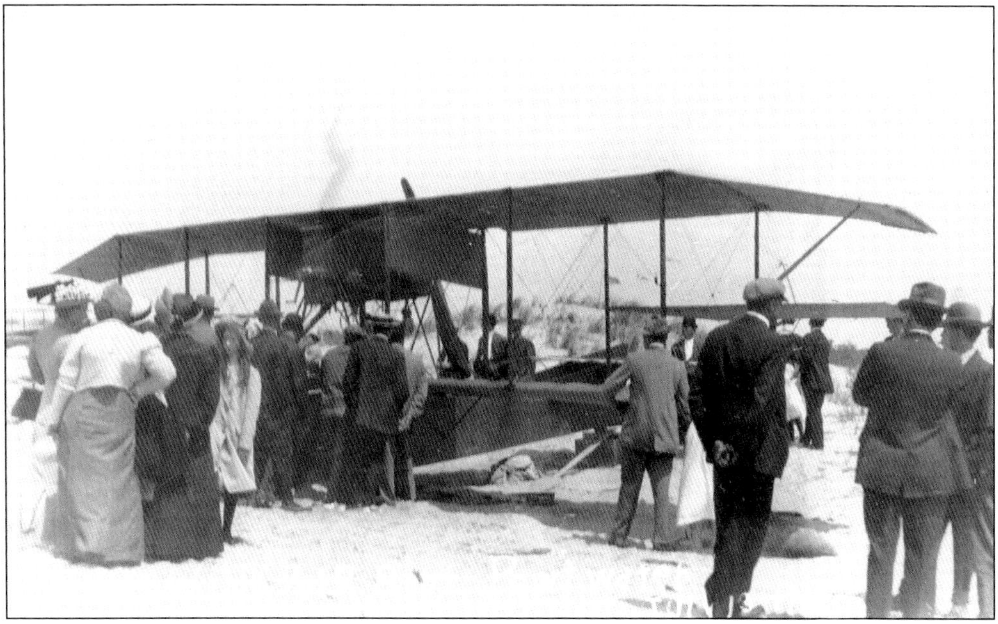

Plane on the Beach. The sight of a plane in the early 1900s was huge news. Early planes were a novelty, and people would come from all over the countryside to watch or pay for the thrill of a ride. Barnstormers, as they were called, performed tricks and aerial feats to the delight of crowds. It was a novel and exciting way for many World War I aviators to make a living after the war.

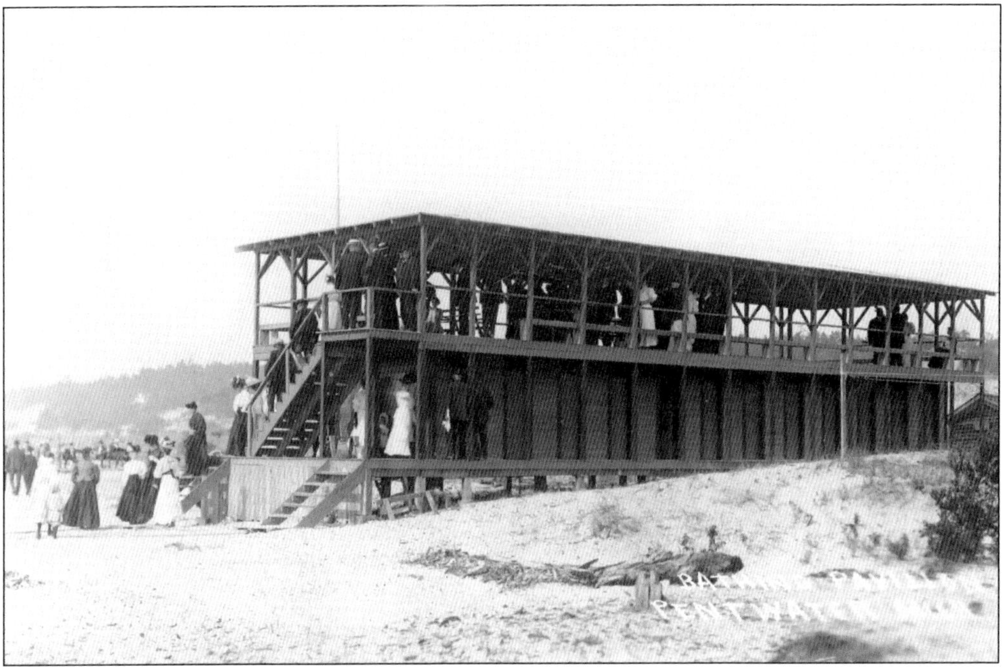

Bathing Pavilion. The bathing pavilion was located on the beach on the north side of the channel and provided a discreet place where Victorian ladies might change into their swim costumes or bathing dresses. Most outfits of the era were modeled after normal clothing and covered most of the body, leaving everything to the imagination.

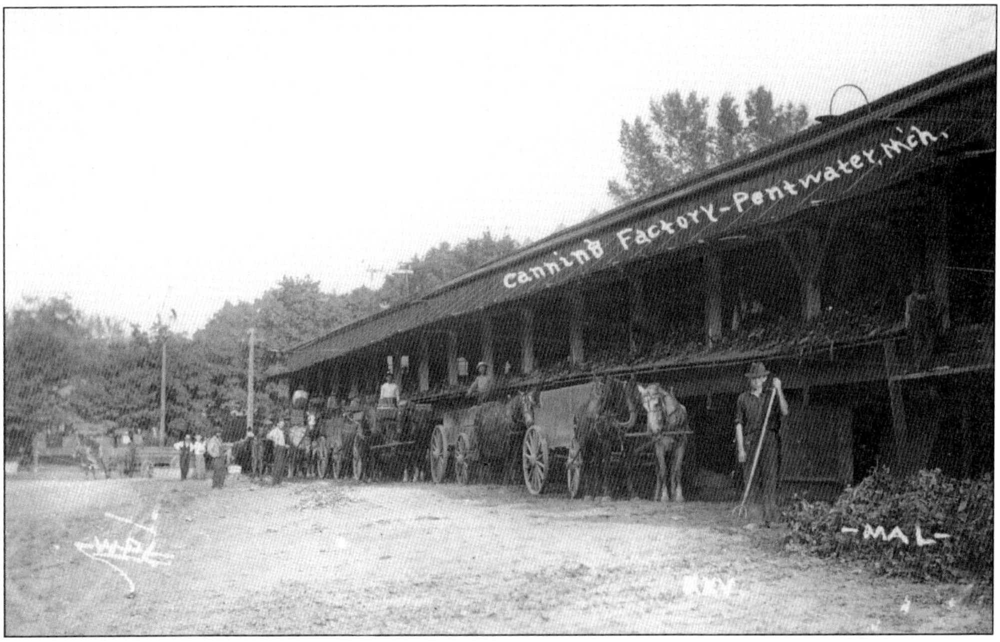

Pentwater Canning Factory. Farmers arrive with wagonloads of produce for the canning factory in this c. 1910 photograph. The first canning factory in America was established in 1812 in New York. It was not until Louis Pasteur proved that microorganisms caused food spoilage 50 years later that people understood why heating and sealing food in containers preserved it.

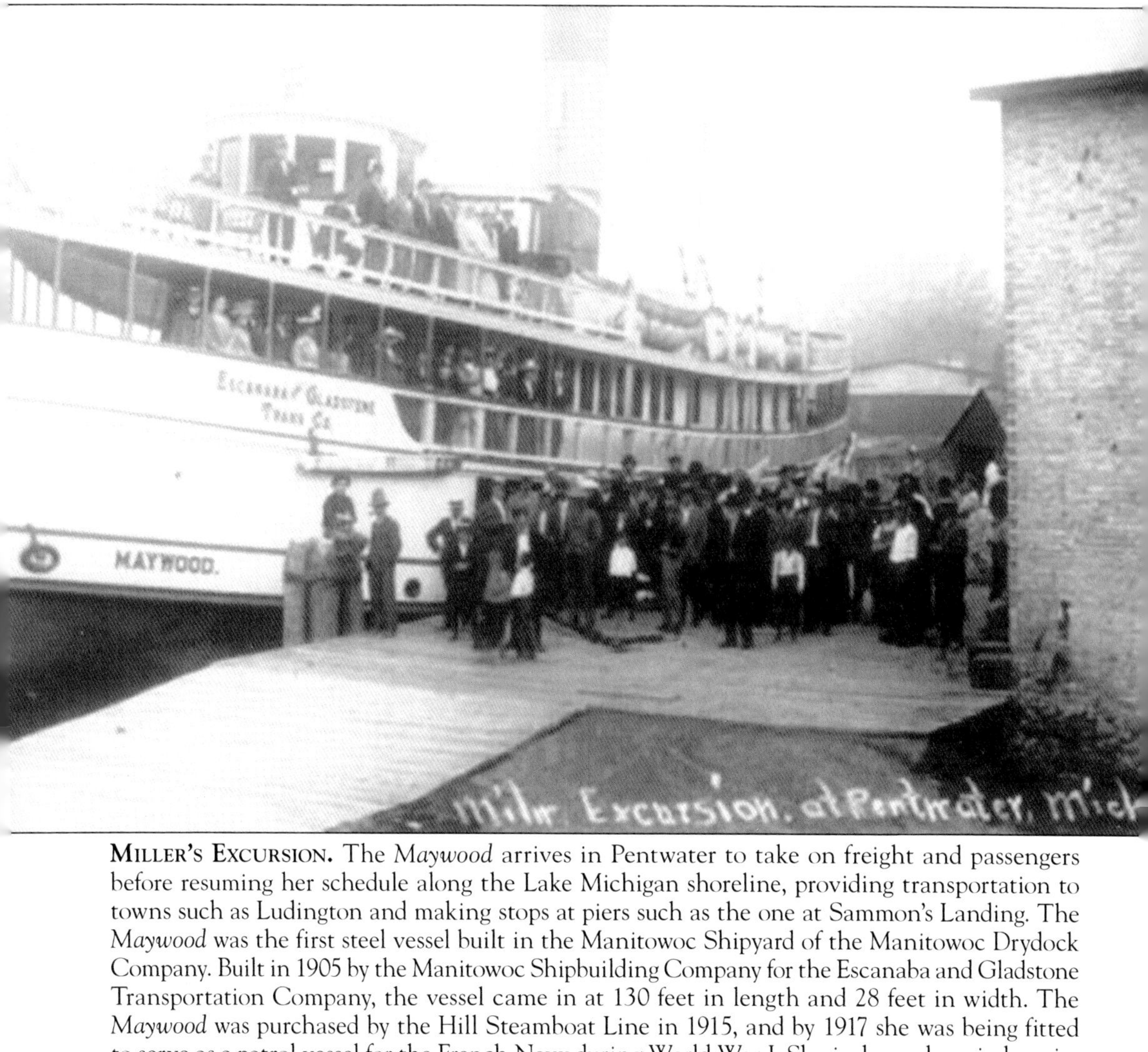

MILLER'S EXCURSION. The *Maywood* arrives in Pentwater to take on freight and passengers before resuming her schedule along the Lake Michigan shoreline, providing transportation to towns such as Ludington and making stops at piers such as the one at Sammon's Landing. The *Maywood* was the first steel vessel built in the Manitowoc Shipyard of the Manitowoc Drydock Company. Built in 1905 by the Manitowoc Shipbuilding Company for the Escanaba and Gladstone Transportation Company, the vessel came in at 130 feet in length and 28 feet in width. The *Maywood* was purchased by the Hill Steamboat Line in 1915, and by 1917 she was being fitted to serve as a patrol vessel for the French Navy during World War I. She is shown here in happier times, taking excited locals on an excursion around 1910.

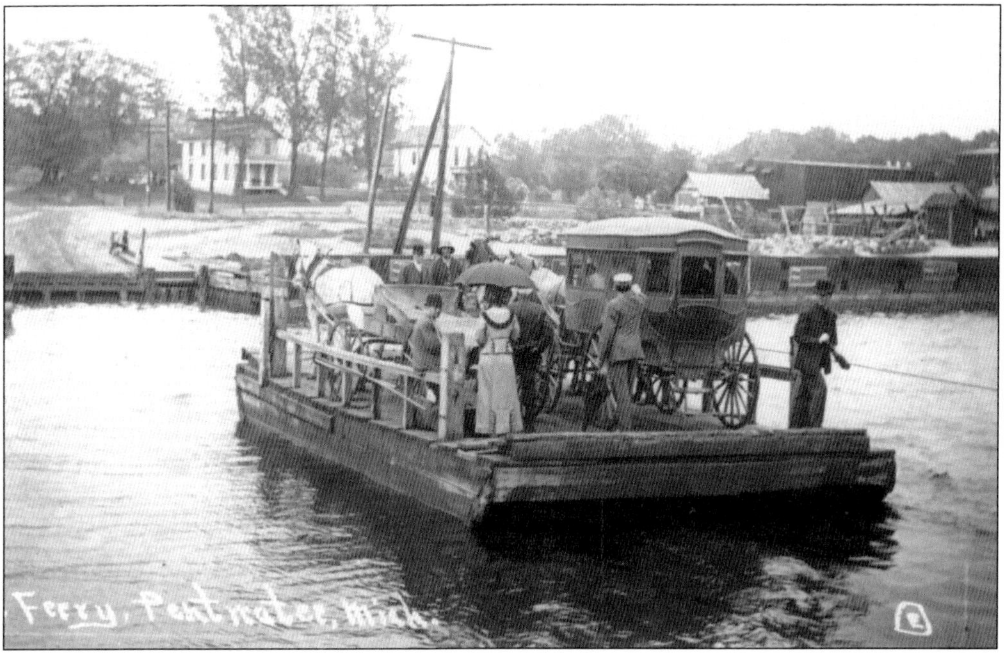

CROSSING ON THE FERRY. The Pentwater Ferry, which was very similar to the one that operated out of Ludington, is shown here heavily patronized by local residents as it crosses the channel. A person would pay 5¢ to make the crossing and an extra nickel if they had a horse. The ferry operated from 1858 to about 1925. It closed down when the Pentwater Bridge was built.

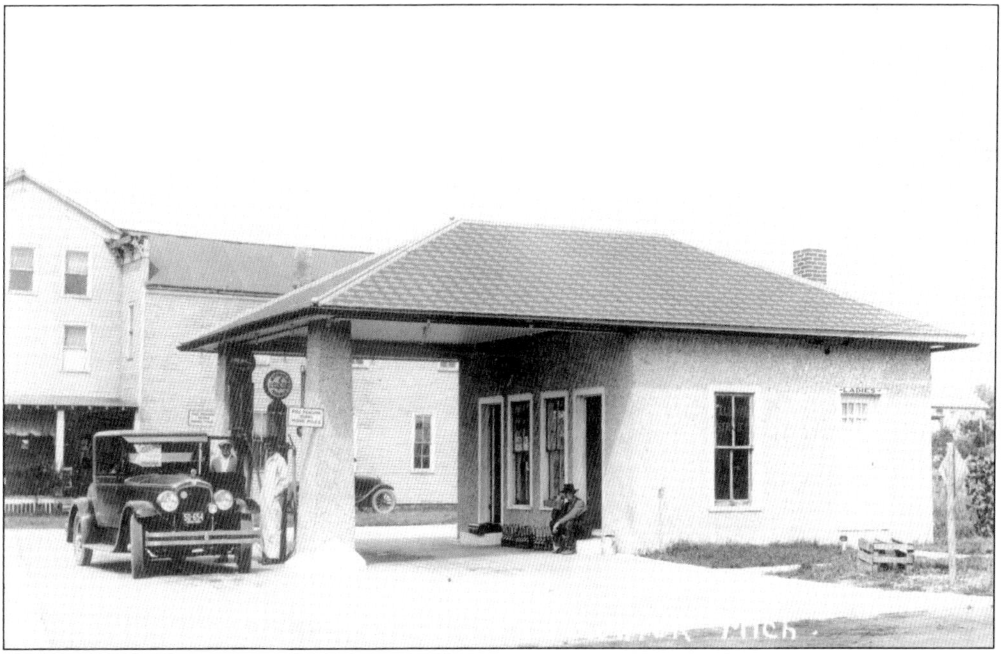

WESTERN OIL STATION. The Western Oil Station offered its customers detailed service anytime they brought their automobile in. The idea of a service station continued to grow, with stations competing with each other; some employed four or five teenagers who would rush out and check the fluids, wash the windshield, and pump the gas.

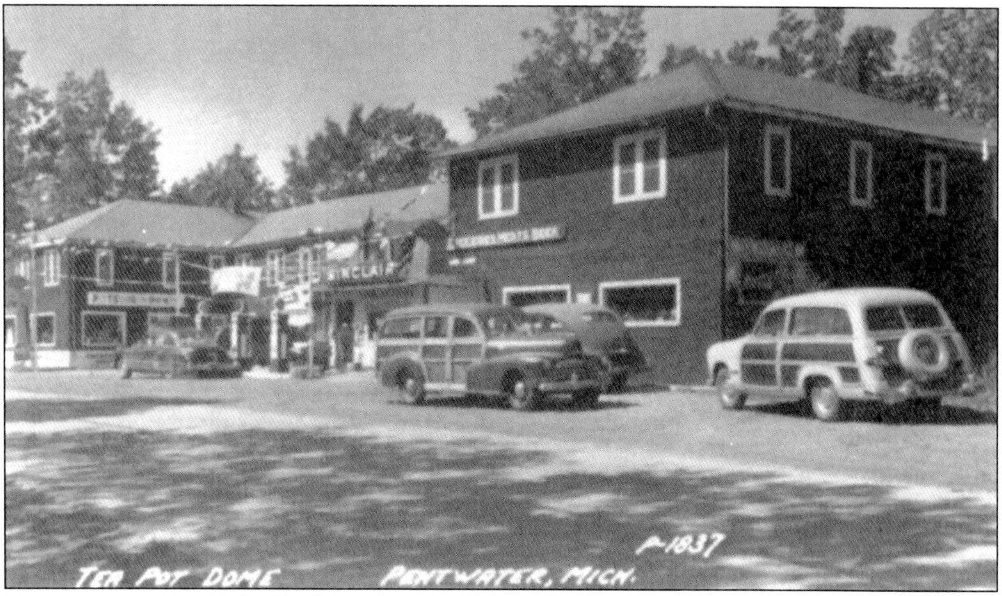

TEAPOT DOME. Established by John Grondsma around 1927, the Teapot Dome consisted of a small store along with a Sinclair Gas Station and was located to the north of Pentwater near Bass Lake. The business was named after the scandal that shook Pres. Warren G. Harding's administration when Secretary of the Interior Albert B. Fall was convicted of taking bribes from oil companies. It was considered the greatest political scandal until Watergate.

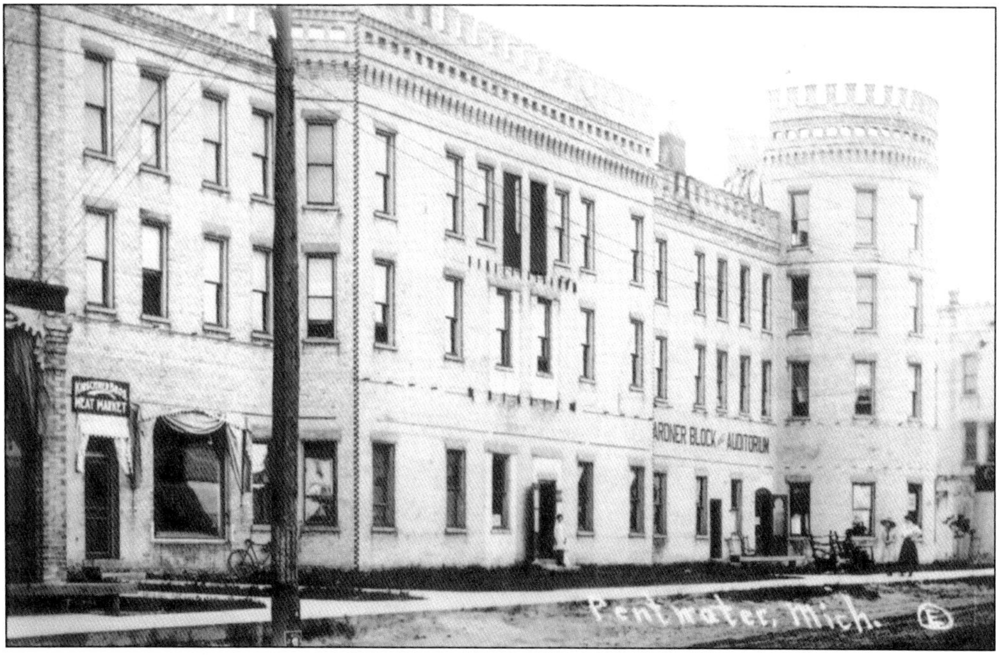

WHITE ELEPHANT GETS ITS NAME. The White Elephant was originally called the Hotel Valeria after the wife of developer G.A. Williams, who envisioned a grand hotel in Pentwater to provide accommodations and amenities to travelers coming north on passenger ships out of Chicago and other locations. Construction began in 1891 and was never completed. The unfinished shell was deemed a white elephant and remained empty until a fire destroyed it in 1927.

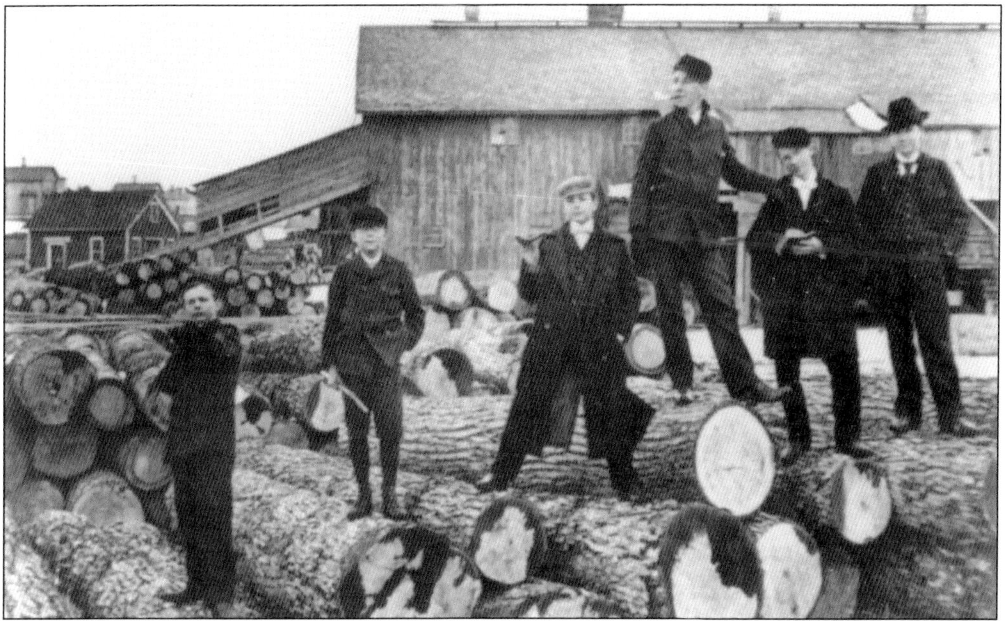

Sands and Maxwell Lumber Company. The Sands and Maxwell Lumber Company, organized in 1885, had an extensive holding in Oceana County. The firm ran sawmills and shingle mills built in Crystal Valley in 1875, Benona in 1876, and also in Pentwater. The firm also had company stores established in each location for the sale of goods and supplies, and its store in Pentwater was said to be the largest between Muskegon and Ludington.

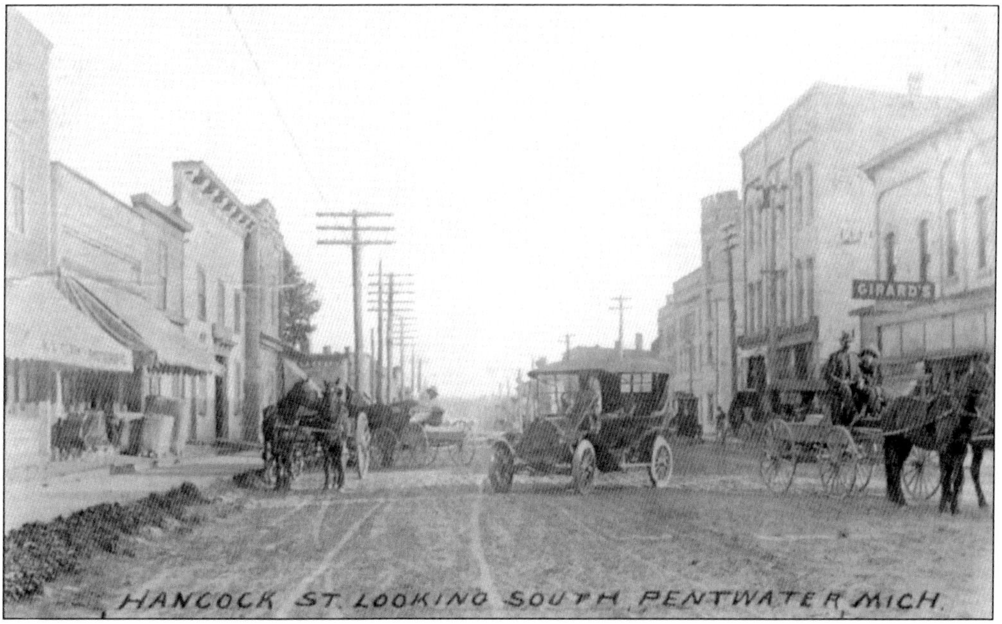

Hancock Street Looking South. Pentwater experienced its great fire in 1889, and like most communities, the fire consumed all of the wooden-structured buildings that housed downtown stores. Afterward, though the wooden buildings were replaced by brick structures that were erected within a few years of each other, the new architecture helped maintain the harmony of the Victorian-themed main streets, considered both charming and inviting.

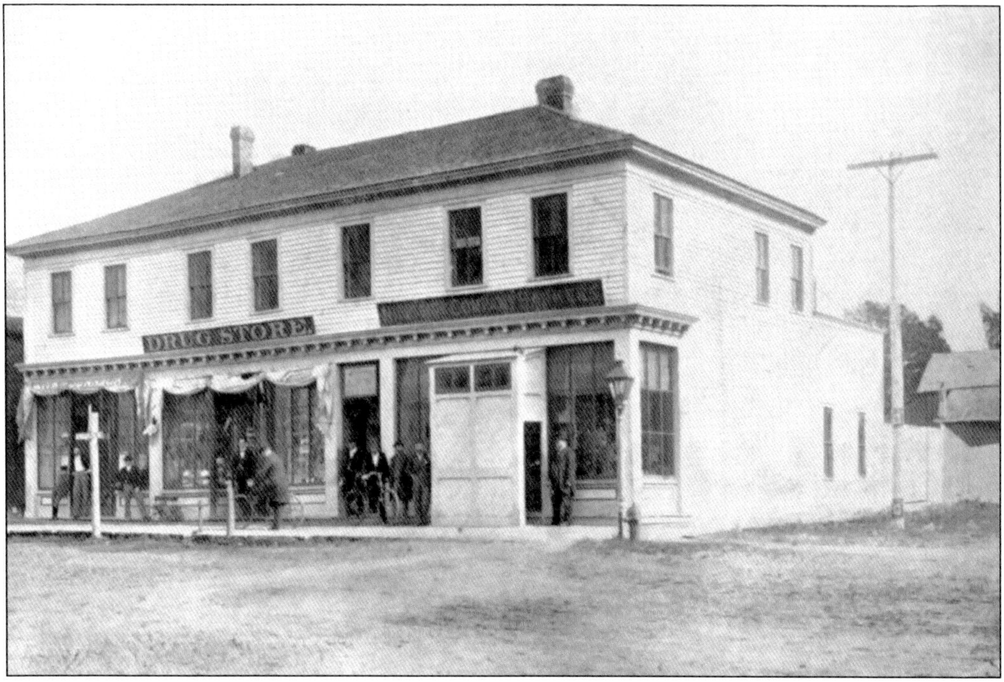

Nielsen and Company. Known as the Bank Block, Nielsen and Company Bankers assumed control in 1877. Originally, the bank was established by Gray and Brothers in 1870, and by 1872 it became the Oceana County Bank. Prior to 1870, money was so scarce, the area lumbering companies printed what was called "Pentwater Orders." These locally produced notes of 5¢ to $1 were used in place of official currency.

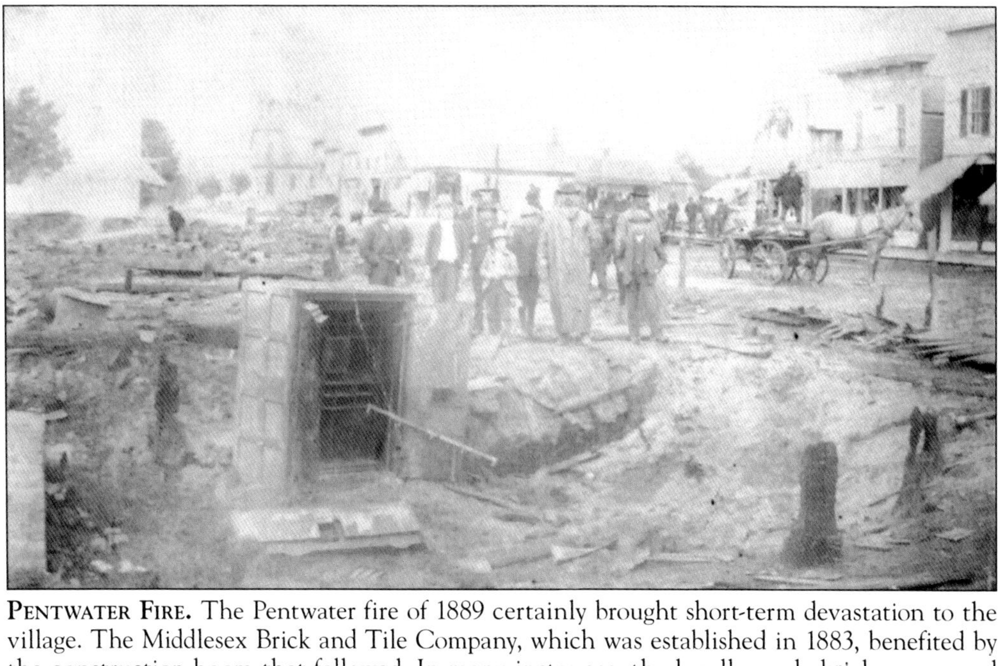

Pentwater Fire. The Pentwater fire of 1889 certainly brought short-term devastation to the village. The Middlesex Brick and Tile Company, which was established in 1883, benefited by the construction boom that followed. In many instances, the locally made bricks were used in construction.

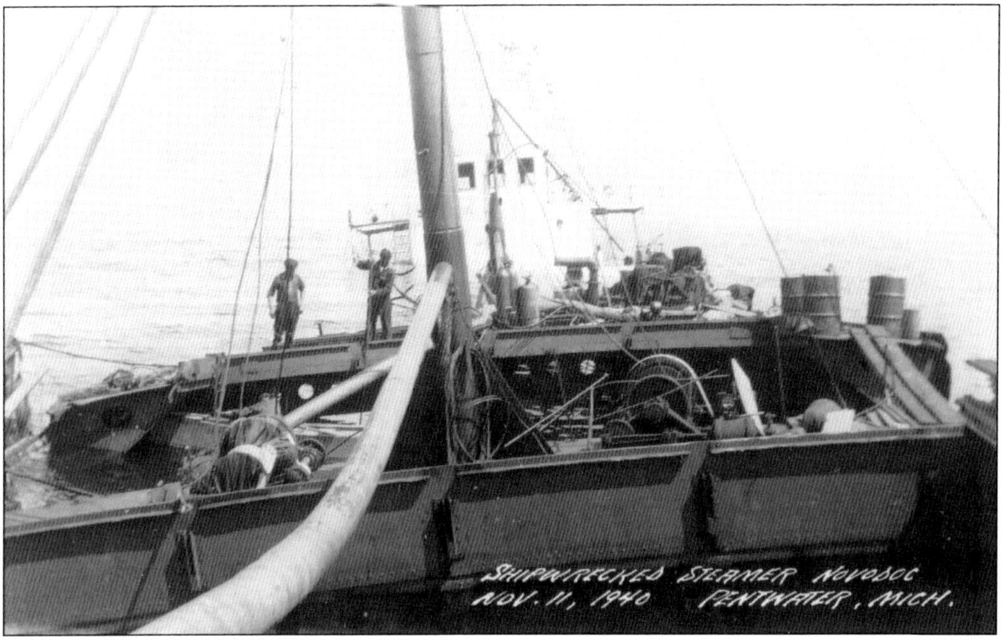

Novadoc on Juniper Beach. Armistice Day 1940 was the day that the "winds of hell," as coined by the locals, broke down the doors of all those living in the Midwest. The storm caused great loss of life and damage to ships on the Great Lakes. The *Novadoc* was one of four ships within 20 miles of Pentwater damaged or sunk. The *William C Davoc* and *Anna Minch*, along with their hands, sunk just a few miles away from the *Novadoc*.

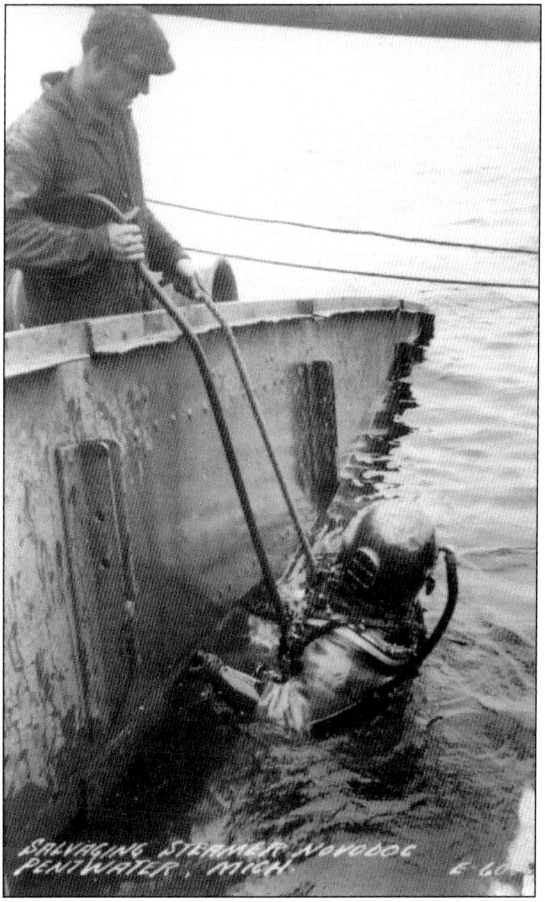

Novadoc after the Storm. The crew of the *Novadoc* experienced some rough hours after the ship beached, finally being rescued by the crew of a local fishing tug *Three Brothers*, guided by Clyde Cross. The *Novadoc* lost two crewmen, who washed overboard in the tragedy, and the remaining crew members were trapped in the cabin by raging waves while awaiting rescue. Just to the north in Ludington, the *Pere Marquette City of Flint* missed the harbor entrance and beached on a sandbar with damage to the ship; luckily, there was no loss of life.

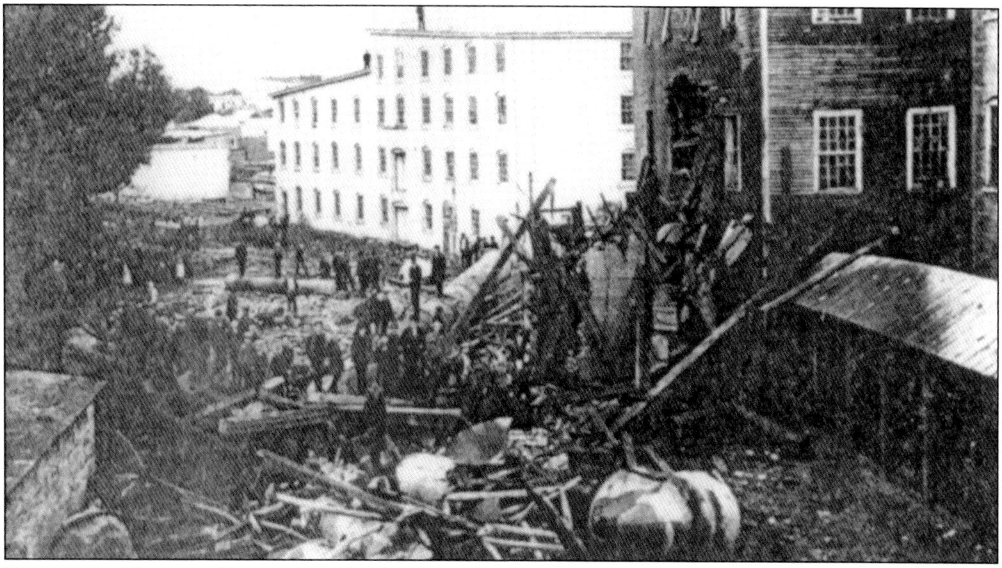

FURNITURE FACTORY EXPLOSION. At the time the furniture factory's boiler exploded in 1898, it was owned by the Sands and Maxwell Company. Originally established as the Pentwater Furniture Factory, the business was renamed the Pentwater Bedstead Company when Sands and Maxwell purchased it to compliment its logging interests. The factory provided much needed employment after the timber gave out and a product that was popular throughout the state.

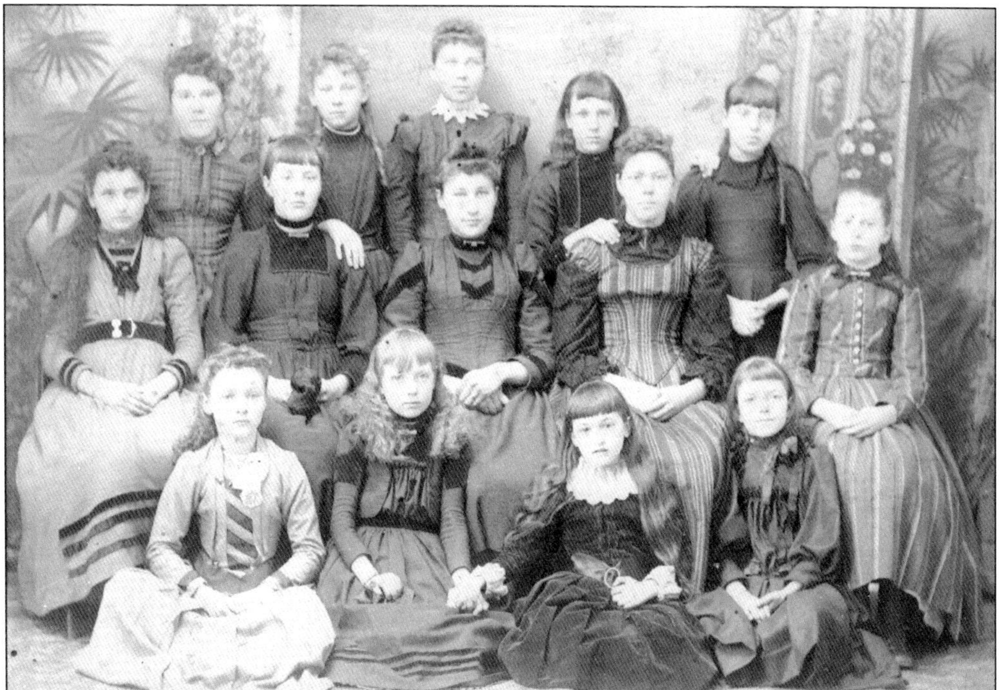

PENTWATER SCHOOLGIRLS. These Pentwater girls pose in their best "goin'-to-meetin' attire." Pentwater's first class began in a local home in 1859, and eight students attended. In 1860, a one-room school was built, and by 1865 a larger building was constructed on the corner of Fourth and Carroll Streets. By 1881, class enrollment had grown to 377 students.

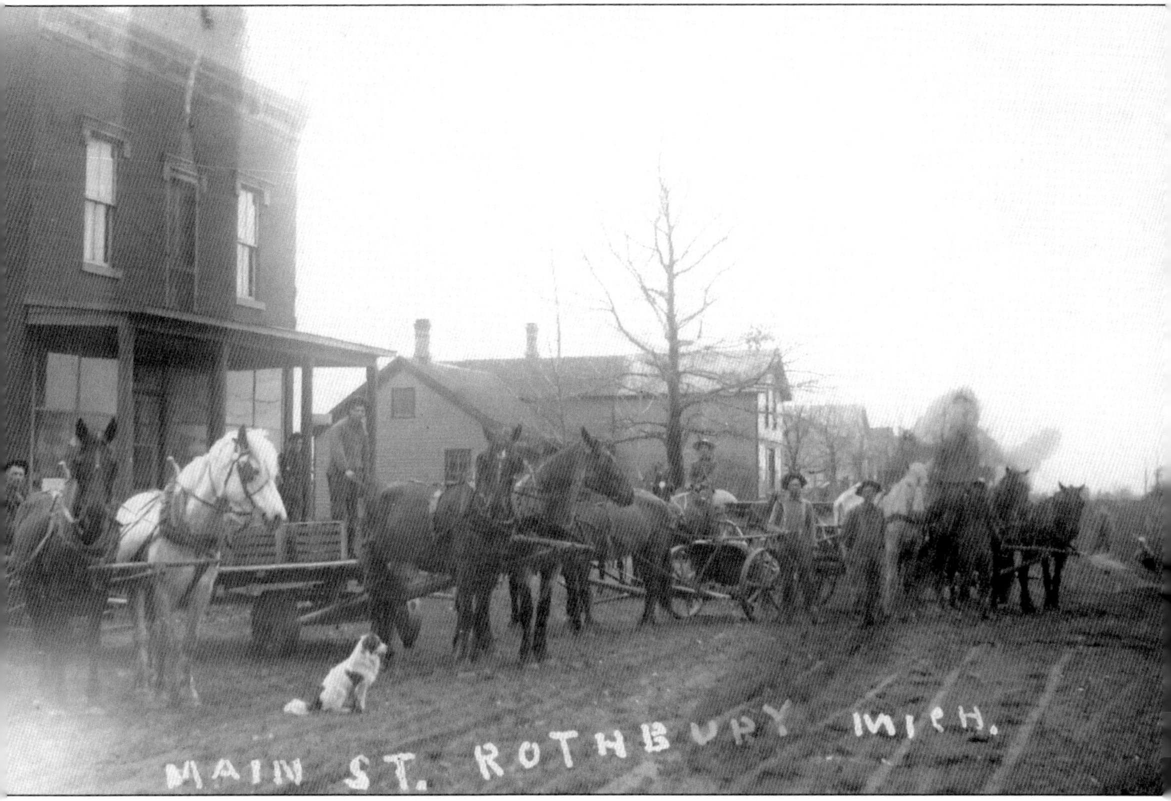

Rothbury Main Street. Originally settled in the 1850s and known as Malta, the community undertook another name change in 1875 when the Chicago & North Western Railroad established a station on Nelson Green's property and named it Greenwood Station. The designation of the post office in early communities often determined the name of the community. Since Greenwood existed in another county of Michigan, a new name was needed, and it was provided by the new postmaster, whose hometown was Rothbury, England. The post office was established as Malta in 1876, closed in 1877, and reopened in 1879 as Rothbury. One of Grant Township's claims to fame was the surprise unearthing of a mastodon in 1963 by Ed Huls. The skull was quite the novelty, as it was found with the jaw and teeth intact. Thousands of people streamed out to the farm to view it. Eventually, it was donated by the family to the Muskegon County Museum.

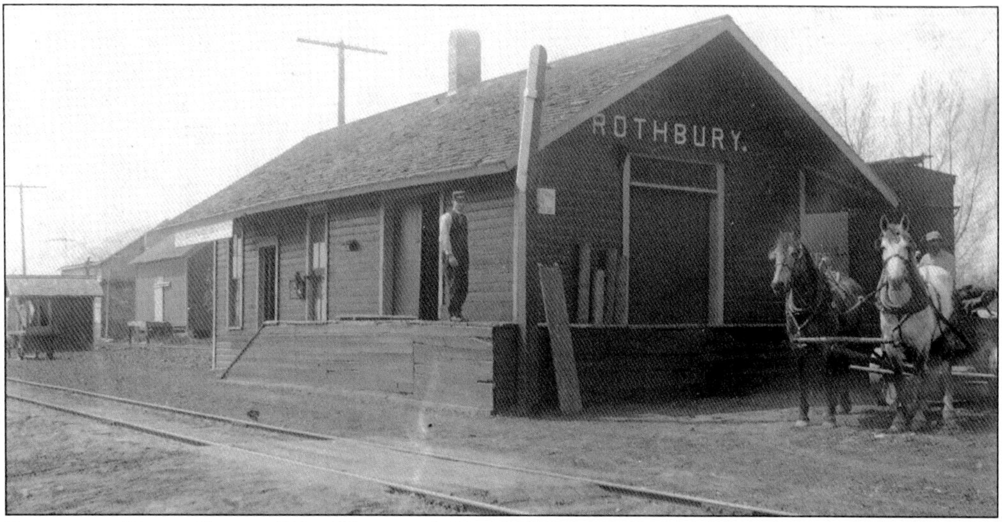

Rothbury Train Depot. The Chicago & North Western Railroad was chartered in 1859 and, through mergers, became one of the largest railroads in the country. By 1900, the company controlled 5,000 miles of track, and by 1970 it had over 12,000 miles of track in seven states, making it one of the longest railroads in the United States.

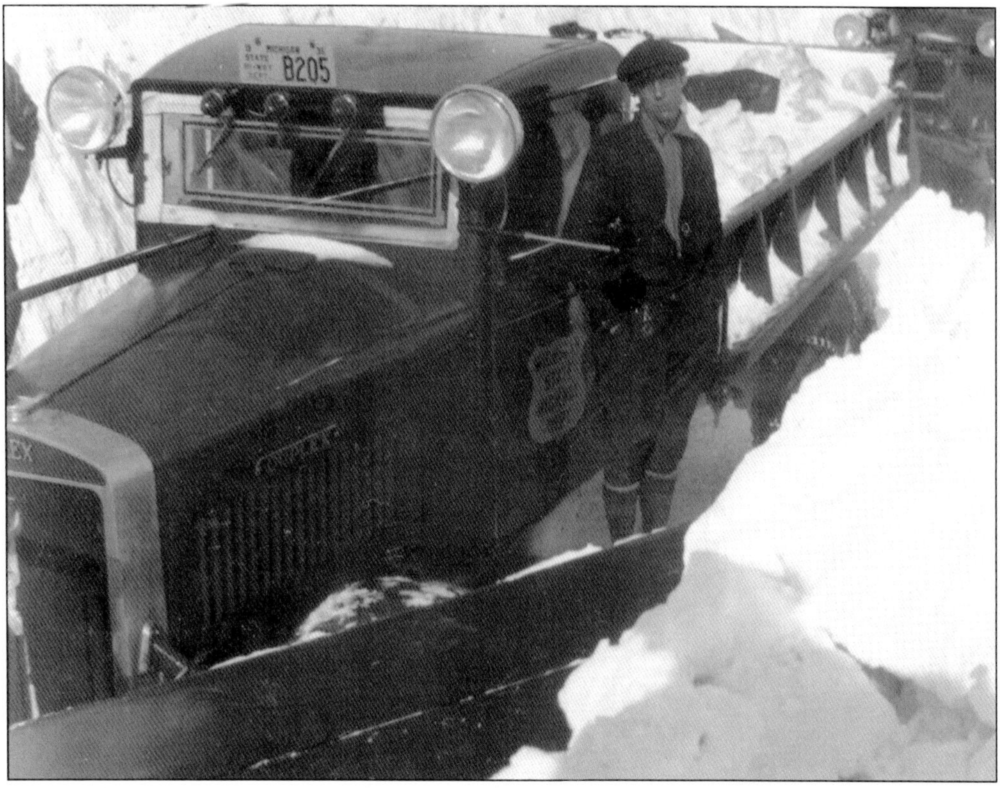

M. Earl Shaw with Snowplow. The winters of 1935 and 1936 were exceptionally harsh, and the road conditions were so bad it was nearly impossible for vehicles to get through. Plows would go out and work around the clock in an effort to keep the roads open; caravans of vehicles followed the plows in order to get through before roads drifted shut again.

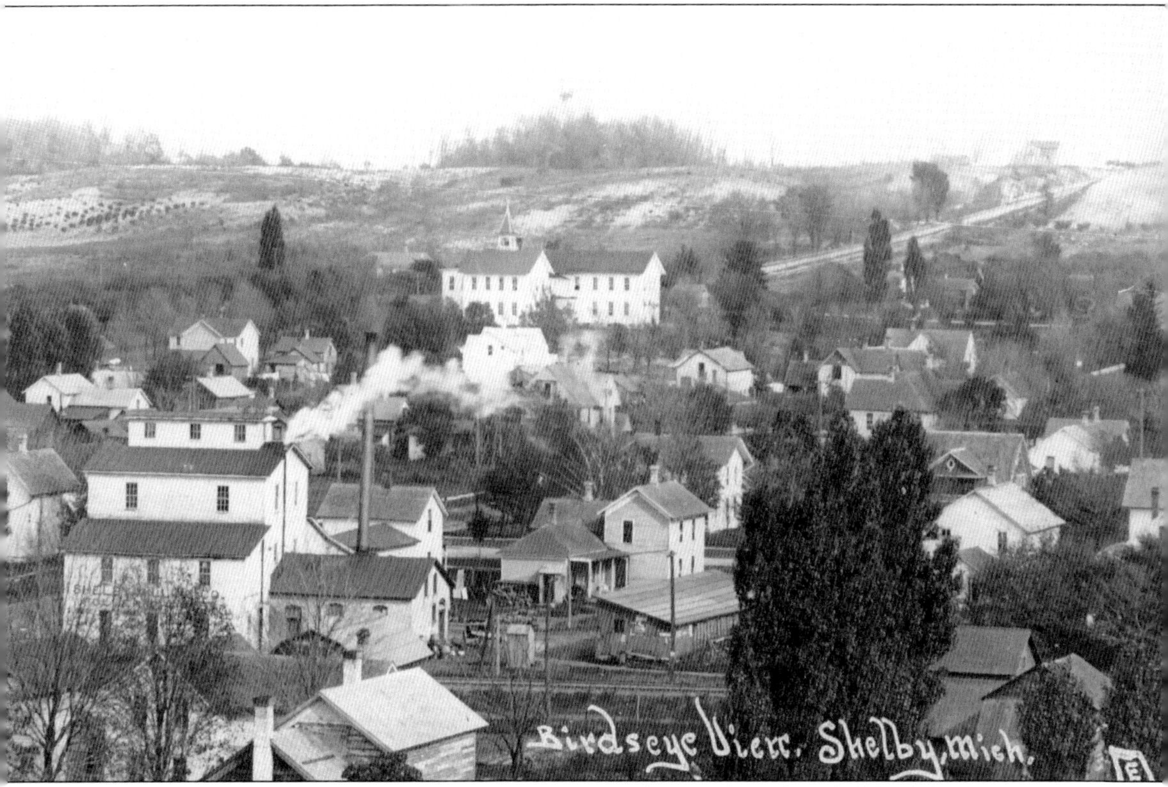

SHELBY BIRD'S-EYE VIEW. Shelby got its start in 1864 when Walter Churchill built his home on what is the corner of Sixth and State Streets. Soon afterwards, Churchill added a hotel and a post office and the area became known as Churchill Corners. Shelby underwent some interesting name changes, as was somewhat common in the early days of settlements. Most unusual was the platting of the town of Barnett, which came about when a brakeman on the railroad agreed to pay the cost of recording the plat of the village if the new village were named after him. Once the plat had been recorded as Barnett, he backed out, so a portion of the village plat still holds the name of the brakeman. Shelby was incorporated as a village in 1885, but if it not for the great flocks of passenger pigeons that came to the area in 1875, bringing hunters, publicity, and revenue, the village may not have developed as it has.

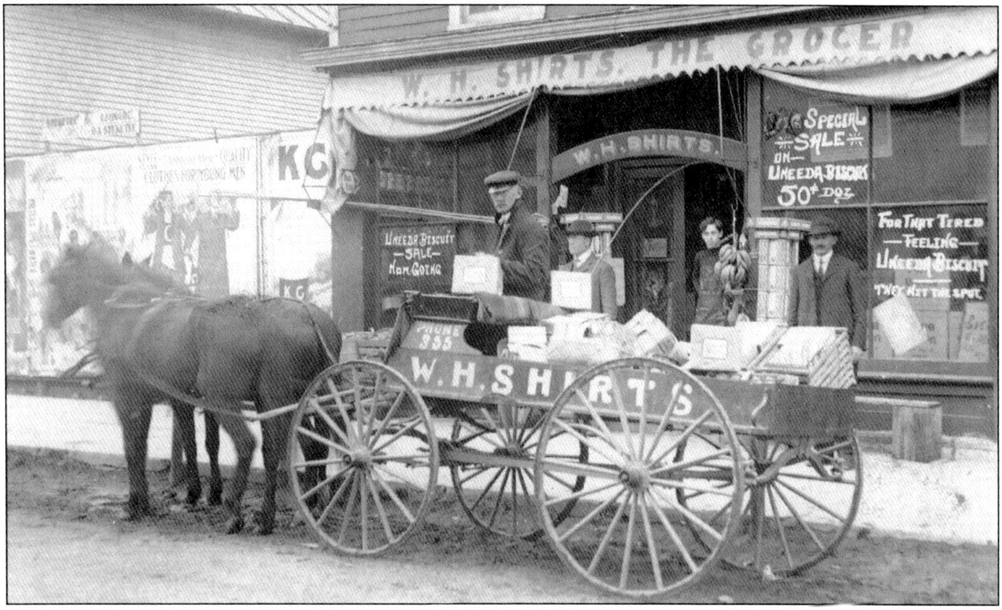

W.H. SHIRTS. W.H. Shirts, "The Grocer," is preparing to make deliveries in this c. 1910 view of his store in Shelby. Judging by the signs in the store window, Uneeda Biscuit is on sale. Prior to 1898, crackers were regionally produced and sold out of barrels; when the National Biscuit Company (Nabisco) began selling crackers nationally, they were wrapped, boxed, and packed for freshness.

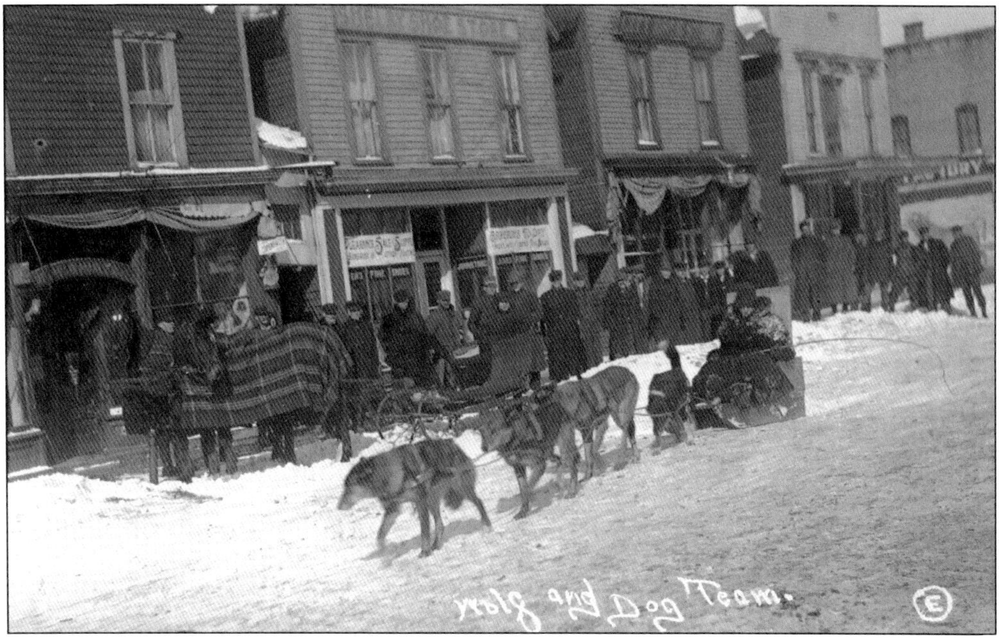

WOLF AND/OR DOG TEAM. This wolf and/or dog team in downtown Shelby illustrates the extent people would go to travel during the winter months when plows were unable to keep up with the weather. It is not possible to discern between whether these are wolves, dogs, or hybrids; however, a couple of the sled dogs seem to have a wild look about them. Wolves are considered more independent thinkers compared to domestic dogs bred for pulling sleds.

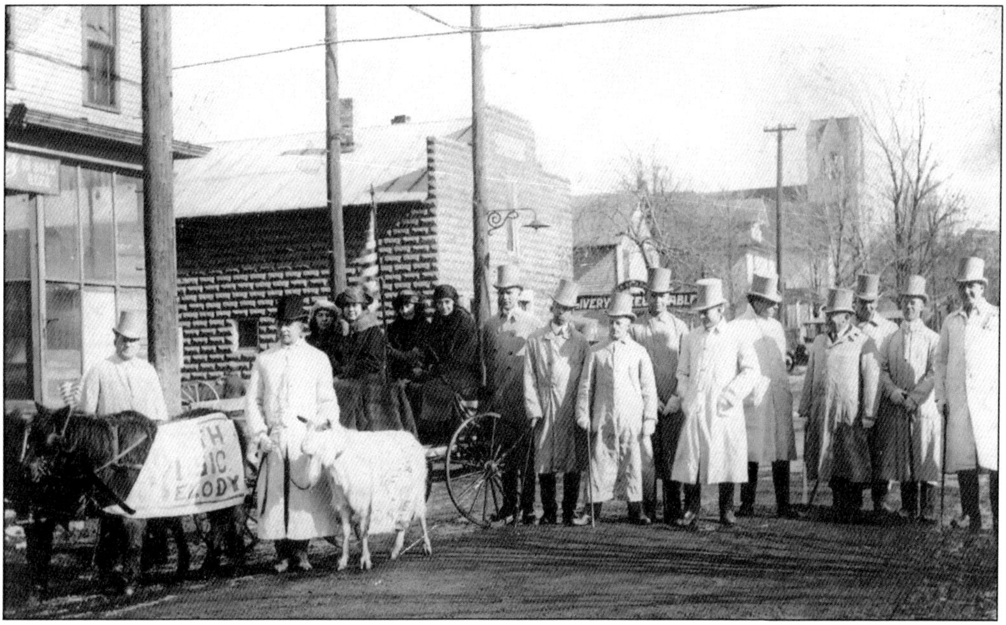

MASONIC MINSTREL PARADE. On February 11, 1921, the Masons gathered for their annual minstrel parade. The lodge in Shelby was chartered on October 7, 1870. The Masons are a fraternal lodge with mythological ties back to the builders of King Solomon's tomb. The goal of the Masons to make good men better, their fundraising efforts, and various projects added to the quality of life in the area.

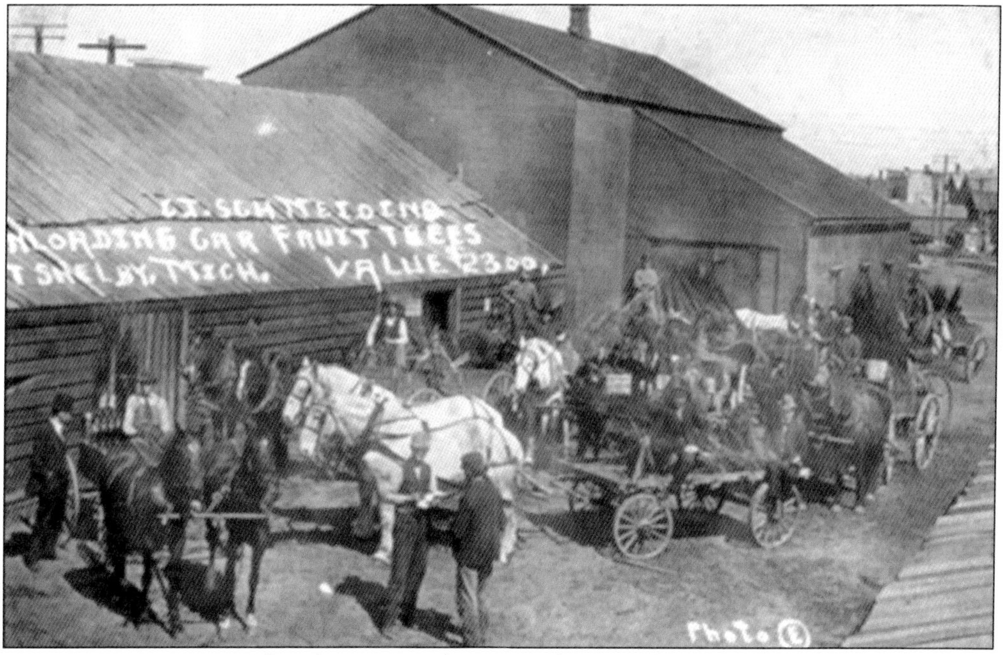

FRUIT TREES ARRIVE. After the pigeons disappeared, it was discovered that the soil was good for growing potatoes and that the hilly area surrounding Shelby was prime for establishing fruit orchards. Each obstacle faced by the community was overcome as new means of generating revenue were found in the natural resources of the area.

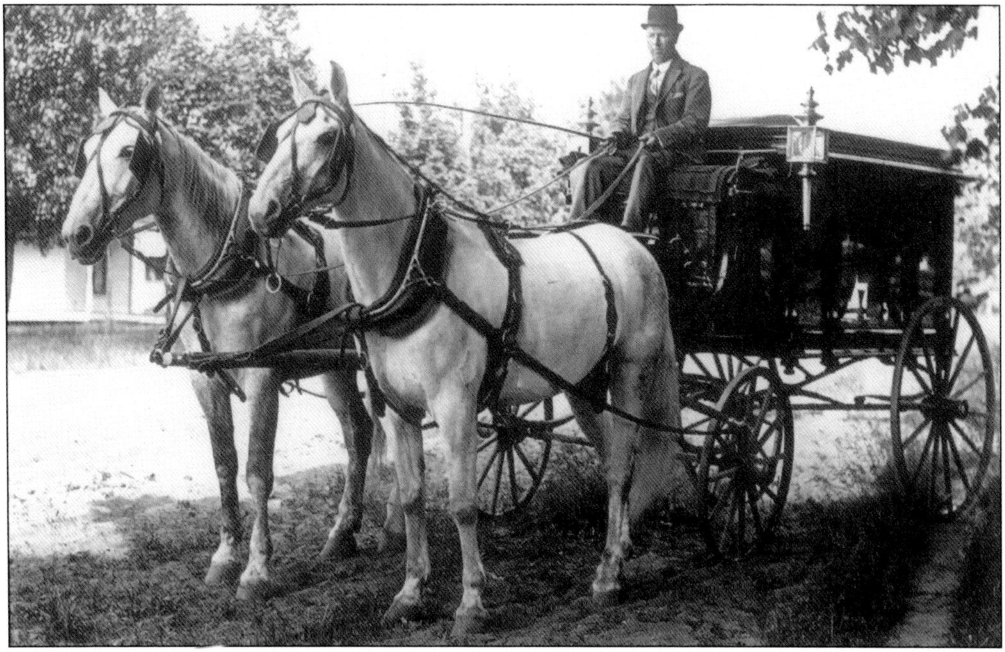

Hearse for Hire. This horse-drawn hearse, seen around 1910, serviced the Shelby area. There were many customs in the past that have changed dramatically over the decades. Funerals were often held at the home with the body displayed in the bay window of the house. Children were seldom delivered at a hospital; from birth to death, the family was intimately involved. (Author's collection.)

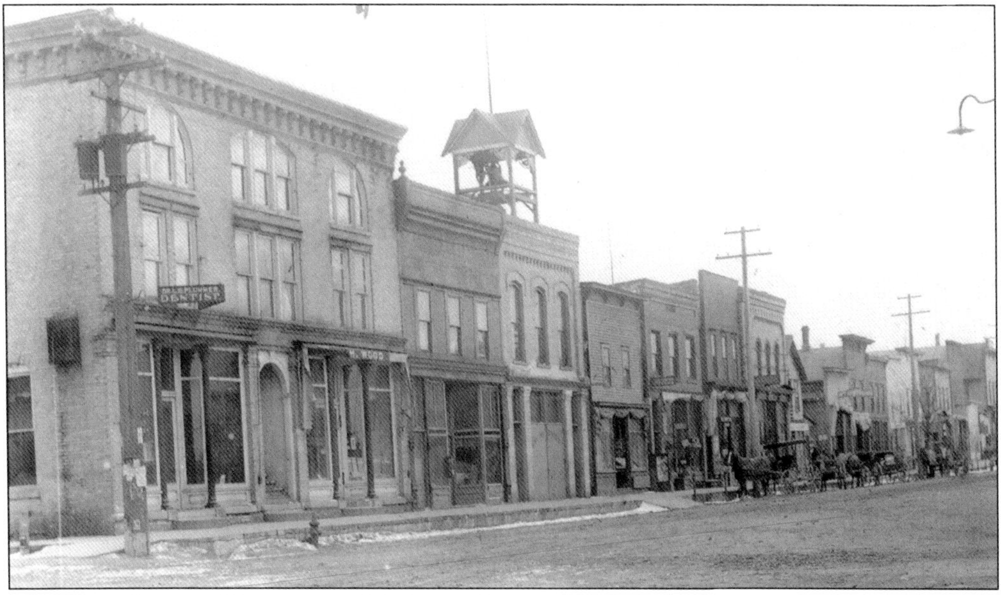

Michigan Avenue Merchants. Michigan Avenue has been home to many businesses, such as the Shelby Pharmacy, which had its start in 1881 when Frank Van Winkel and James Flood established a pharmacy at 199 North Michigan Avenue. Over the years, the pharmacy was owned by the Hoffman brothers, Collin Betchell, Paul Livingston, and the Wheelers. It was the Wheelers who renamed the business Shelby Pharmacy.

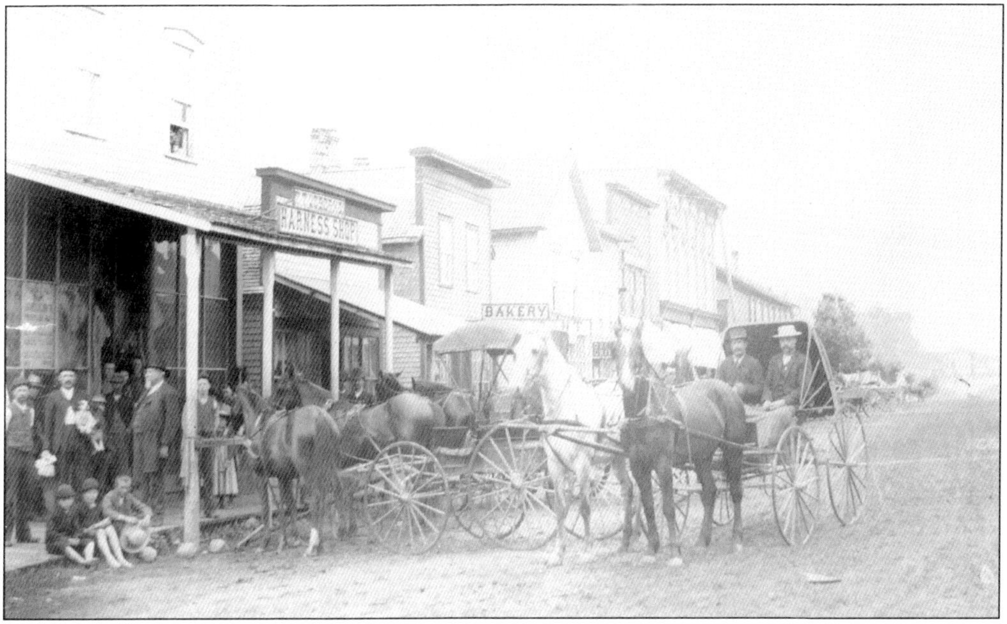

SHELBY MAIN STREET. When Shelby Township organized in 1862, there were but eight settlers to cast votes. By 1910, Shelby was a well-established and bustling community. The T.T. Usbrone Harness Shop on Main Street remained a viable business in 1910, but one that would be short lived as the "horseless carriage" took over; harness shops were replaced by service stations within a few short years.

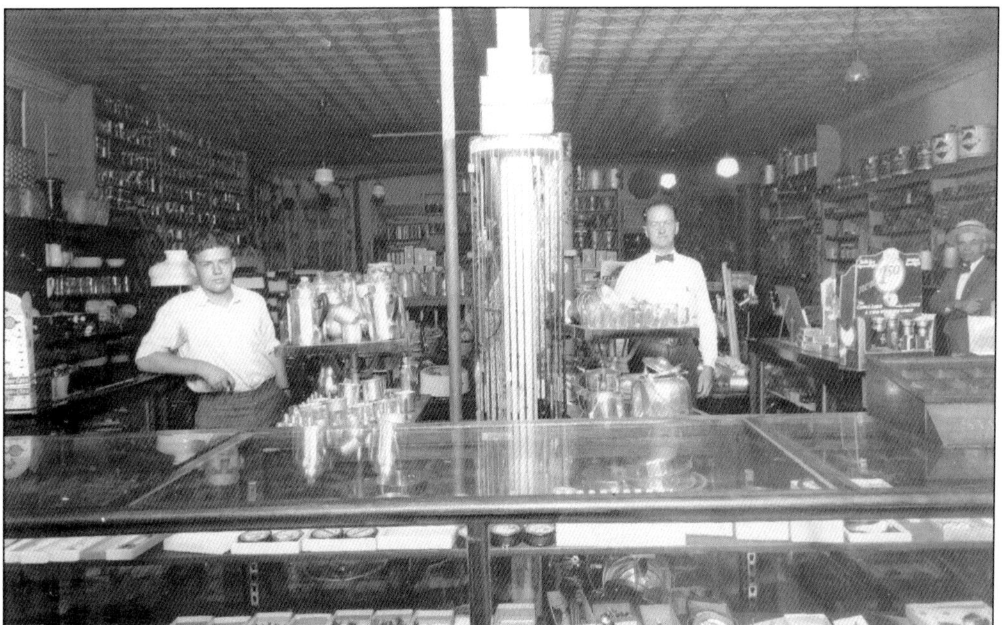

SAYLES AND LEWIS HARDWARE. William Ely Sayles was born in Pentwater in 1882 and worked in his father's hardware store before buying a half interest in a hardware store in Shelby. In 1924, he formed the partnership of Sayles and Lewis. Sayles was active in community politics, elected register of deeds, and also served as postmaster.

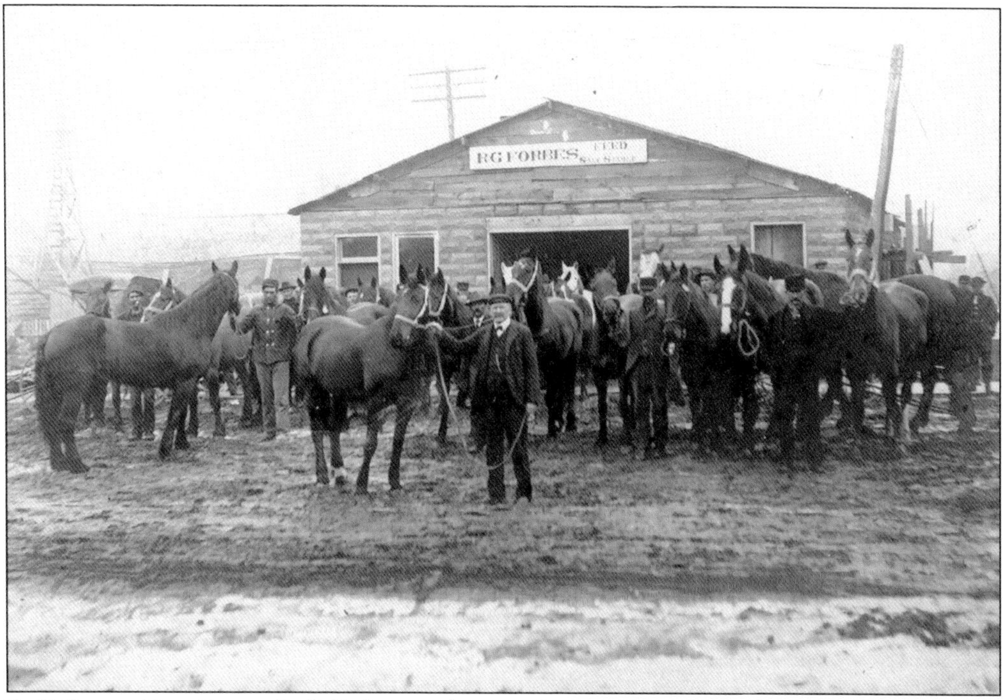

R.G. Forbes Feed Store. R.G. Forbes was born in Ontario, Canada, and came to the area about 1870. He was first the owner of a livery business and was later involved in lumbering. He had a great interest in horses and eventually settled into a business of dealing in quality horse stock on a large scale.

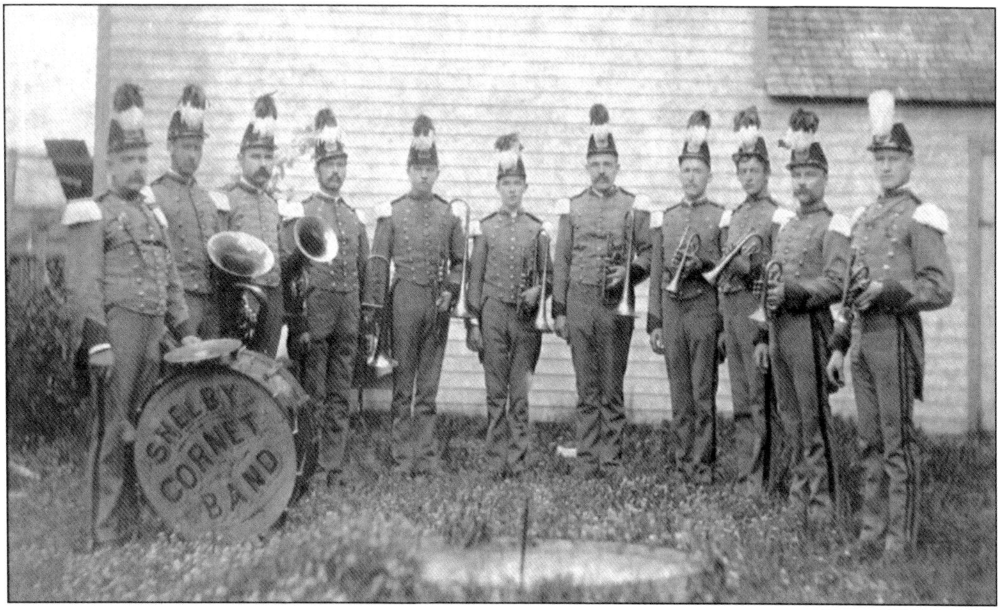

Shelby Cornet Band. The Shelby Coronet Band takes a break from playing a concert in order to have a picture taken. Community bands such as this formed during the Gilded Age were popular and welcome at all community functions. Generally, the bands consisted of cornets and other brass instruments, as pictured here.

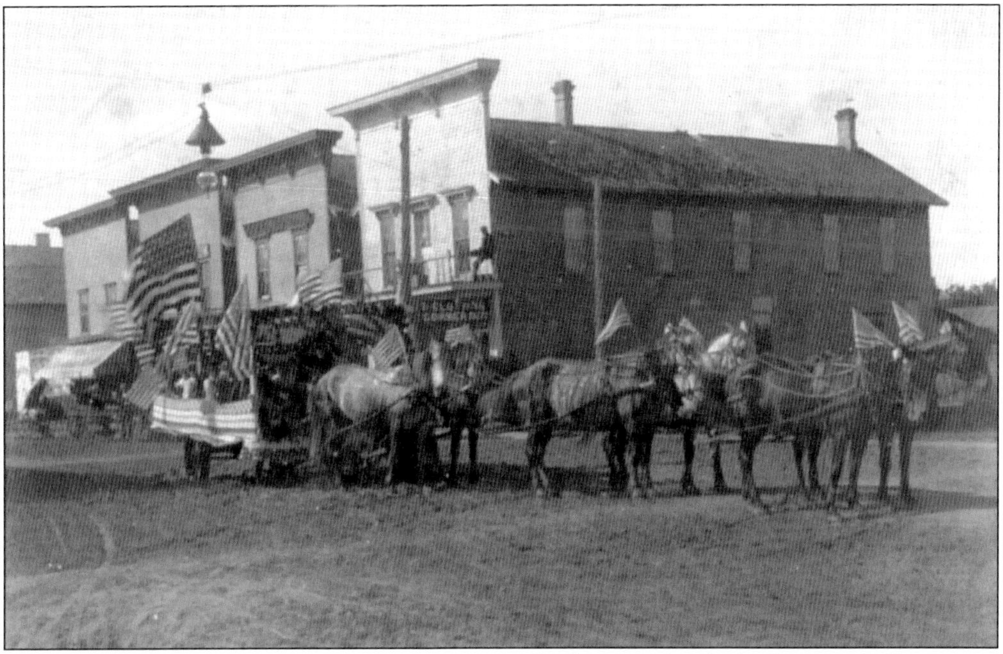

FOURTH OF JULY PARADE. A team of six horses pulls this Fourth of July float in Shelby around 1910. Celebrations during this era were grand events filled with a parade, contests of all types, a dance, reenactments by veterans, and other activities designed to bring in and include all aspects of the community.

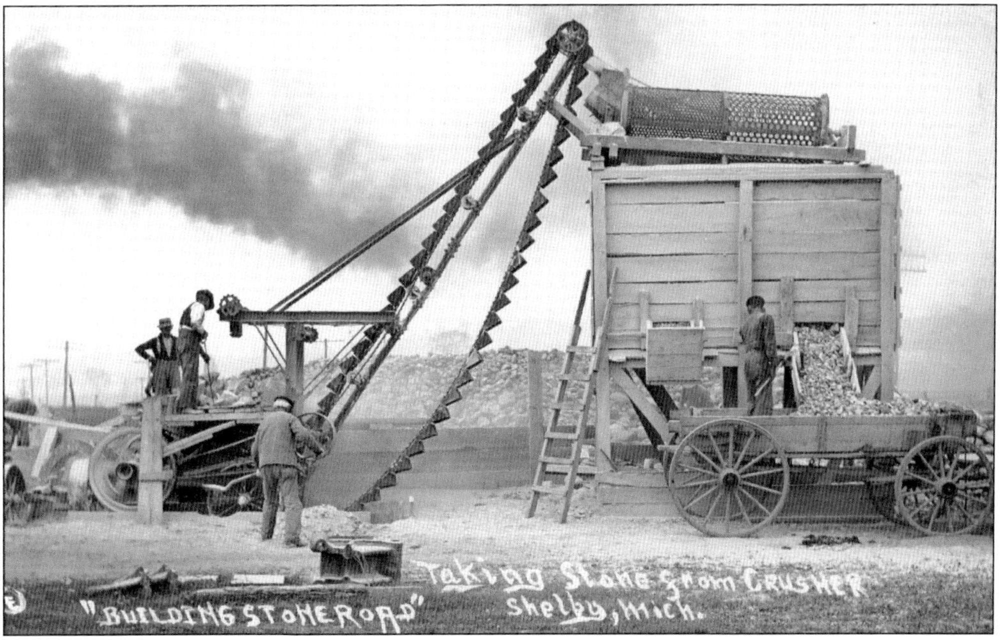

BUILDING STONE ROAD. Although it may sound strange to today's travelers, the building of a concrete or stone road was an affair of great importance. Roads in the early part of the 20th century were still in poor condition in many Michigan localities, and the improvements were considered a great accomplishment that meant ease and comfort even while traveling.

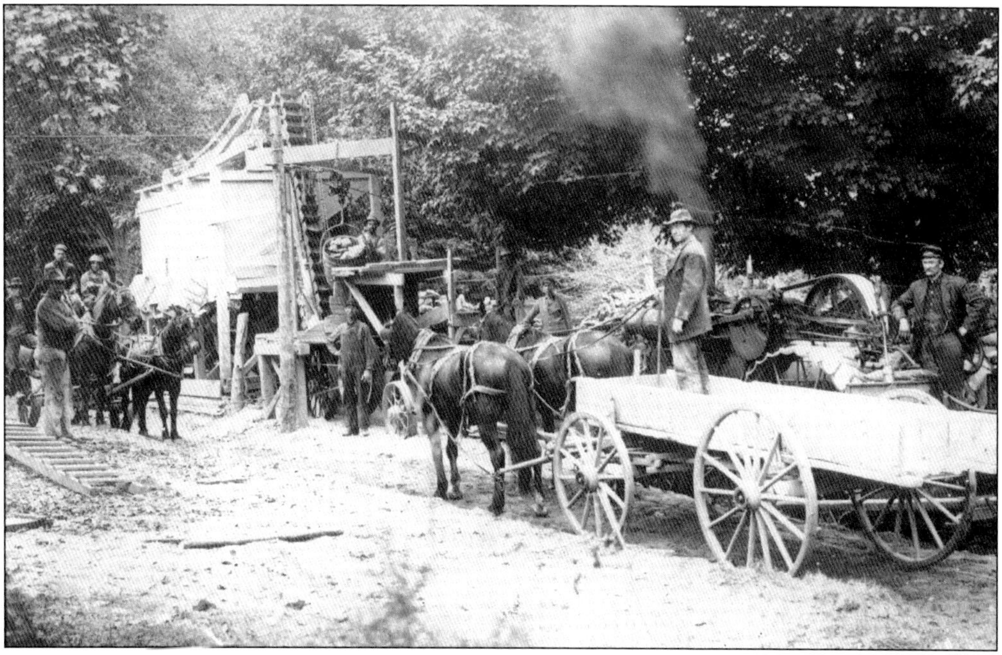

BUILDING STONE ROAD. The new roads were such a novelty, local residents with cars would come out on a Sunday afternoon and drive back and forth on the new surface just for the fun of it. Local farmers found a use for some of the rocks dug out of their fields; they received about $2 per wagonload.

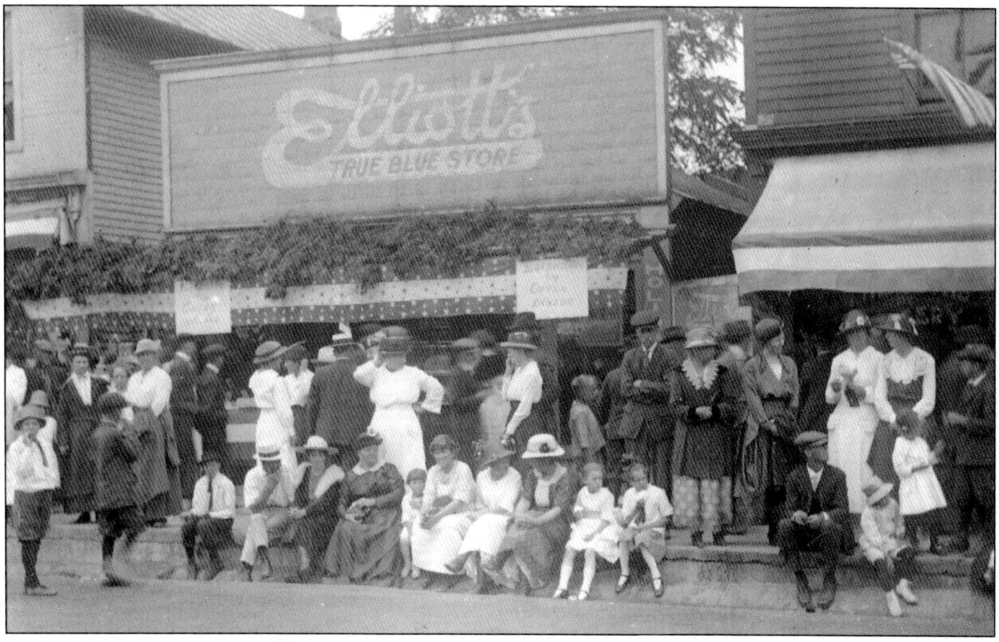

THE TRUE BLUE STORE. Elliott's True Blue Store is decked out for the Fourth of July in this c. 1910 view. One of the signs in this image reads, "Sandwiches and coffee inside." The crowd, however, seems to be focusing on the next float in the parade rather than paying attention to Elliott's attempt to entice them into the store.

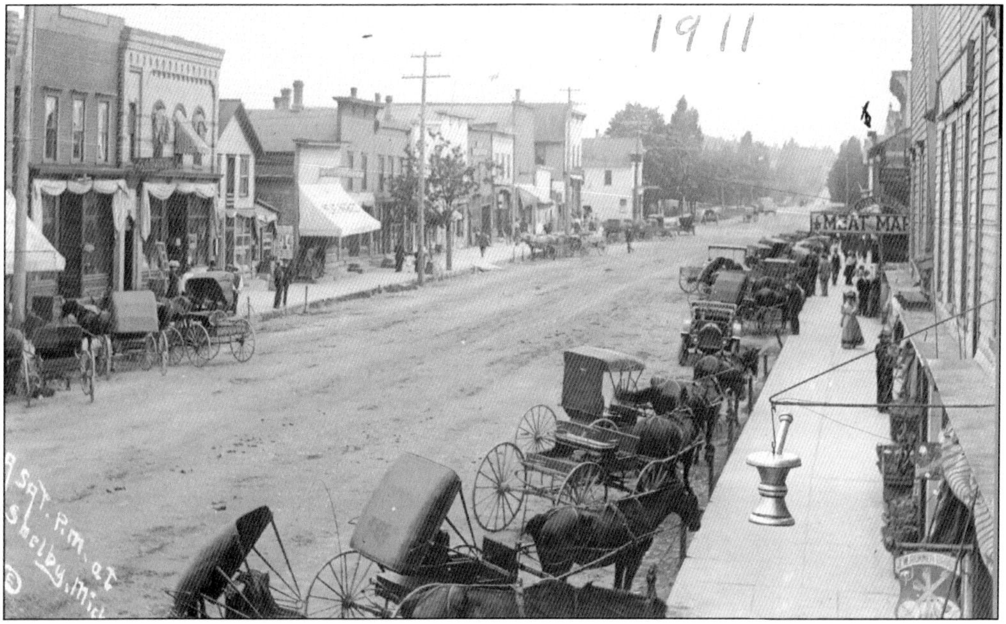

Michigan Avenue. This 1911 photograph, taken during a Saturday afternoon in Shelby, shows a bustling main street with many farmers coming to town for supplies. By 1914, the Gem Theatre opened, bringing a new form of entertainment: moving pictures. The projector used at the time had to be fed film by hand, and the movie's musical accompaniment was provided by piano or organ.

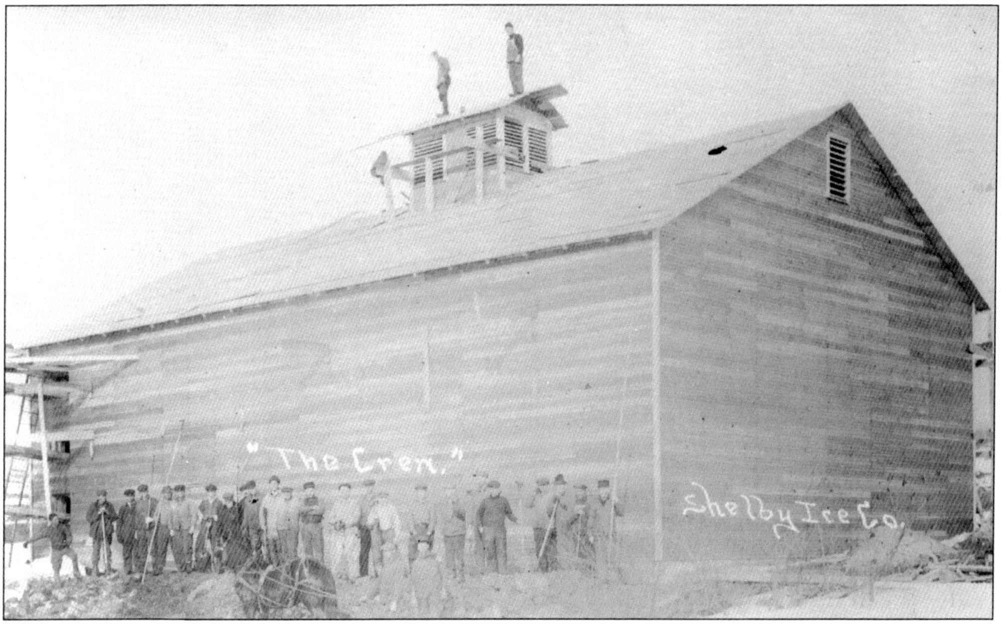

Shelby Ice Company. The ice-cutting crew is pictured outside of the icehouse in Shelby. In the days before electric refrigeration, ice was harvested from many of the lakes and ponds in the country. The only way ice was available in the summer for preserving food and cooling drinks was if someone took the time during the winter to harvest and store it, insulating it with straw for future use.

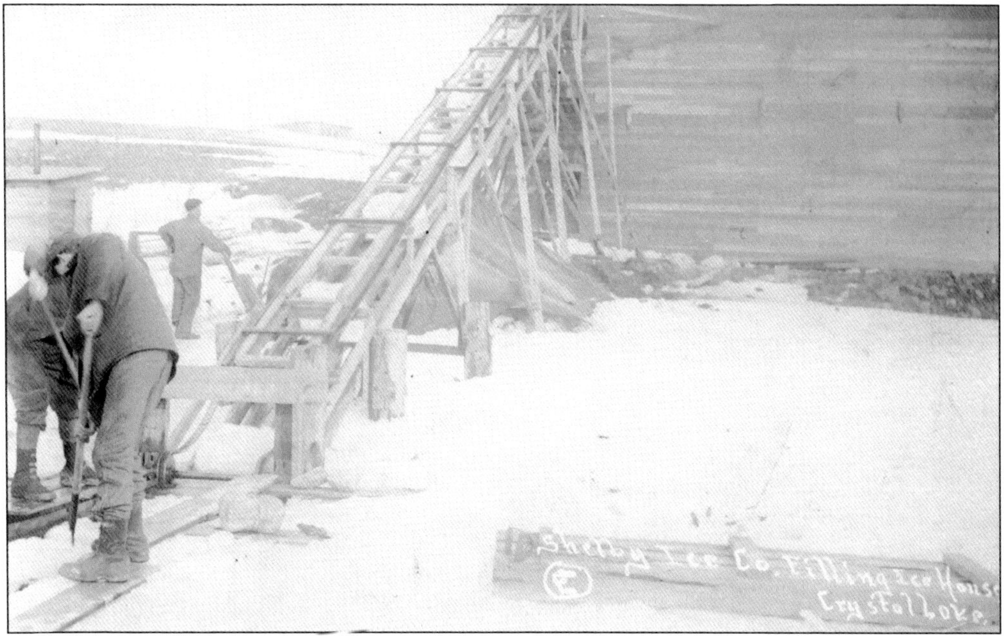

SHELBY ICE COMPANY. Ice is being sent up the conveyor belt for safe packing. Crews would head out onto the frozen lakes with saws and spuds to cut the blocks of ice into manageable sizes that could be handled. The ice was then transported for storage and eventually delivered to customers for their home ice boxes during the hot summer months.

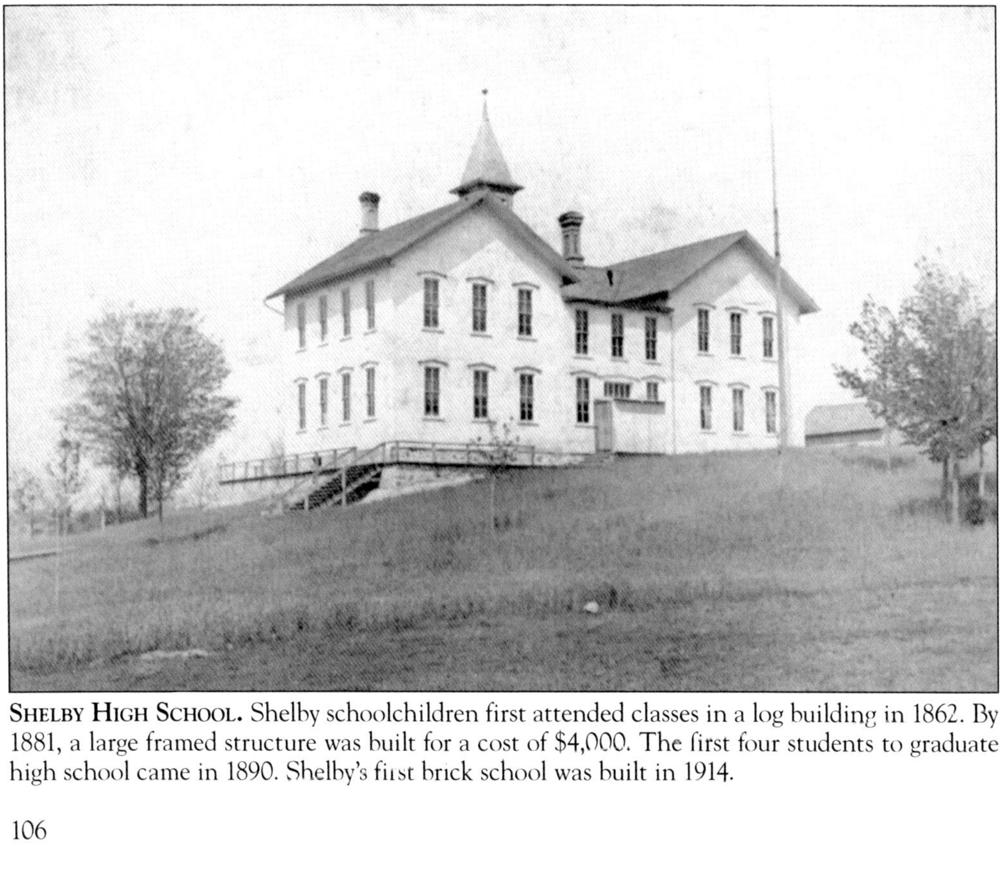

SHELBY HIGH SCHOOL. Shelby schoolchildren first attended classes in a log building in 1862. By 1881, a large framed structure was built for a cost of $4,000. The first four students to graduate high school came in 1890. Shelby's first brick school was built in 1914.

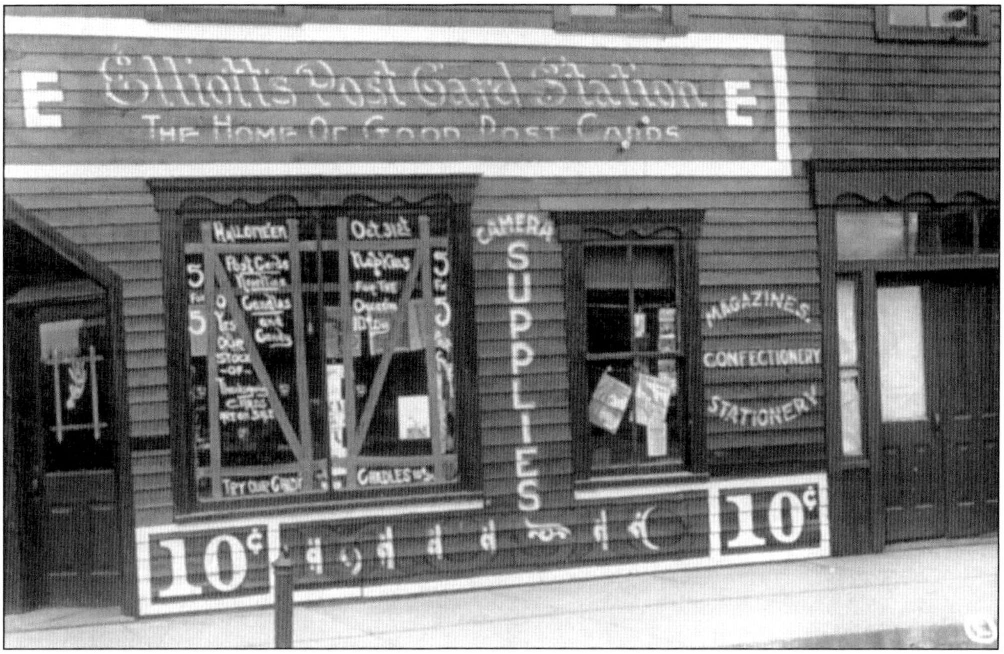

POSTCARD STATION. Harlo Elliott is a familiar name to postcard collectors; his views of the past fetch upwards of $100 or more for rarer images. Elliott, born in 1878, established his True Blue Photographic Studio and Store in 1908 to sell postcards and other goods. Elliott's images are featured throughout this book and capture many of the areas significant historical events and landmarks.

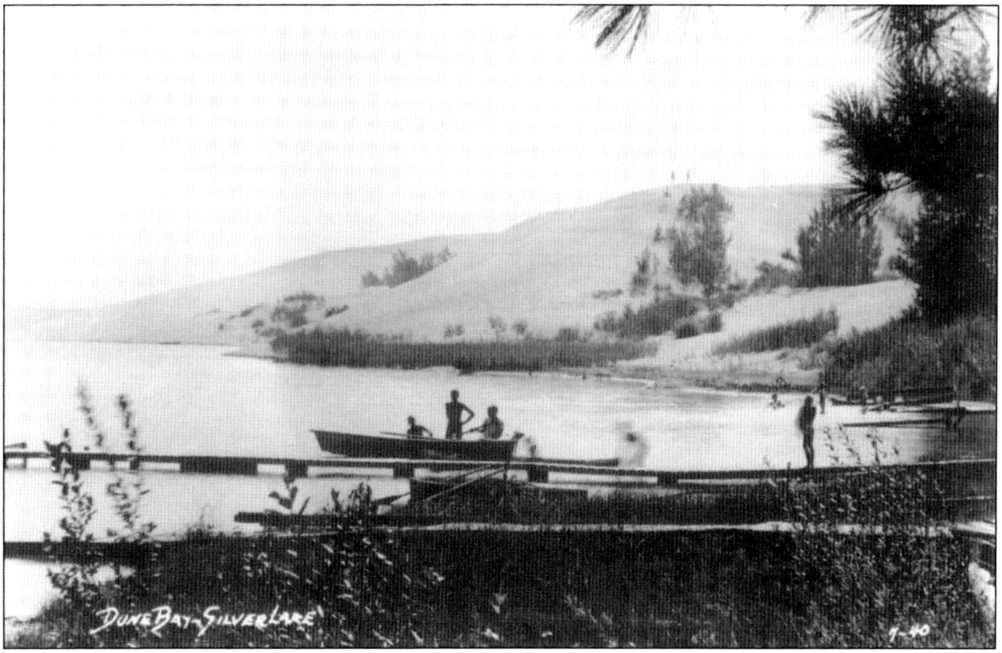

SILVER LAKE VACATION. The Silver Lake area has been a nationally known vacation spot since the mid-1920s with summer and year-round cottages flourishing. The new construction was not without risk, as more than a dozen of the cottages were swallowed up by the encroaching dunes on the north end of Silver Lake.

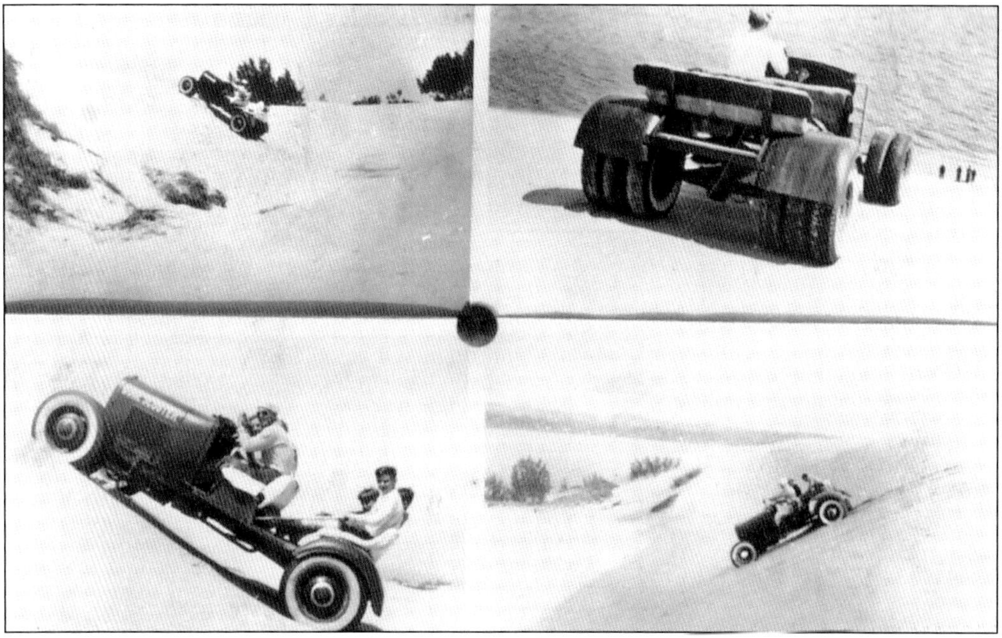

Dune Scooter Rides. Mac Woods was renowned for his dune scooters, which traversed the sandy dunes near Silver Lake and provided vacationers with a thrilling ride across the sand. His discovery of the ability to drive across the dunes happened by accident when he drove across the them on tires that were almost flat. He realized that vacationers might enjoy a ride across the dunes and launched a new business that quickly became popular.

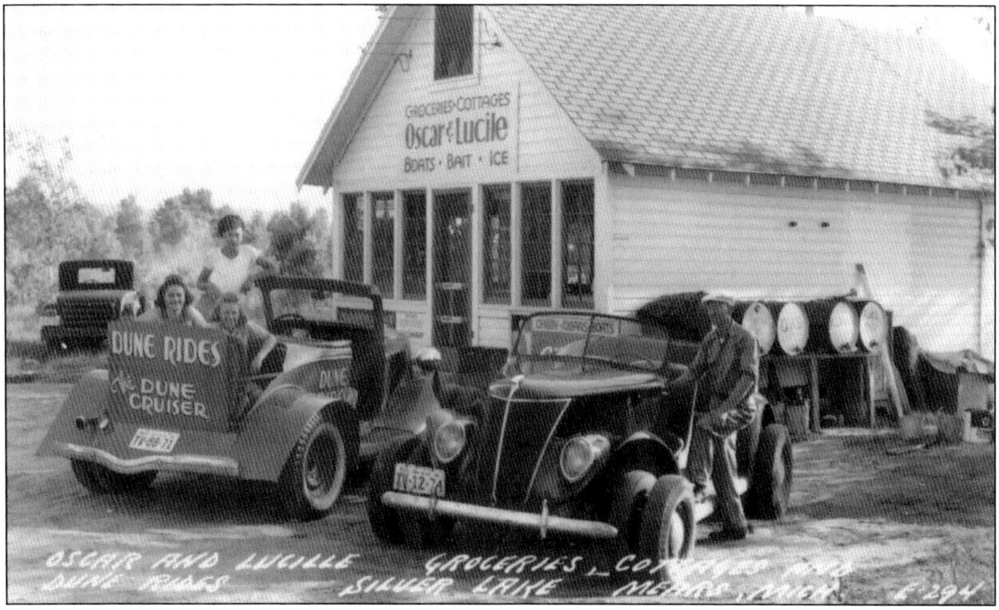

Oscar and Lucile Shogren. The Silver Lake sand dunes are about 11 miles wide and 21 miles long, stretching between Silver Lake and Lake Michigan. Dune scooter rides became a local attraction in 1927 and were enjoyed by many visitors who came to vacation around Silver Lake. When Oscar Shogren did get started in the dune scooter business in 1938, he operated two cars in addition to the store.

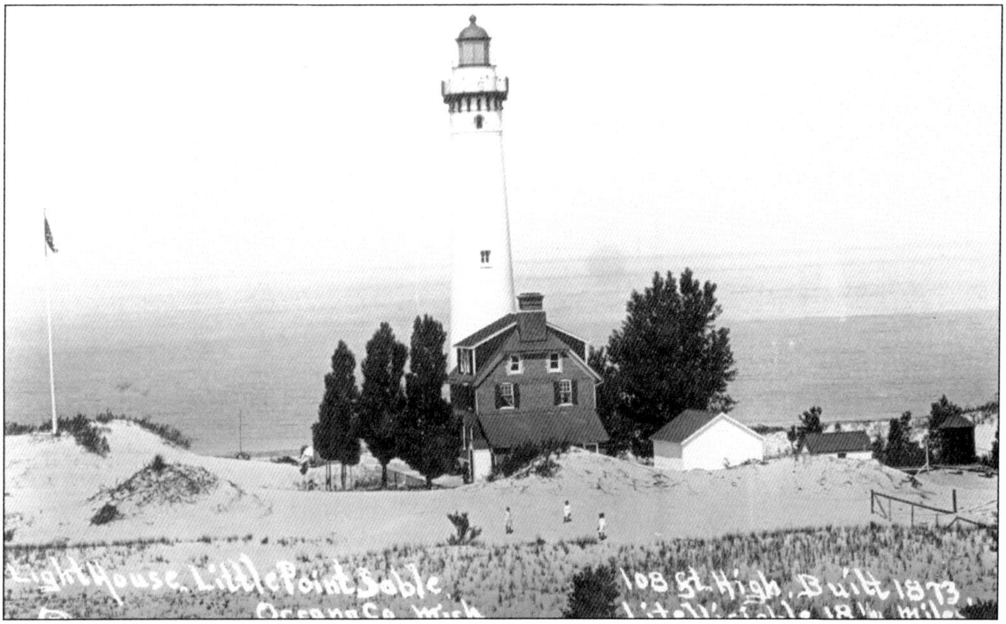

Little Sable Lighthouse. The lack of a good access road initially hindered construction of the lighthouse, but work was finally completed in 1873, and the light was activated in 1874. The base of the lighthouse is five feet thick. The 107-foot-tall tower features a third-order Fresnel lens. Panted white in 1900, the lighthouse was sandblasted and returned to its natural brick exterior in 1975. (Courtesy of Carole Elve.)

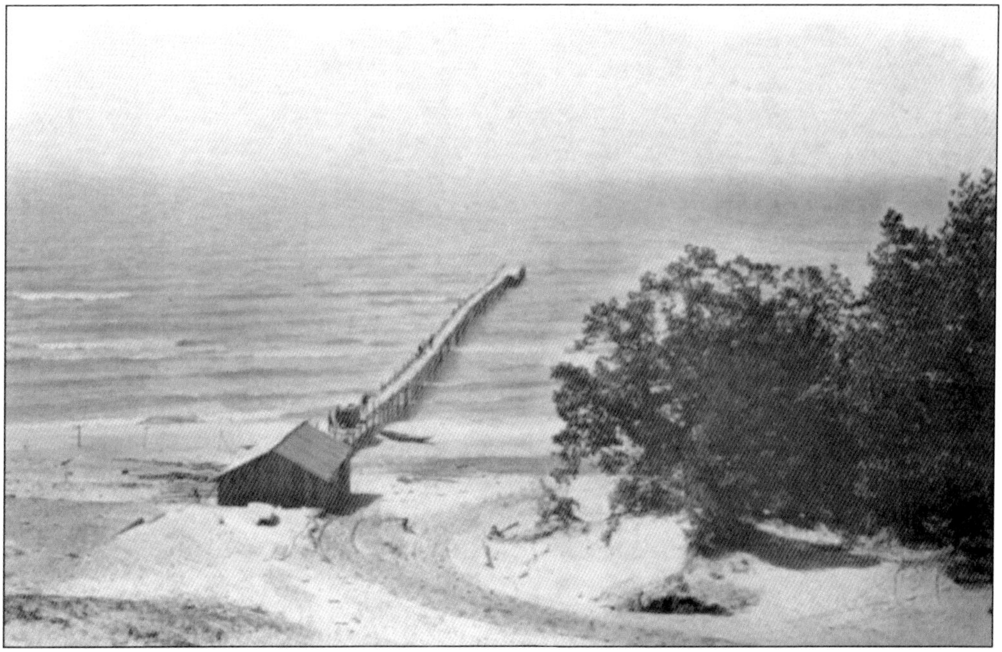

Sammon's Landing. In 1880, a pier was constructed near Little Sable Lighthouse that was known as Sammon's Landing. Pilings were driven into the lake in order to extend wooden piers to a depth capable of servicing break-bulk ships. These piers, stretching 300 feet into the lake, were loaded and unloaded by day; laborers were referred to as dock-wallopers.

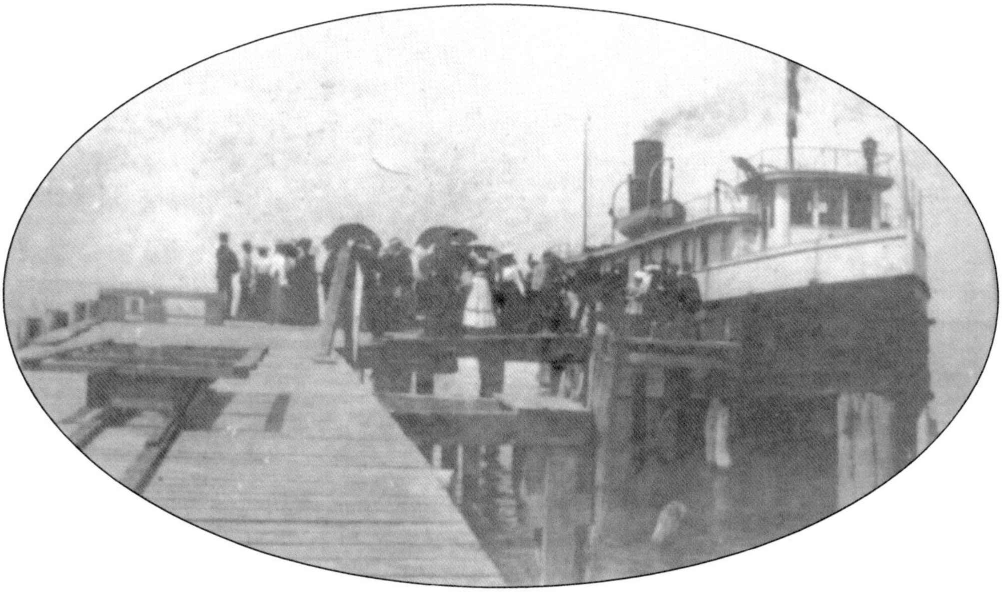

Passenger Ship at Stony Creek. In 1865, construction began on a pier that extended 1,300 feet out into Lake Michigan. It was completed in 1867, allowing passenger steamers to dock and bring supplies and visitors. Later, many local resort communities had docks that extended out into Lake Michigan, which allowed easy access for summer folk from remote parts of counties along the Lake Michigan shoreline. A steamer is shown here taking on a group of passengers near the Stony Creek outlet. (Courtesy of Lance Heitz.)

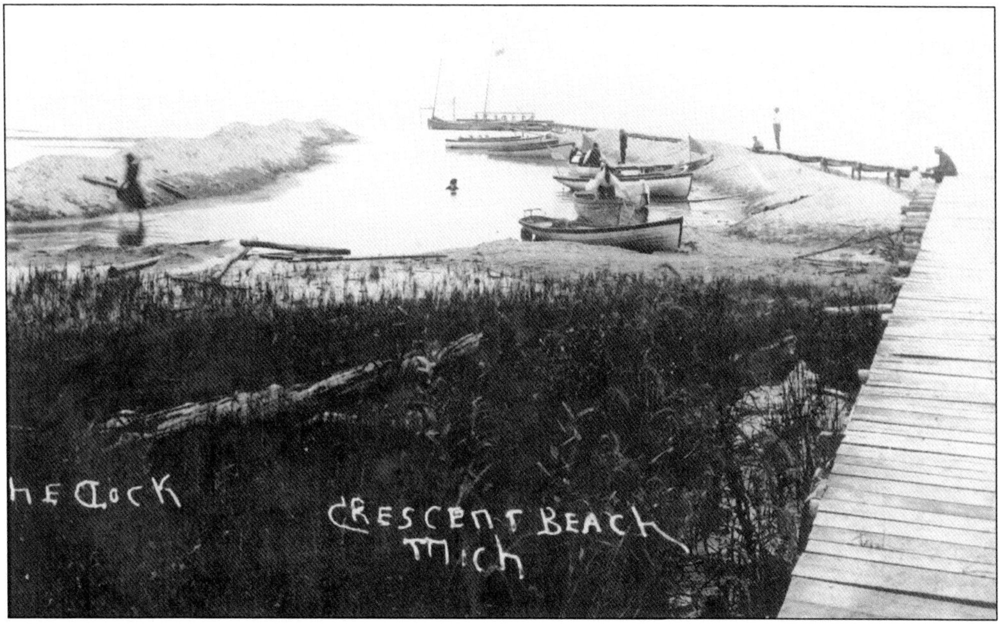

Crescent Beach Dock. Sand is piled up to create an impromptu harbor. It could provide some temporary protection for boats and schooners moored on the dock, but it would not last in inclement weather. Fishermen needed a safe place to moor their boats and unload their daily catch. They were forced to improvise, as Pentwater had the only safe harbor on the Oceana County shoreline.

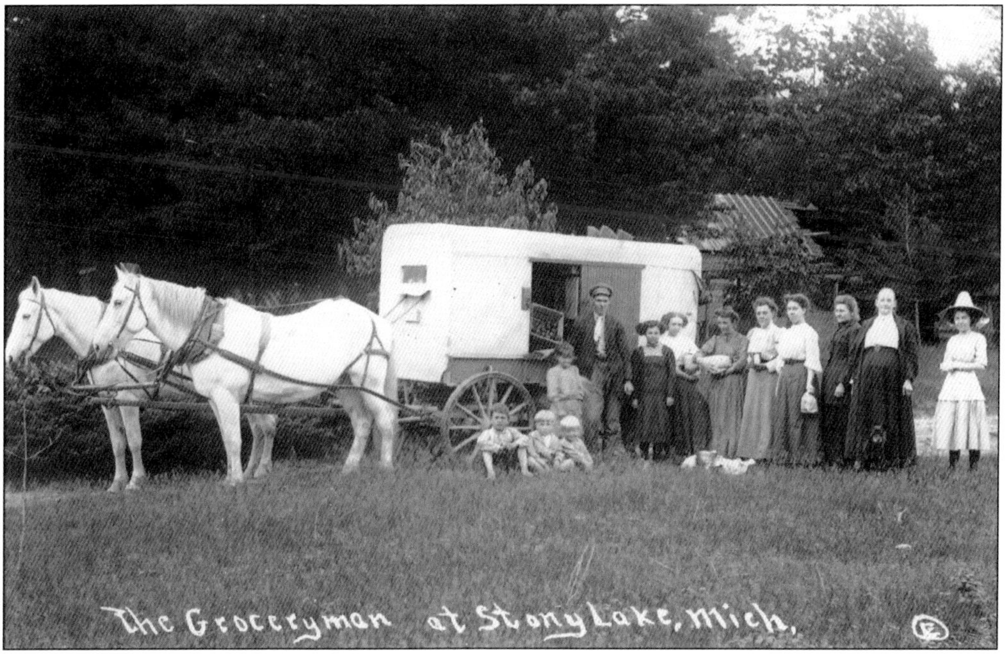

The Grocery Man. The grocery man was a lifeline for the visitors who depended on him to bring supplies out to Stony Lake and other resort communities. In 1910, it was not possible to just jump in the car and make a quick run into town to grab a couple things for dinner. When people came to vacation in the early 1900s, they were somewhat isolated and without modern gadgets and conveniences.

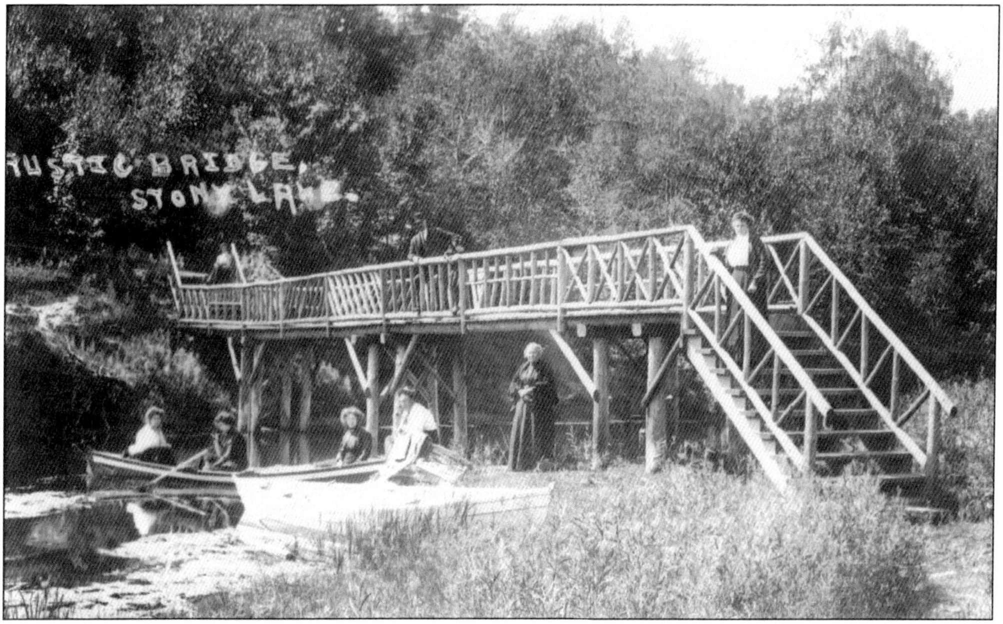

Rustic Bridge at Stony Lake. Four brothers of Norwegian descent by the name of Brady settled near Stony Creek. The area continues to be known as Bradyville. This picturesque rustic bridge over the channel provided a convenient manner in which the ladies could cross over the channel without getting wet.

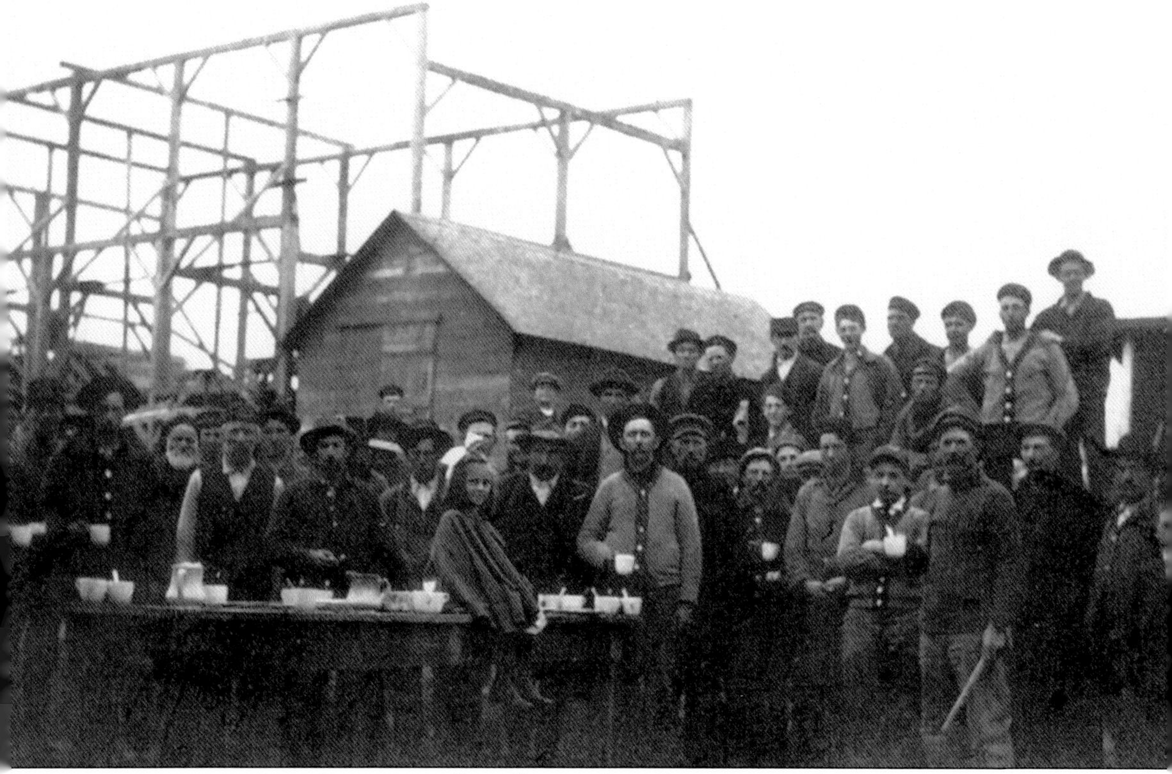

WALKERVILLE BARN RAISING. Walkerville was platted by Fayette Walker in 1883. By all accounts, going ahead with the project was a leap of faith, as there were two existing country stores a short distance away. Alvin Stetson had established a store and a post office in 1882 but did not take action to plat a village. The site picked by Walker lacked water for powering mills, and it was near a swamp. Yet once the village was laid out, settlers came and established homes and businesses, and in 1888 the Mason & Oceana Railroad (M&O) came to Walkerville on its intended route to Grand Rapids. Fayette Walker came from Warsaw, New York, to Oceana County in 1869 with his new bride. They initially lived in Leavitt Township and moved to Colfax a short time afterwards. After Fayette's wife contracted tuberculosis and died, the family moved back to Leavitt Township in 1880. By 1883, Walker had come to the conclusion that a village could thrive there, so he went forward with his plans. Walker's faith was rewarded as settlers came and Walkerville prospered.

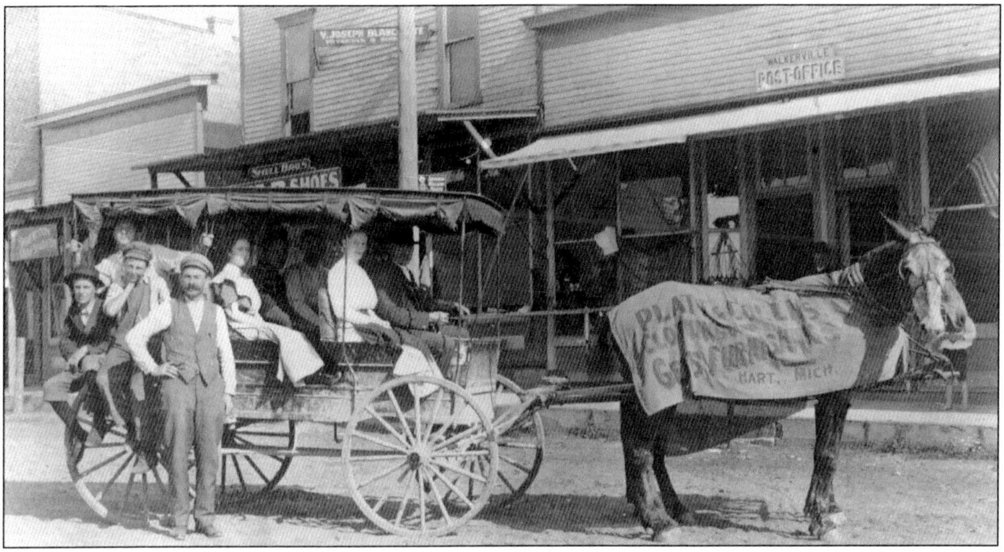

MAIL SERVICE. In 1875, Carpenter's store was the site of the first post office in the area, with Rufus Carpenter appointed postmaster. Additionally, another post office was established in Stetson's store in 1881, a short distance away, with Alvin Stetson as the appointed postmaster. In 1885, the post office moved into the village of Walkerville. The daily mail service is shown ready to make the rounds in this c. 1910 view.

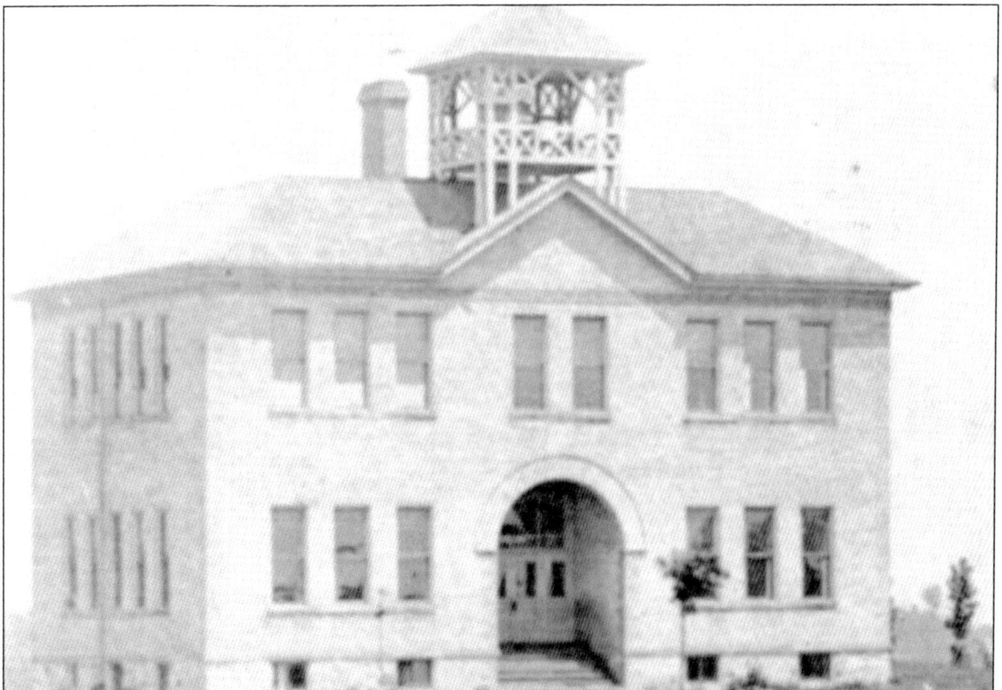

HIGH SCHOOL. In 1905, Walkerville built a new two-story brick school behind the bank for $5,000. Unfortunately, the structure was not completed in time for the new school year, and students attended classes in the town hall. The district ran out of money and could not finish the building, but it raised an additional $1,000 to complete the second floor the following year.

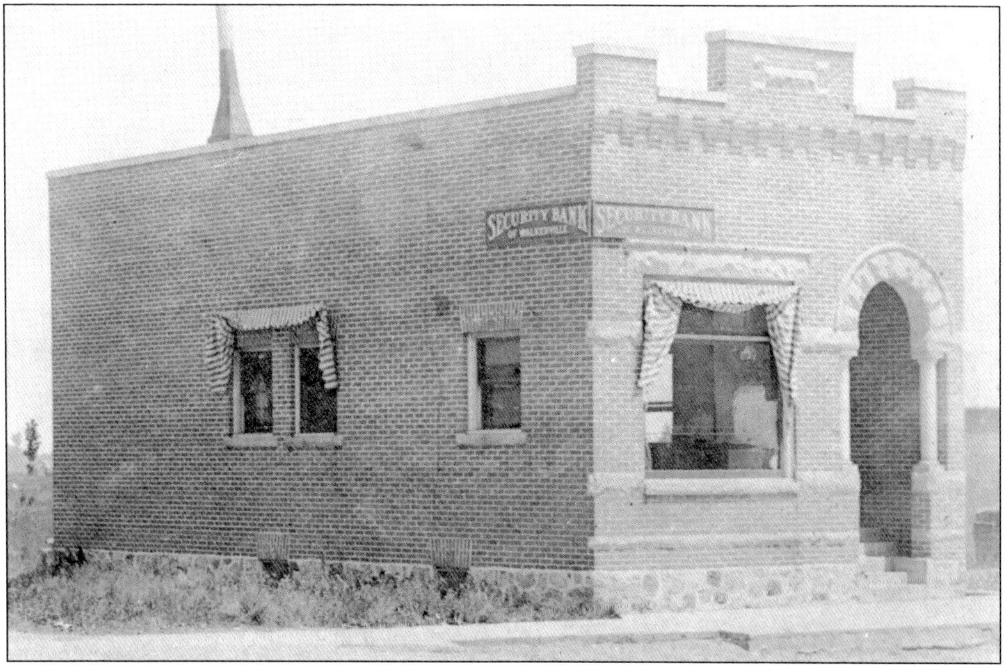

BANK OF WALKERVILLE. The Security Bank of Walkerville was established in 1908 by three men who went by the last names of McPhail, Cole, and Bloomer. The bank operated for a time in a house before moving into its new brick building in 1910. The bank was operated efficiently, remained solvent, and was able to reopen immediately after the bank holiday, when banks in the state failed in 1933.

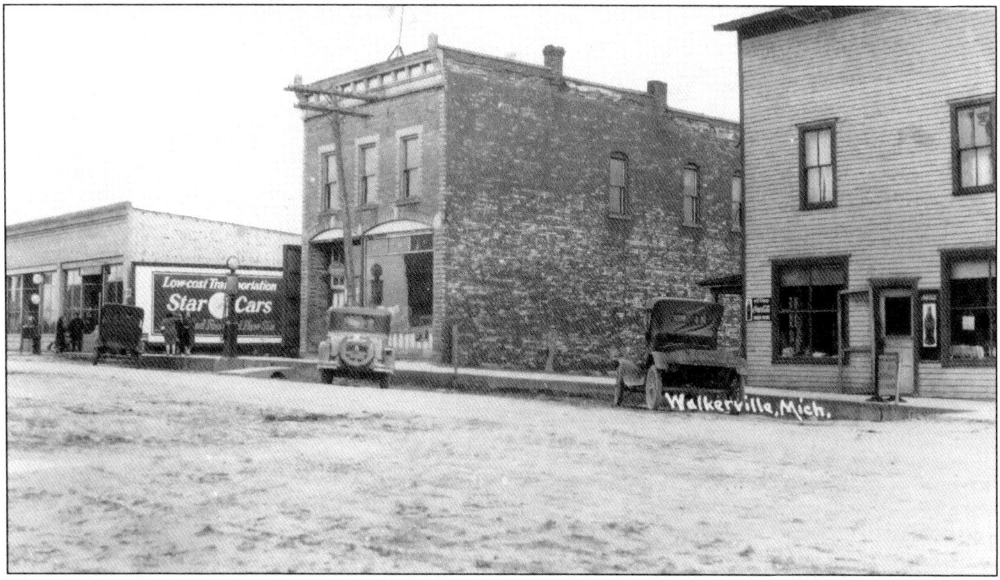

WALKERVILLE MAIN STREET. In this 1920 photograph, Walkerville's Main Street boasts several brick buildings that were constructed after the big fires of 1891 and 1914. Fires were a scourge of early settlements, and Walkerville experienced several fires over the years. The 1891 fire burned both sides of Main Street, but the community was rebuilt within two years. Seven buildings were lost in 1914, and fire struck again in 1941.

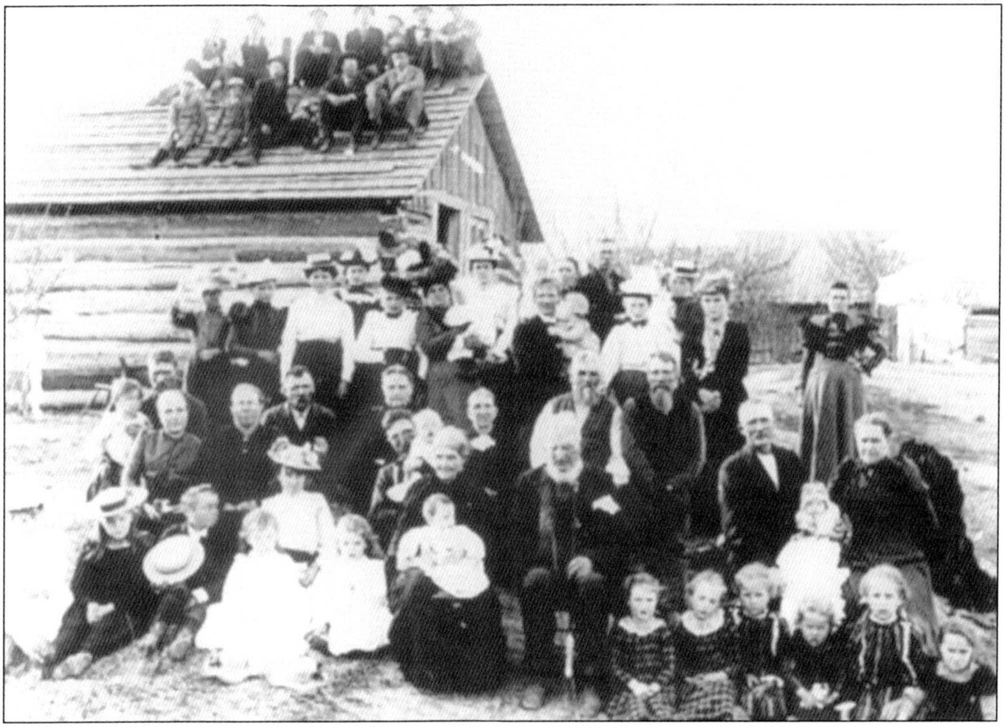

Bromley Clan Gathering. The Bromley clan of Oceana County is pictured here near Walkerville for a celebration of the family of Ami Chittenden Bromley. The woman standing alone to the far right and in the back is Alice Bromley, wife of William C. Bromley. There were 10 children born to this family that included William, Perle, Otis, Henry, George, Moni, Ada, Earl, Beatrice, and Ralph.

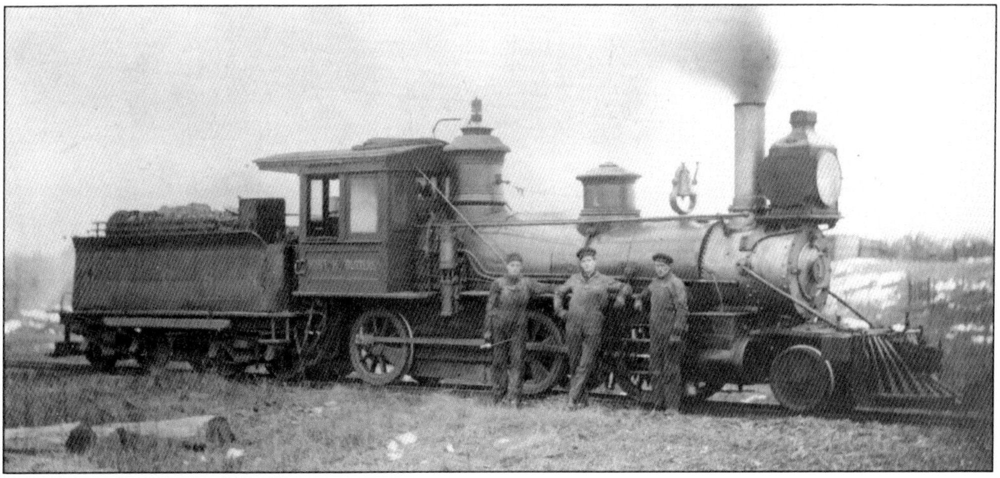

Butters's M&O Railroad. The Mason & Oceana Railroad (also known by crewmen as the "Miserable and Ornery" due to the noises its trains' engines made) was established by Mason County lumberman Horace Butters. The narrow-gauge rail line wound down into Oceana County through Peachville on its intended route to Grand Rapids, Michigan. The lumber gave out, and the railroad failed to reach its destination. In its short time of operation, logs were cut and transported to a mill in Buttersville to be sawn and shipped out to southern markets.

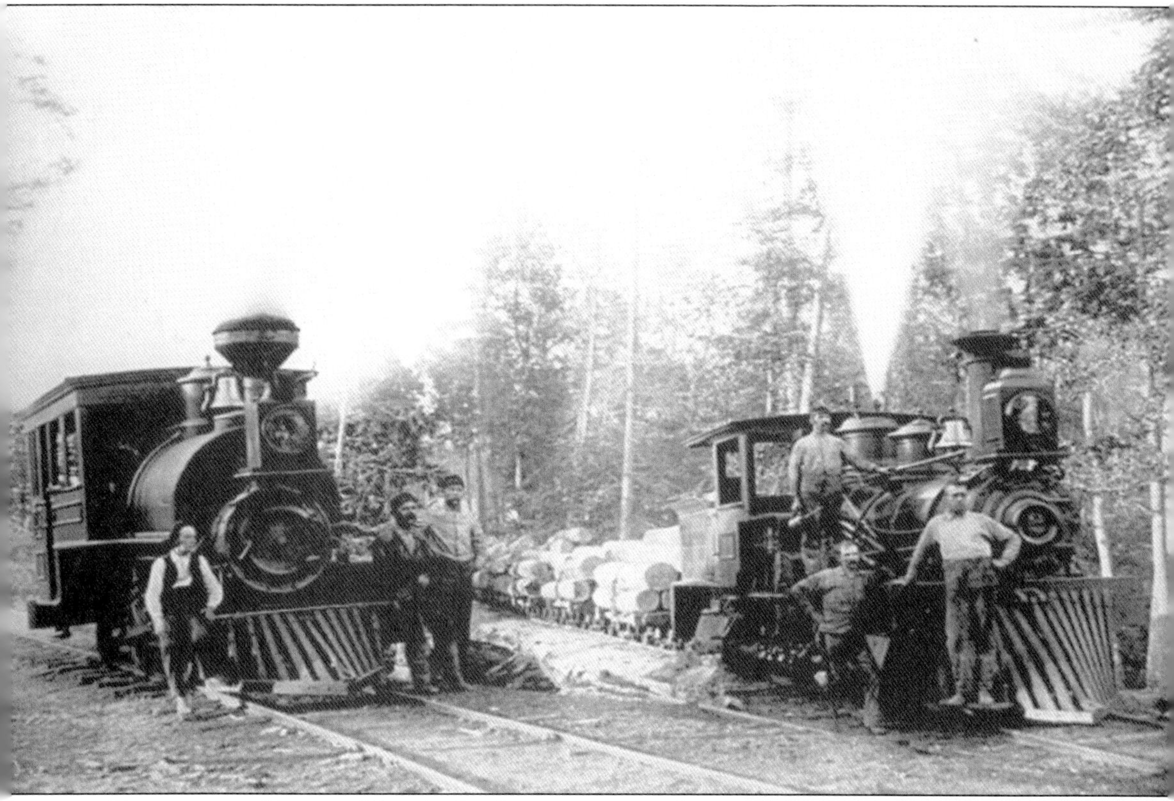

Butters and Peters. After the lumbering era started to wind down, Marshall F. Butters took charge of the operation and had a vision of extending the railroad to Grand Rapids. There was a great deal of support for the plan, which would have established Walkerville as an important link in the railroad line. Farmers were already shipping produce on the train to Ludington, where it was loaded and shipped to Milwaukee by the next morning, which opened new markets for their crops. Many local farmers and businesses contributed to the effort to extend the line south to Grand Rapids, as they realized that it would not only benefit their village, but it would also be of economic benefit to them all. The overall prosperity and condition of the area improved, and Walkerville's future was ensured.

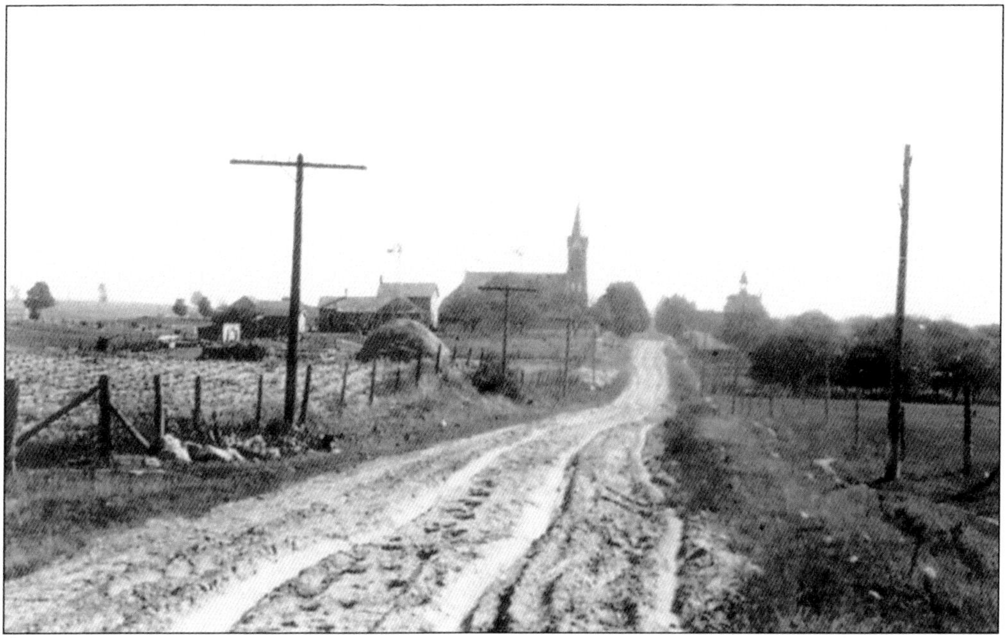

St. Joseph Catholic Church. The first church at this location was built in 1884. Construction of the present church, pictured here, began in 1909 and was dedicated in October 1912. The new church carried some of the history of the old with it: the bell from the first church was installed in the new one. By 1920, the country roads were still in poor shape; getting there was, by itself, a show of faith.

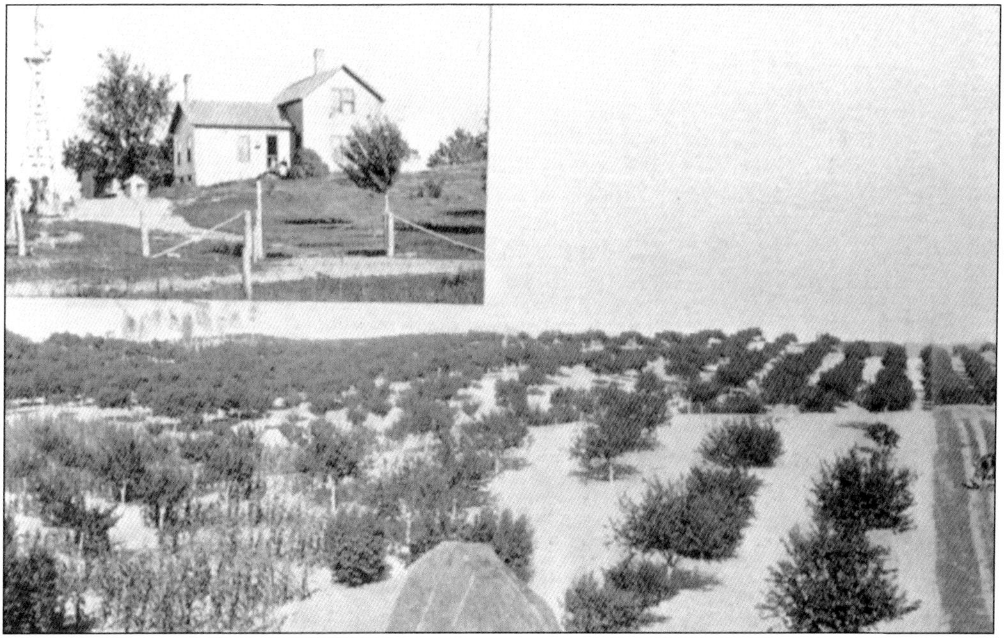

Lakeview Fruit Farm of Weare. E.D. Richmond settled in Weare Township and established a 40-acre fruit farm named the Lakeview Fruit Farm. The orchard consisted of 4,000 apple, peach, apricot, and cherry trees.

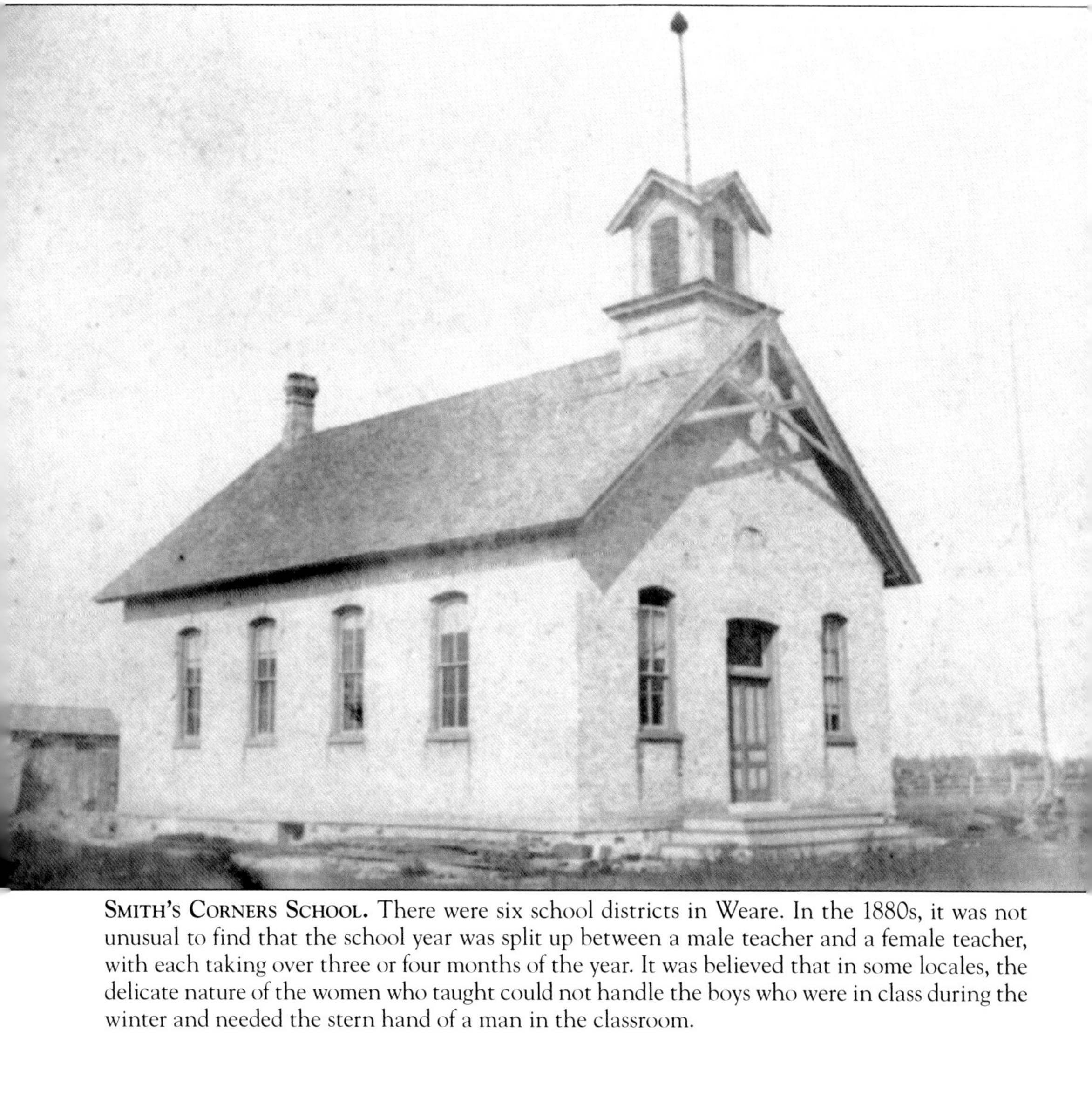

Smith's Corners School. There were six school districts in Weare. In the 1880s, it was not unusual to find that the school year was split up between a male teacher and a female teacher, with each taking over three or four months of the year. It was believed that in some locales, the delicate nature of the women who taught could not handle the boys who were in class during the winter and needed the stern hand of a man in the classroom.

Four

Pioneer Portraits

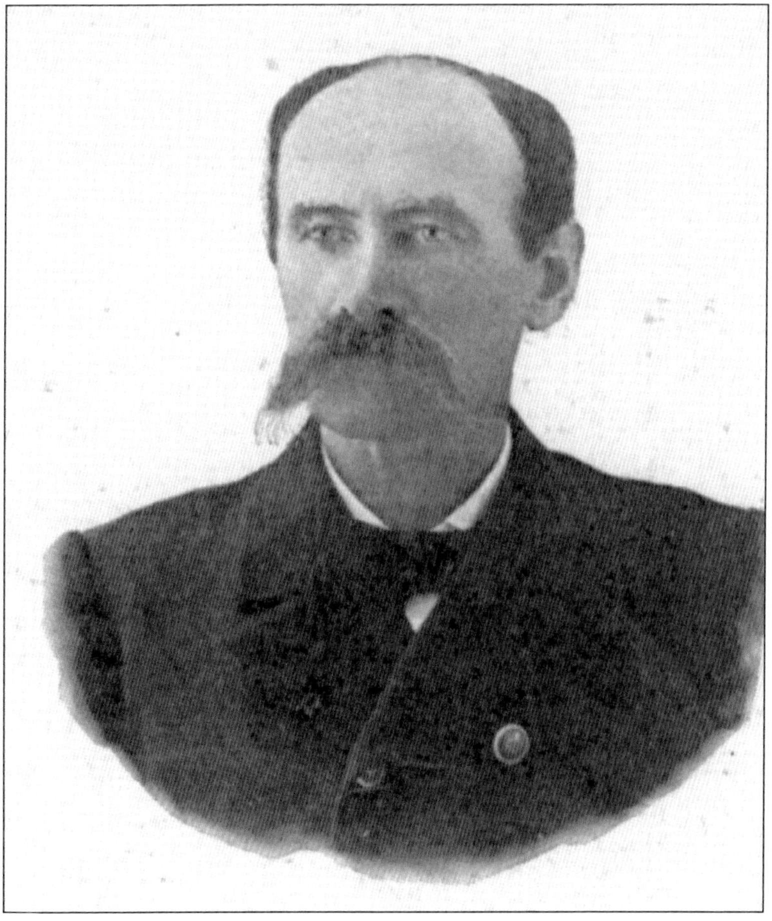

Lifesaving Keeper of Pentwater. Martin Ewald was born in Germany in 1857 and came to America as a child, settling first in Wisconsin and then in Grand Haven. Martin initially found employment on the water in the fishing tugs that were operating out of Grand Haven. In 1880, he was employed as a surfman in the Manistee Lifesaving Station, and from there he was promoted to keeper of the Pentwater Lifesaving Station.

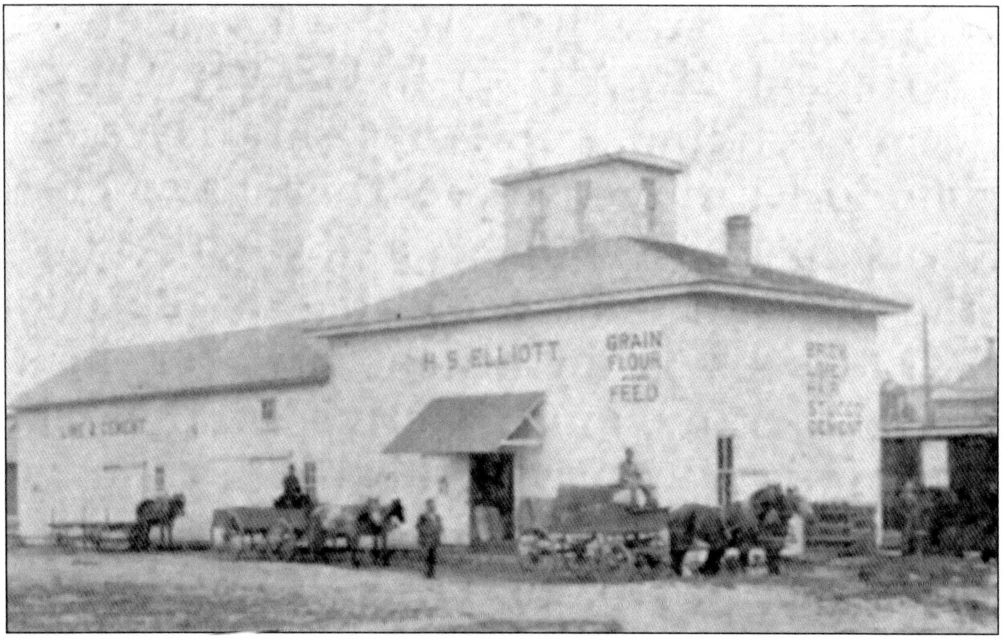

Elliott's Improved Fruit Basket. Harmon Elliott was a fruit grower and commission merchant in the Shelby area who arrived in 1869. By 1891, Elliott had built a large warehouse to handle grains, flour, and feed, as well as shingles, lumber, and logs. More importantly, Elliott received a patent for an improved fruit basket, which was claimed would revolutionize the packing of fruit.

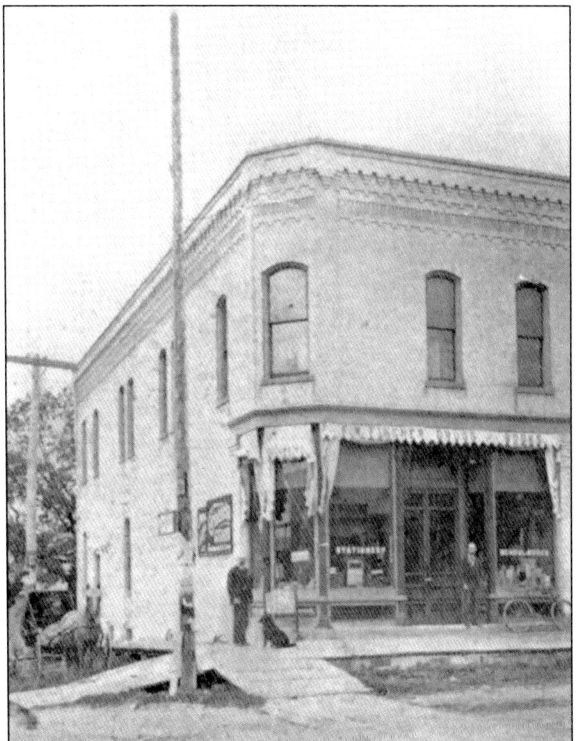

Fincher Drug Store. Francis Fincher was born in Hudson in May 1855, and after moving to New York, he found work on local farms. As a young man of 17, Francis came to Pentwater and went to work in the mills while attending school. He left Pentwater to attend lectures in the Chicago College of Pharmacy and work in a Muskegon drugstore. After a year, he returned to Pentwater to work in the Page and Jesson Drug Store, and by 1880 he purchased the business.

LOUIS M. HARTWICK, PROSECUTOR. Coming from Indiana, Louis Hartwick attended the University of Michigan and eventually settled in Pentwater in 1872 after passing the bar. He was very active in the community and in county politics, serving as justice of the peace, village president, and village attorney; in 1892, he was elected prosecutor. In 1880, Hartwick purchased the *Pentwater News*, where he, along with his brother-in-law William Tuller, published *Oceana County Pioneers and Businessmen*.

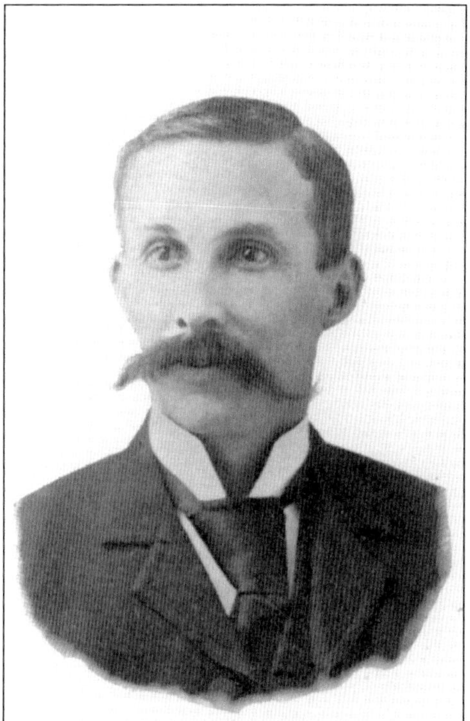

L. M. HARTWICK.

J.W. RUNNER. The Runner home was located at the corner of Fifth and Maple Streets in Shelby. Wallace J. Runner came to Oceana County with his parents from New York in 1864. He gained his education and began to teach in a local school at age 17. In 1887, in partnership with his brother and Dr. Kerzartee, he purchased the Bert Royal Drug Store.

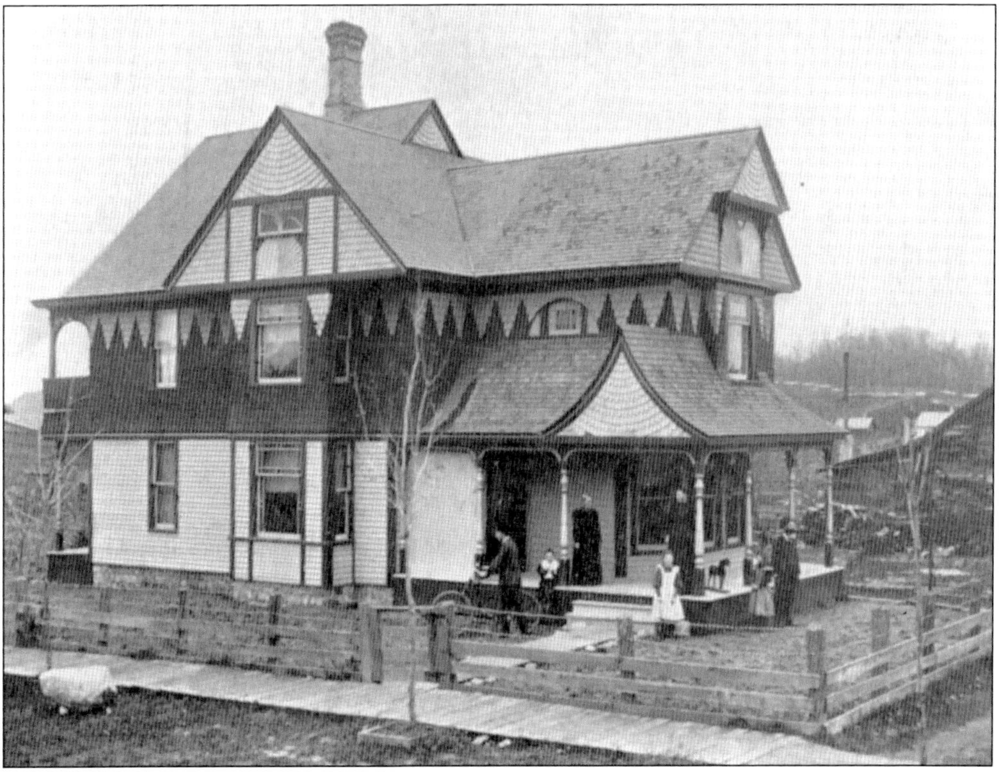

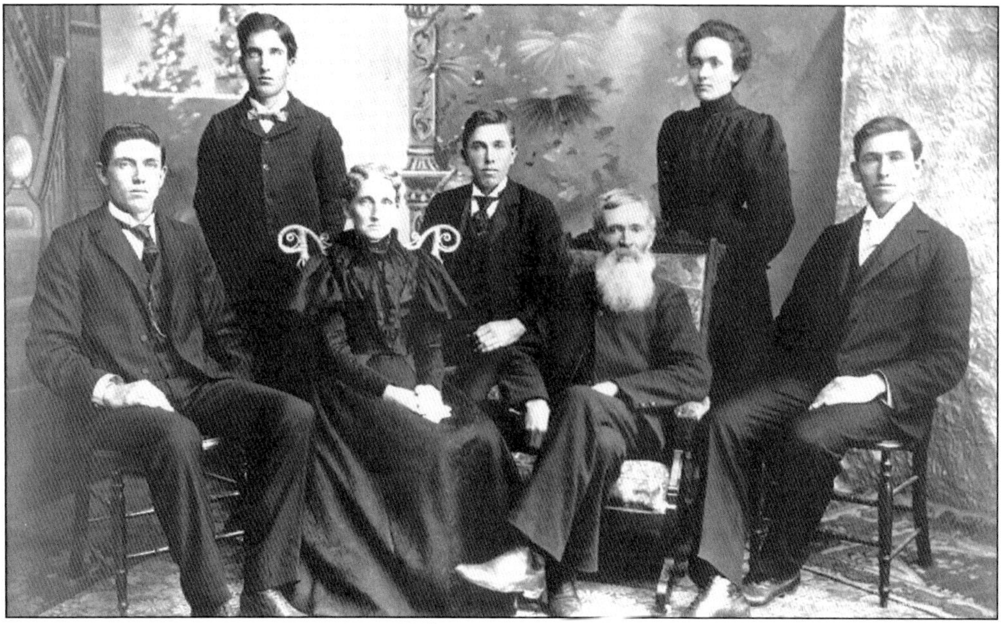

William H.H. Purdy. Coming from Hillsdale County in lower Michigan, William H.H. Purdy was typical of the early settlers who came to the Oceana County countryside to farm and raise a family. William was married to Alice Tuller in Hillsdale and raised five children: Maude Purdy Beech, Edwin, Bert, H.H., and Arthur Bouton Purdy. Maude and her husband, Alva Beech, left the area for California, and the men remained to raise their families in Oceana County, where the Purdy name continues.

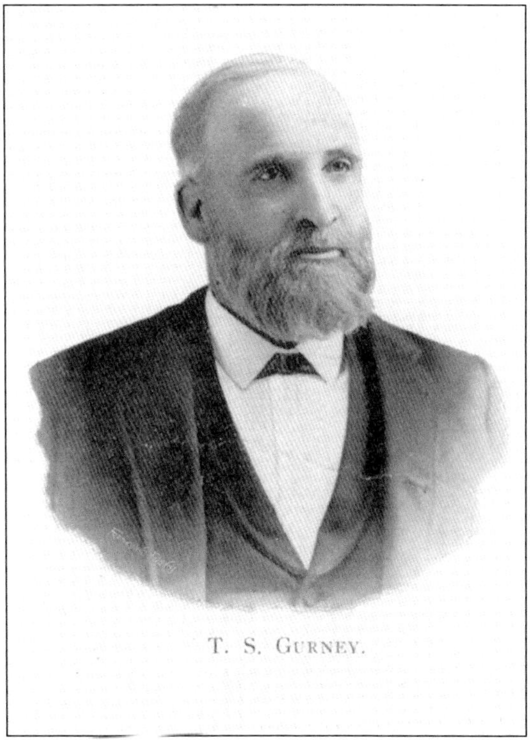

T. S. Gurney.

Theron Gurney. Theron S. Gurney came to Hart in 1867 from Ohio, where he had been the principal of the Charden Ohio Union School. Once he arrived in Hart, he set up a law practice and began to buy and sell land. Gurney was involved in local politics, and in 1889 he was elected to the Michigan State Senate. He operated his fruit farm under the name of Highland Valley Fruit Farm and was heavily vested in a number of businesses, such as the Hart Roller Mills.

J.H. Bouton Sheriff. Born in New York in 1848, John Bouton moved to the Pentwater area in about 1872, working for several local businesses such as Pentwater Lumber Company and the Pentwater Furniture Company. He married Cynthia Tuller in 1875 and continued clerking until he was elected as sheriff in 1894.

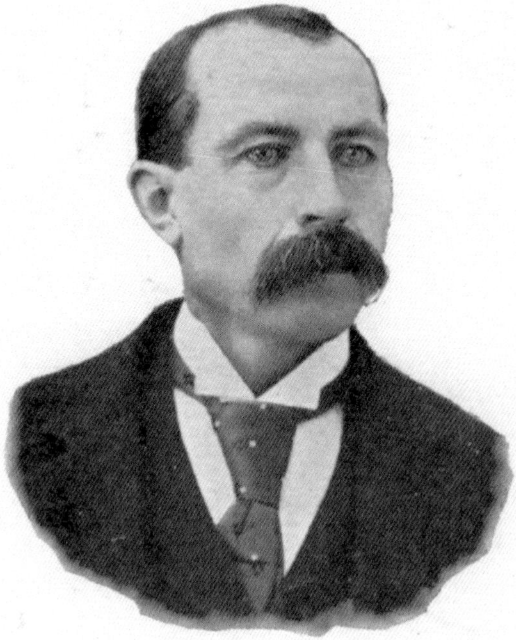

J. H. Bouton,
Sheriff.

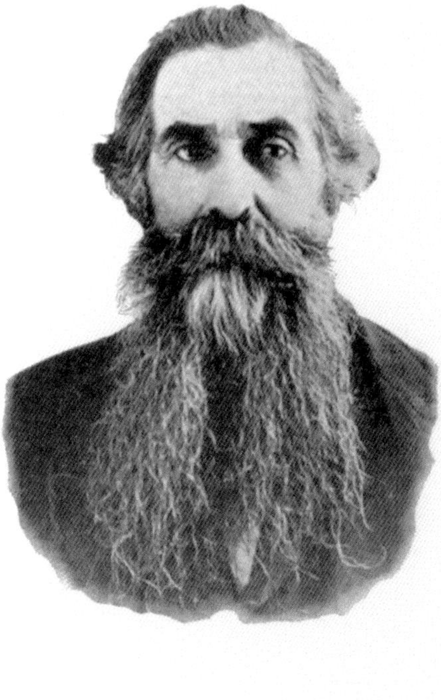

James Gibbs Pioneer. Gibbs was a farmer in Benona Township who had initially come to the area to work in the pineries and mills at White Lake. He earned a reputation as a jobber after taking a crew of men and clearing all of the overhanging trees and submerged logs out of the White River up to Hesperia. After returning from the Civil War in 1865, he returned to work at the 240-acre farm and orchard he had left behind.

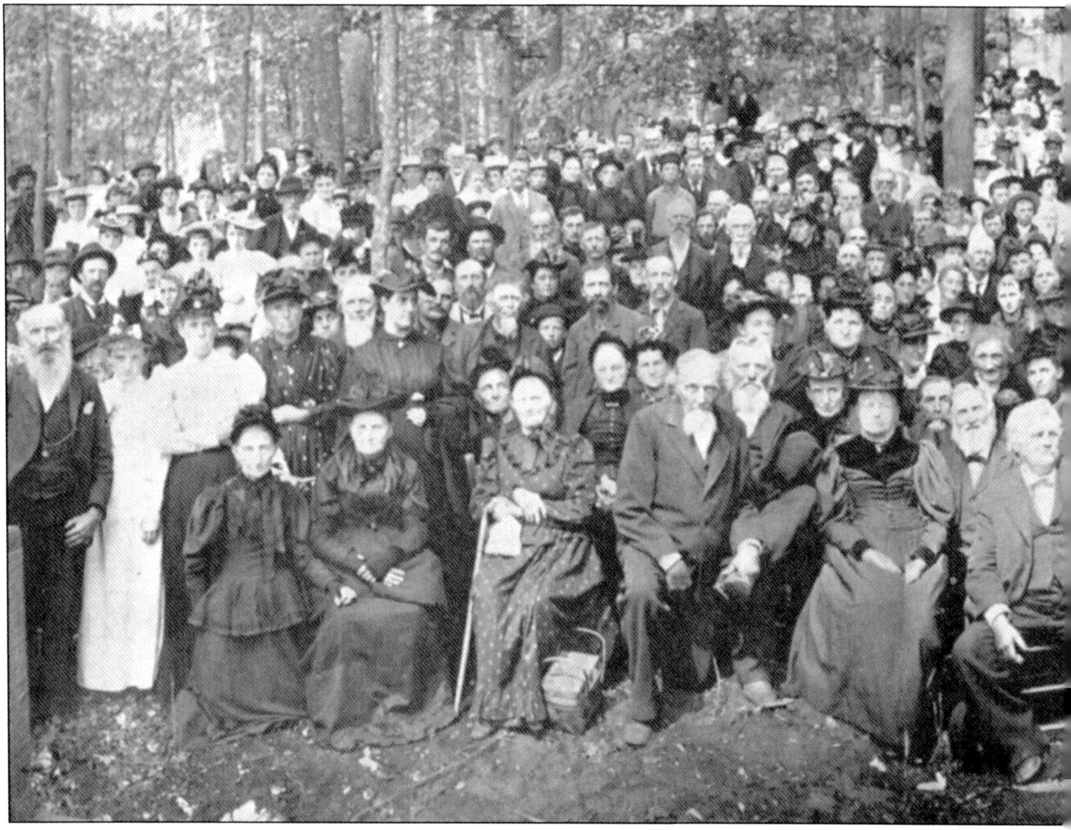

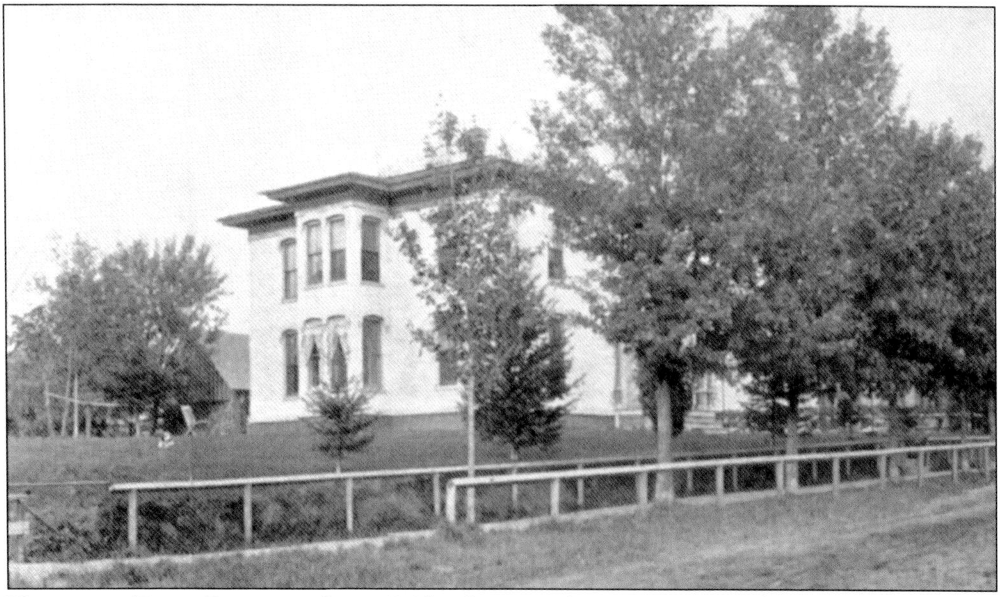

Honorable Flood Residence. James K. Flood came to Oceana County and settled in Pentwater in 1864, taking employment in the mills there. From that humble beginning, he was able to invest in a drugstore in Hart, and from there he became postmaster from 1881 to 1886. His involvement in local politics led him to run for the state house of representatives, where he was elected in 1894.

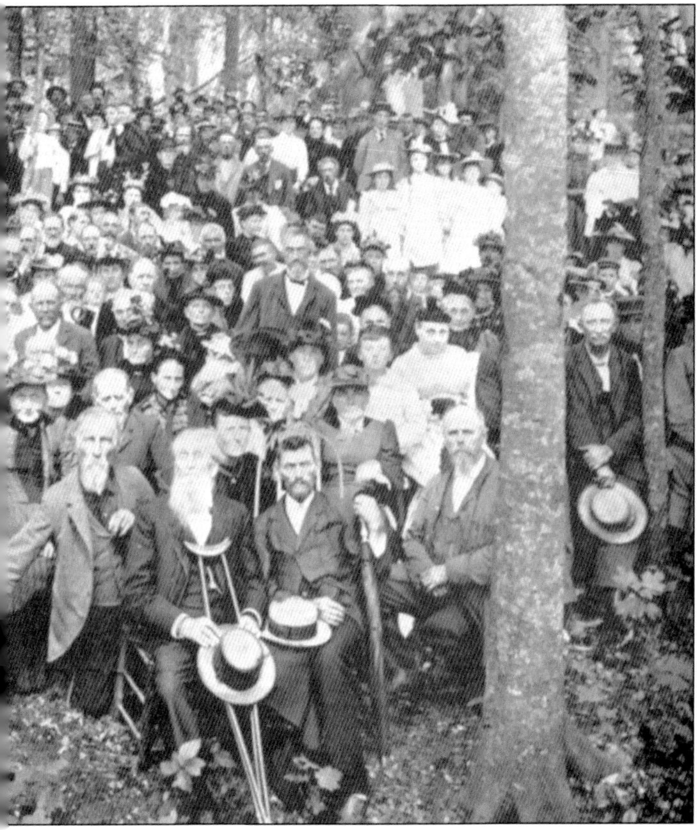

OLD SETTLERS REUNION. On August 8, 1895, Getty's Grove was the scene of the Old Settlers Reunion. There were bonds of blood, sweat, and friendship that were forged between families in the early settlement of these communities that would last for generations. The families often depended upon each other for survival; they helped build homes in a rugged wilderness, raise barns, bring in crops, and as their children grew and married, they mixed friendships with blood in a manner that few might understand in the 21st century. Those same names still exist in the county roll of residents, and families remain involved and a part of the county's past, present, and future. Celebrations were a time to renew friendships and recall times past.

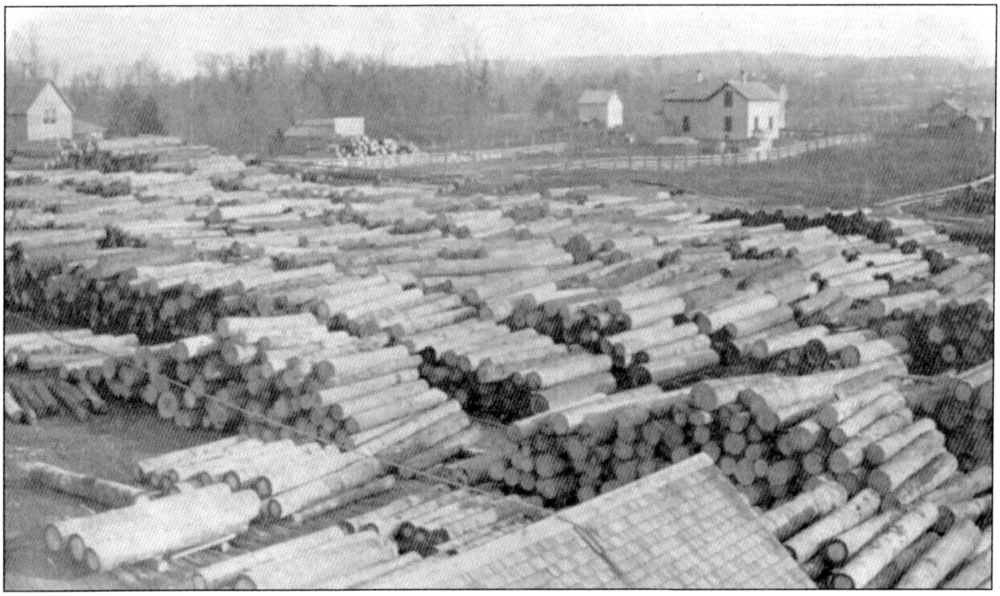

FRANK M. GALLUP. Coming to Hart from Ohio in 1891, Gallup became the general manager of the Sandusky Manufacturing Company. The company made lumber and hardwood articles, such as the stock needed by the Sandusky Tool Company for the production of its line of wood-handled tools.

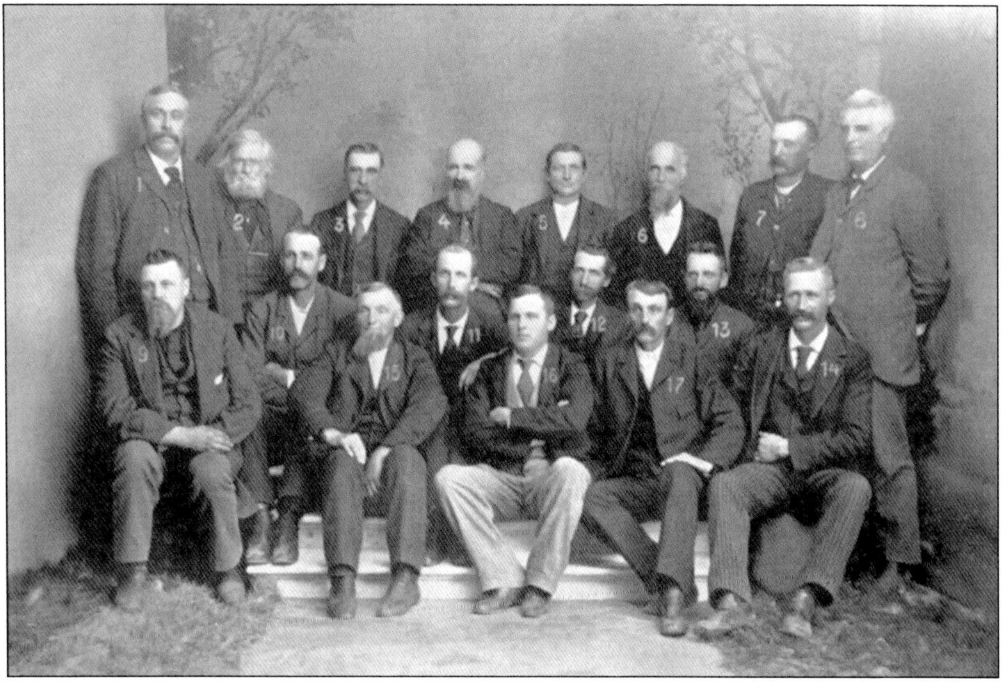

Board of Supervisors, 1895. In 1895, a 17-member board of supervisors governed the affairs of the county and represented their individual communities and townships. Identified only by their last names, from left to right are (first row) Harwood, Lake, Farrell, Powers, Randall, Mason, Philo, Tennant, and Genung; (second row) Carr, Potter, Wright, Everden, Artlip, Clark, Moore, and Butler.

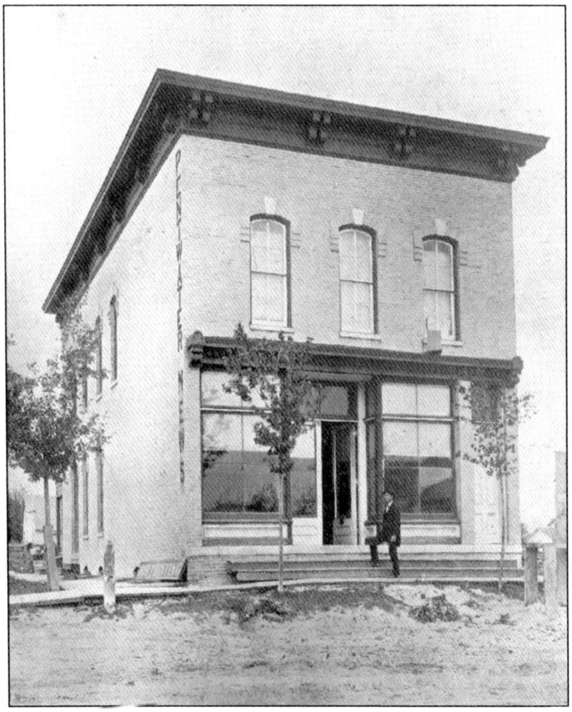

E.L. Bates's *Pentwater News*. E.L. Bates took over operation of the *Pentwater News* in January 1893. The newspaper had been under the direction of Louis Hartwick since 1880, and with Hartwick's election as county prosecutor a new editor was needed. The newspaper occupied the basement and the first floor of the news block.

About the Oceana County Historical and Genealogical Society

The Oceana County Historical and Genealogical Society was organized in 1967 with an organizational meeting in Pentwater. In 1974, the Swift Lathers home in Mears, Michigan, was donated by the family for use as a museum. Since that small beginning, the museum has grown into a historical park, which includes five buildings and one storage building.

In addition, the society now is the proud owner of the historic Swedish Mission Church. In 1984, the society purchased the Chadwick-Munger house from the county to be used as its headquarters. A dedicated staff of volunteers maintains genealogical material and collected artifacts. Volunteers also conduct tours of the museum, answer questions about Oceana history, and conduct fundraisers. The society is a nonprofit organization, relying totally on dues from its memberships, gifts from individuals, and fundraisers such as the Buy a Brick Program. A brick permanently engraved with your name or a loved one's can be a lasting part of the walkway in our memorial garden, which will be constructed on the west side of the historic Swedish Mission Church between the ramp and the church building at the Museum Park in Mears. Just fill out the form available online at www.oceanahistory.org/images/buy-a-brick.jpg, and we will do the rest. A contribution of $100 will buy a four-inch-by-eight-inch brick engraved with up to three lines. Proceeds will be used to complete the restoration of the church and provide funds for the maintenance of the museum park.

Our research and library headquarters is located at 114 Dryden Street in Hart, Michigan (49420). If you are unable to visit us, you may send us requests for genealogical or historical information. Our volunteers will do their best to find the information you have requested. Contact us for information on fees for this service. We can be contacted by phone at 231-873-2600 or on the web at www.oceanahistory.org. We are open on Wednesdays from 10:00 a.m. to 5:00 p.m. We are here to help you with your research, whether you query onsite, contacting us by email at info@oceanahistory.org, or by mail to our Dryden Street address.